Total Quality Management
text with cases

Second edition

John S. Oakland
PhD, CChem, MRSC, FIQA, FSS, MASQ, FinstD, FRSA

Professor of Business Excellence and Quality Management
University of Leeds Business School

Executive Chairman, Oakland Consulting plc

BUTTERWORTH
HEINEMANN

OXFORD AUCKLAND BOSTON JOHANNESBURG MELBOURNE NEW DELHI

Butterworth-Heinemann
Linacre House, Jordan Hill, Oxford OX2 8DP
225 Wildwood Avenue, Woburn, MA 01801-2041
A division of Reed Educational and Professional Publishing Ltd

 A Member of the Reed Elsevier plc group

First published 1995
Reprinted 1996, 1997, 1998
Second edition 2000
Reprinted 2000, 2001

British Library Cataloguing in Publication Data
Oakland, John S.
   Total quality management: text with cases – 2nd ed.
   1. Total quality management
   I. Title
   658.4'013

ISBN 0 7506 3952 0

Library of Congress Cataloguing in Publication Data
A catalogue record for this book is available from the Library of Congress

ISBN 0 7506 3952 0

Composition by Genesis Typesetting, Rochester, Kent
Printed and bound in Great Britain

Contents

Preface

When I wrote the first edition of *Total Quality Management* in 1988, there were very few books on the subject. Since its publication, the interest in TQM and business process improvement has exploded. There are now many texts on TQM and its various aspects, including Business Excellence.

So much has been learned during the last ten years of TQM implementation that it has been necessary to rewrite the book and revise it again. This student edition is based on the first, but its content and case studies have changed to reflect the developments, current understanding, and experience gained of TQM.

Continuous cost reduction, productivity and quality improvement have proved essential for organizations to stay in operation. We cannot avoid seeing how quality has developed into the most important competitive weapon, and many organizations have realized that TQM is *the* way of managing for the future. TQM is far wider in its application than assuring product or service quality – it is a way of managing organizations to improve every aspect of performance, both internally and externally.

This book is about how to manage in a total quality way. It is structured around five parts of a model for TQM. The core of the model is the *customer–supplier* interfaces, both externally and internally, and the fact that at each interface there lies a number of *processes*. This sensitive core must be surrounded by *commitment* to quality and meeting the customer requirements, *communication* of the quality message, and recognition of the need to change the *culture* of most organizations to create total quality. These are the soft FOUNDATIONS, to which must be added the SYSTEMS, the TOOLS, and the TEAMS – the hard management necessities.

Under these headings the essential steps for the successful IMPLEMENTATION of TQM are set out in what I hope is a meaningful and practical way. The book should guide the reader through the language of TQM and sets down a clear way to proceed for organizations.

Many of the management 'gurus' appear to present different theories. In reality they are talking the same 'language' but they use different dialects; the basic principles of defining quality and taking it into account throughout all the activities of the 'business' are common. Quality has to be managed – it does not just happen. Understanding and commitment by senior management, effective leadership and teamwork are fundamental parts of the recipe for success. I have tried to use my extensive research and consultancy experience to take what is to many a jigsaw puzzle and assemble a comprehensive, practical, working model for total quality – the rewards of which are greater efficiencies, lower costs, improved reputation and greater market share.

The book should meet the requirements of the increasing number of students who need to understand the part TQM may play in their courses on science, engineering, or management. I hope that those engaged in the pursuit of professional qualifications in the management of quality assurance, such as memberships of the Institute of Quality Assurance, the American Society for Quality, or the Australian Organization for Quality, will make this book an essential part of their library. With its companion book, *Statistical Process Control* (now in its fourth edition), *Total Quality Management* documents a comprehensive approach, one that has been used successfully in many organizations throughout the world.

I would like to thank my colleagues in the European Centre for Business Excellence and Oakland Consulting plc for the sharing of ideas and help in their development. The book is the result of many years' collaboration in assisting organizations to introduce good methods of management and embrace the concepts of total quality. I am most grateful to Jan Selby who converted a patchwork quilt of scribble and typescript into error-free electronic form.

John Oakland

Reading, using and analyzing the cases

The cases in this book provide a description of what occurred in nine different organizations, regarding various aspects of their quality improvement efforts. They may each be used as a learning vehicle as well as providing information and description which demonstrate the application of the concepts and techniques of TQM.

The objective of writing the cases has been to offer a resource through which the student of TQM (including the practising manager) understands how TQM companies operate. It is hoped that the cases provide a useful and distinct contribution to TQM education and training.

The case material is suitable for practising managers, students on undergraduate and postgraduate courses, and all teachers of the various aspects of business management and TQM. The cases have been written so that they may be used in three ways:

1 As orthodox cases for student preparation and discussion.
2 As illustrations, which teachers may also use as support for their other methods of training and education.
3 As supporting/background reading on TQM.

If used in the orthodox way, it is recommended that firstly the case is read to gain an understanding of the issues and to raise questions which may lead to a collective and more complete understanding of the company, TQM and the issues in the particular case. Secondly, case discussion or presentations in groups will give practice in putting forward thoughts and ideas persuasively.

The greater the effort put into case study, preparation, analysis and discussions in groups, the greater will be the individual benefit. There are, of course, no 'correct' and tidy cases in any subject area. What the directors and managers of an organization actually did is not necessarily the best way forward. One object of the cases is to make the reader think about the situation, the problems and the progress made, and what improvement or developments are possible.

The writing of each case emphasizes particular problems or issues which were apparent for the organization. This may have obscured other more important ones. Imagination, innovation and intuition should be as much a part of the study of a case as observation and analysis of the facts and any data available.

TQM cases, by their nature, will be very complicated and, to render the cases in this book useful for study, some of the complexity has been omitted. This simplification is accompanied by the danger of making the implementation seem clear-cut and obvious – that is never the case with TQM!

TQM case analysis

The main objective of each description is to enable the reader to understand the situation and its implications, and to learn from the particular experiences. The cases are not, in the main, offering specific problems to be solved. In using the cases, the reader/student should try to:

- *recognize or imagine* the situation in the organization
- *understand* the context and objectives of the process(es) described
- *analyse* the different parts of the case (including any data) and their interrelationships
- *determine* the overall structure of the situation/problem(s)/case
- *consider* the different options facing the organization
- *evaluate* the options and the course of action chosen, using any results stated
- *consider any recommendations* which should be made to the organization for further work, action, or implementation.

The set of cases has been chosen to provide a good coverage across different types of industry and organization, including those in the service, manufacturing and public sectors. Somewhat artificially, cases have been arranged at the end of the book in a sequence which follows the various parts of the Oakland Model of TQM:

- the foundations
- the role of the quality systems
- the role of tools, techniques and measurement
- the organization, communication and teamwork aspects
- the implementation and integration into strategy.

The value of illustrative cases in an area such as TQM is that they inject reality into the conceptual frameworks developed by authors on the subject. The cases are all based on real situations and are designed to illustrate certain aspects of managing change in organizations, rather than to reflect good or poor management practice. The cases may be used for analysis, discussion, evaluation, and even decision-making within groups, without risk to the individuals, groups, or organization(s) involved. In this way students of TQM may become 'involved' in many different organizations and their approaches to TQM implementation, over a short period and in an efficient and effective way.

The organizations described here have faced translating TQM theory into practice, and the description of their experiences should provide an opportunity for the reader of TQM literature to test his/her preconceptions and understanding of this topic. All the cases describe real TQM processes in real organizations and the author is grateful to the people involved for their contribution to this book.

Further reading

Easton, G., *Learning from Case Studies* (3rd edition), Prentice-Hall, UK, 1998.

The Foundations – A Model for TQM

Good order is the foundation of all good things.
 Edmund Burke, 1729–1797, from 'Reflections on the Revolution in France'

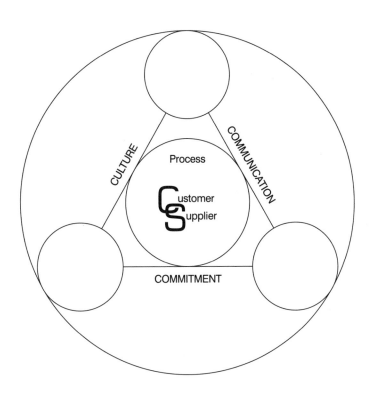

Chapter 1

Understanding quality

Quality, competitiveness and customers

Whatever type of organization you work in – a hospital, a university, a bank, an insurance company, local government, an airline, a factory – competition is rife: competition for customers, for students, for patients, for resources, for funds. Any organization basically competes on its *reputation* – for quality, reliability, price and delivery – and most people now recognize that quality is the most important of these competitive weapons. If you doubt that, just look at the way some organizations, even whole industries in certain countries, have used quality to take the heads off their competitors. Not only Japanese companies, but also British, American, French, German, Italian, Spanish, Swiss, Swedish organizations, and organizations from other countries, have used quality strategically to win customers, steal business resources or funding, and be competitive. Moreover, this sort of attention to quality improves performance in reliability, delivery and price.

For any organization, there are several aspects of reputation which are important:

1 It is built upon the competitive elements of quality, reliability, delivery and price, of which quality has become strategically the most important.
2 Once an organization acquires a poor reputation for quality, it takes a very long time to change it.
3 Reputations, good or bad, can quickly become national reputations.
4 The management of the competitive weapons, such as quality, can be learned like any other skill, and used to turn round a poor reputation, in time.

Before anyone will buy the idea that quality is an important consideration, they would have to know what was meant by it.

What is quality?

'Is this a quality watch?' Pointing to my wrist, I ask this question of a class of students – undergraduates, postgraduates, experienced managers – it matters not who. The answers vary:

- 'No, it's made in Japan.'
- 'No, it's cheap.'
- 'No, the face is scratched.'
- 'How reliable is it?'
- 'I wouldn't wear it.'

My watch has been insulted all over the world – London, New York, Paris, Sydney, Brussels, Amsterdam, Leeds! Very rarely am I told that the quality of the watch depends on what the wearer requires from it – perhaps a piece of jewellery to give an impression of wealth; a timepiece that gives the required data, including the date, in digital form; or one with the ability to perform at 50 metres under the sea? Clearly these requirements determine the quality.

Quality is often used to signify 'excellence' of a product or service – people talk about 'Rolls-Royce quality' and 'top quality'. In some engineering companies the word may be used to indicate that a piece of metal conforms to certain physical dimensional characteristics often set down in the form of a particularly 'tight' specification. In a hospital it might be used to indicate some sort of 'professionalism'. If we are to define quality in a way that is useful in its *management*, then we must recognize the need to include in the assessment of quality the true requirements of the 'customer' – the needs and expectations.

Quality then is simply *meeting the customer requirements*, and this has been expressed in many ways by other authors:

- 'Fitness for purpose or use' – Juran.
- 'The totality of features and characteristics of a product or service that bear on its ability to satisfy stated or implied needs' – BS 4778: 1987 (ISO 8402, 1986) *Quality Vocabulary*: Part 1, *International Terms*.
- 'Quality should be aimed at the needs of the consumer, present and future' – Deming.
- 'The total composite product and service characteristics of marketing, engineering, manufacture and maintenance through which the product and service in use will meet the expectation by the customer' – Feigenbaum.
- 'Conformance to requirements' – Crosby.

Another word that we should define properly is *reliability*. 'Why do you buy a BMW car?' 'Quality and reliability' comes back the answer. The two are used synonymously, often in a totally confused way. Clearly, part of the acceptability of a product or service will depend on its ability to function satisfactorily *over a period of time*, and it is this aspect of performance that is given the name *reliability*. It is the ability of the product or service to *continue* to meet the customer requirements. Reliability ranks with quality in importance, since it is a key factor in many purchasing decisions where alternatives are being considered. Many of the general management issues related to achieving product or service quality are also applicable to reliability.

It is important to realize that the 'meeting the customer requirements' definition of quality is not restricted to the functional characteristics of products or services. Anyone with children knows that the quality of some of the products they purchase is more associated with *satisfaction in ownership* than some functional property. This is also true of many items, from antiques to certain items of clothing. The requirements for status symbols account for the sale of some executive cars, certain bank accounts and charge cards, and even hospital beds! The requirements are of paramount importance in the assessment of the quality of any product or service.

By *consistently* meeting customer requirements, we can move to a different plane of satisfaction – *delighting the customer*. There is no doubt that many organizations have so well ordered their capability to meet their customers' requirements, time and time again, that this has created a reputation for 'excellence'. A development of this thinking regarding customers and their satisfaction is *customer loyalty*, an important variable in an organization's success. Research shows that focus on customer loyalty can provide several commercial advantages:

- Customers cost less to retain than to acquire.
- The longer the relationship with the customer, the higher the profitability.
- A loyal customer will commit more spend to its chosen supplier.
- About half of new customers come through referrals from existing clients (indirectly reducing acquisition costs).

Companies like 3M use measures of customer loyalty to identify customers who are 'completely satisfied', would 'definitely recommend' 3M, and would 'definitely repurchase'.

Understanding and building the quality chains

The ability to meet the customer requirements is vital, not only between two separate organizations, but within the same organization.

When the air stewardess pulled back the curtain across the aisle and set off with a trolley full of breakfasts to feed the early morning travellers on the short domestic flight into an international airport, she was not thinking of quality problems. Having stopped at the row of seats marked 1ABC, she passed the first tray onto the lap of the man sitting by the window. By the time the second tray had reached the lady beside him, the first tray was on its way back to the hostess with a complaint that the bread roll and jam were missing. She calmly replaced it in her trolley and reached for another – which also had no roll and jam.

The calm exterior of the girl began to evaporate as she discovered two more trays without a complete breakfast. Then she found a good one and, thankfully, passed it over. This search for complete breakfast trays continued down the aeroplane, causing inevitable delays, so much so that several passengers did not receive their breakfasts until the plane had begun its descent. At the rear of the plane could be heard the mutterings of discontent: 'Aren't they slow with breakfast this morning?' 'What is she doing with those trays?' 'We will have indigestion by the time we've landed.'

The problem was perceived by many to be one of delivery or service. They could smell food but they weren't getting any of it, and they were getting really wound up! The air hostess, who had suffered the embarrassment of being the purveyor of defective product and service, was quite wound up and flushed herself, as she returned to the curtain and almost ripped it from the hooks in her haste to hide. She was heard to say through clenched teeth, 'What a bloody mess!'

A problem of quality? Yes, of course, requirements not being met, but where? The passengers or customers suffered from it on the aircraft, but down in the bowels of the organization there was a man whose job it was to assemble the breakfast trays. On this day the system had broken down – perhaps he ran out of bread rolls, perhaps he was called away to refuel the aircraft (it was a small airport!), perhaps he didn't know or understand, perhaps he didn't care.

Three hundred miles away in a chemical factory . . . 'What the hell is Quality Control doing? We've just sent 15,000 litres of lawn weedkiller to CIC and there it is back at our gate – they've returned it as out of spec.' This was followed by an avalanche of verbal abuse, which will not be repeated here, but poured all over the shrinking Quality Control Manager as he backed through his office door, followed by a red-faced Technical Director advancing menacingly from behind the bottles of sulphuric acid racked across the adjoining laboratory.

'Yes, what is QC doing?' thought the Production Manager, who was behind a door two offices along the corridor, but could hear the torrent of language now being used to beat the QC man into an admission of guilt. He knew the poor devil couldn't possibly do anything about the rubbish that had been produced except test it, but why should he volunteer for the unpleasant and embarrassing ritual now being experienced by his colleague – for the second time this month. No wonder the QC manager had been studying the middle pages of the *Telegraph* on Thursday – what a job!

Do you recognize these two situations? Do they not happen every day of the week – possibly every minute somewhere in manufacturing or the service industries? Is it any different in banking, insurance, the health service? The inquisition of checkers and testers is the last bastion of desperate systems trying in vain to catch mistakes, stop defectives, hold lousy materials, before they reach the external customer – and woe betide the idiot who lets them pass through!

Two everyday incidents, but why are events like these so common? The answer is the acceptance of one thing – *failure*. Not doing it right the first time at every stage of the process.

Why do we accept failure in the production of artefacts, the provision of a service, or even the transfer of information? In many walks of life we do not accept it. We do not say, 'Well, the nurse is bound to drop the odd baby in a thousand – it's just going to happen.' We do not accept that!

In each department, each office, even each household, there are a series of suppliers and customers. The typist is a supplier to the boss. Are the requirements being met? Does the boss receive error-free word-processing set out as it is wanted, when it is wanted? If so, then we have a quality typing service. Does the air steward receive from the supplier in the airline the correct food trays in the right quantity?

Throughout and beyond all organizations, whether they be manufacturing concerns, banks, retail stores, universities, hospitals or hotels, there is a series of *quality chains* of customers and suppliers (Figure 1.1) that may be broken at any point by one person

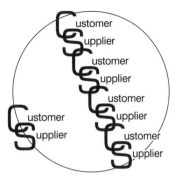

Figure 1.1 *The quality chains*

or one piece of equipment not meeting the requirements of the customer, internal or external. The interesting point is that this failure usually finds its way to the interface between the organization and its outside customers, and the people who operate at that interface – like the air hostess – usually experience the ramifications. The concept of internal and external customers/suppliers forms the *core* of total quality.

A great deal is written and spoken about employee motivations as a separate issue. In fact the key to motivation *and* quality is for everyone in the organization to have well-defined customers – an extension of the word beyond the outsider that actually purchases or uses the ultimate product or service to anyone to whom an individual gives a part, a service, information; in other words the results of his or her work.

Quality has to be managed – it will not just happen. Clearly it must involve everyone in the process and be applied throughout the organization. Many people in the support functions of organizations never see, experience or touch the products or services that their organizations buy or provide, but they do handle or produce things like purchase orders or invoices. If every fourth invoice carries at least one error, what image of quality is transmitted?

Failure to meet the requirements in any part of a quality chain has a way of multiplying and a failure in one part of the system creates problems elsewhere, leading to yet more failure, more problems and so on. The price of quality is the continual examination of the requirements and our ability to meet them. This alone will lead to a 'continuing improvement' philosophy. The benefits of making sure the requirements are met at every stage, every time, are truly enormous in terms of increased competitiveness and market share, reduced costs, improved productivity and delivery performance, and the elimination of waste.

Meeting the requirements

If quality is meeting the customer requirements, then this has wide implications. The requirements may include availability, delivery, reliability, maintainability and cost-effectiveness, among many other features. The first item on the list of things to do is find out what the requirements are. If we are dealing with a customer–supplier relationship crossing two organizations, then the supplier must establish a 'marketing' activity charged with this task.

The marketers must of course understand not only the needs of the customer but also the ability of their own organization to meet them. If my customer places a requirement on me to run 1,500 metres in 4 minutes, then I know I am unable to meet this demand, unless something is done to improve my running performance. Of course I may never be able to achieve this requirement.

Within organizations, between internal customers and suppliers, the transfer of information regarding requirements is frequently poor to totally absent. How many executives really bother to find out what their customers' – their secretaries' – requirements are? Can their handwriting be read, do they leave clear instructions, do the secretaries always know where the boss is? Equally, do the secretaries establish what their bosses need – error-free word processing, clear messages, a tidy office? Internal supplier–customer relationships are often the most difficult to manage in terms of establishing the requirements. To achieve quality throughout an organization, each person in the quality chain must interrogate every interface as follows:

Customers

- Who are my immediate customers?
- What are their true requirements?
- How do or can I find out what the requirements are?
- How can I measure my ability to meet the requirements?
- Do I have the necessary capability to meet the requirements? (If not, then what must change to improve the capability?)
- Do I continually meet the requirements? (If not, then what prevents this from happening, when the capability exists?)
- How do I monitor changes in the requirements?

Suppliers

- Who are my immediate suppliers?
- What are my true requirements?
- How do I communicate my requirements?
- Do my suppliers have the capability to measure and meet the requirements?
- How do I inform them of changes in the requirements?

The measurement of capability is extremely important if the quality chains are to be formed within and without an organization. Each person in the organization must also realize that the supplier's needs and expectations must be respected if the requirements are to be fully satisfied.

To understand how quality may be built into a product or service, at any stage, it is necessary to examine the two distinct, but interrelated aspects of quality:

- Quality of design
- Quality of conformance to design.

Quality of design

We are all familiar with the old story of the tree swing (Figure 1.2), but in how many places in how many organizations is this chain of activities taking place? To discuss

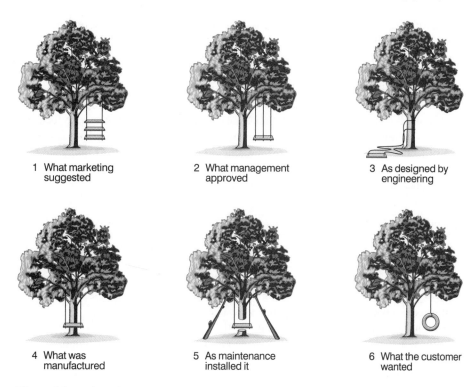

1 What marketing
   suggested

2 What management
   approved

3 As designed by
   engineering

4 What was
   manufactured

5 As maintenance
   installed it

6 What the customer
   wanted

Figure 1.2 *Quality of design*

the quality of, say, a chair it is necessary to describe its purpose. What it is to be used for? If it is to be used for watching TV for 3 hours at a stretch, then the typical office chair will not meet this requirement. The difference between the quality of the TV chair and the office chair is not a function of how it was manufactured, but its *design.*

Quality of design is a measure of how well the product or service is designed to achieve the agreed requirements. The beautifully presented gourmet meal will not necessarily please the recipient if he or she is travelling on the motorway and has stopped for a quick bite to eat. The most important feature of the design, with regard to achieving quality, is the specification. Specifications must also exist at the internal supplier–customer interfaces if one is to achieve total quality. For example, the company lawyer asked to draw up a contract by the sales manager requires a specification as to its content:

1 Is it a sales, processing or consulting type of contract?
2 Who are the contracting parties?
3 In which countries are the parties located?
4 What are the products involved (if any)?
5 What is the volume?
6 What are the financial, e.g. price, escalation, aspects?

The financial controller must issue a specification of the information he or she needs, and when, to ensure that foreign exchange fluctuations do not cripple the company's finances. The business of sitting down and agreeing a specification at every interface will clarify the true requirements and capabilities. It is the vital first stage for a successful total quality effort.

There must be a corporate understanding of the organization's quality position in the market place. It is not sufficient that marketing specifies the product or service 'because that is what the customer wants'. There must be an agreement that the operating departments can achieve that requirement. Should they be incapable of doing so, then one of two things must happen: either the organization finds a different position in the market place or it substantially changes the operational facilities.

Quality of conformance to design

This is the extent to which the product or service achieves the quality of design. What the customer actually receives should conform to the design, and operating costs are tied firmly to the level of conformance achieved. Quality cannot be inspected into products or services; the customer satisfaction must be designed into the whole system. The conformance check then makes sure that things go according to plan.

A high level of inspection or checking at the end is often indicative of attempts to inspect-in quality. This may well result in spiralling costs and decreasing viability. The area of conformance to design is concerned largely with the quality performance of the actual operations. It may be salutary for organizations to use the simple matrix of Figure 1.3 to assess how much time they spend doing the right things right. A lot of people, often through no fault of their own, spend a good proportion of the available time doing the right things wrong. There are people (and organizations) who spend time doing the wrong things very well, and even those who occupy themselves doing the wrong things wrong, which can be very confusing!

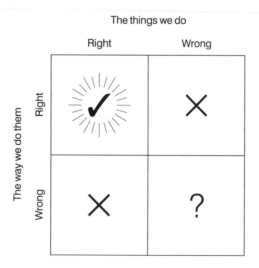

Figure 1.3 *How much time is spent doing the right things right?*

Managing processes

Every day two men who work in a certain factory scrutinize the results of the examination of the previous day's production, and begin the ritual battle over whether the material is suitable for despatch to the customer. One is called the Production Manager, the other the Quality Control Manager. They argue and debate the evidence before them, the rights and wrongs of the specification, and each tries to convince the other of the validity of his argument. Sometimes they nearly start fighting.

This ritual is associated with trying to answer the question, '*Have we done the job correctly?*', correctly being a flexible word, depending on the interpretation given to the specification on that particular day. This is not quality *control*, it is *detection* – wasteful detection of bad product before it hits the customer. There is still a belief in some quarters that to achieve quality we must check, test, inspect or measure – the ritual pouring on of quality at the end of the process. This is nonsense, but it is frequently practised. In the office one finds staff checking other people's work before it goes out, validating computer data, checking invoices, word processing, etc. There is also quite a lot of looking for things, chasing why things are late, apologizing to customers for lateness, and so on. Waste, waste, waste!

To get away from the natural tendency to rush into the detection mode, it is necessary to ask different questions in the first place. We should not ask whether the job has been done correctly, we should ask first, '*Are we capable of doing the job correctly?*' This question has wide implications, and this book is devoted largely to the various activities necessary to ensure that the answer is yes. However, we should realize straight away that such an answer will only be obtained by means of satisfactory methods, materials, equipment, skills and instruction, and a satisfactory 'process'.

What is a process?

As we have seen, quality chains can be traced right through the business or service processes used by any organization. A process is the transformation of a set of inputs, which can include actions, methods and operations, into outputs that satisfy customer needs and expectations, in the form of products, information, services or – generally – results. Everything we do is a process, so in each area or function of an organization there will be many processes taking place. For example, a finance department may be engaged in budgeting processes, accounting processes, salary and wage processes, costing processes, etc. Each process in each department or area can be analysed by an examination of the inputs and outputs. This will determine some of the actions necessary to improve quality. There are also cross-functional processes.

The output from a process is that which is transferred to somewhere or to someone – the *customer*. Clearly, to produce an output that meets the requirements of the customer, it is necessary to define, monitor and control the inputs to the process, which in turn may be supplied as output from an earlier process. At every supplier–customer interface then there resides a transformation process (Figure 1.4), and every single task throughout an organization must be viewed as a process in this way.

Many organizations now seek to understand their inner workings from a 'horizontal', customer-facing core process viewpoint, rather than from a 'vertical' functional viewpoint (Figure 1.5).

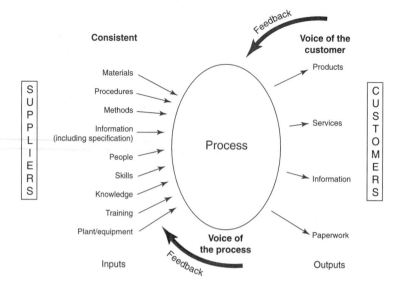

Figure 1.4 *A process*

Once we have established that our process is capable of meeting the requirements, we can address the next question, '*Do we continue to do the job correctly?*', which brings a requirement to monitor the process and the controls on it. If we now re-examine the first question, 'Have we done the job correctly?, we can see that, if we have been able to answer the other two questions with a yes, we *must* have done the

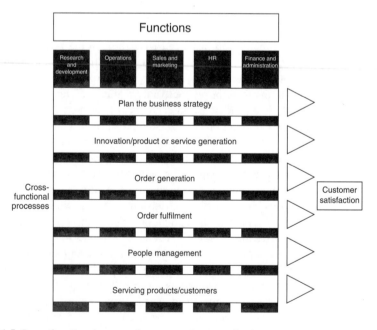

Figure 1.5 *Cross-functional approach to managing core business processes*

job correctly. Any other outcome would be illogical. By asking the questions in the right order, we have moved the need to ask the 'inspection' question and replaced a strategy of *detection* with one of *prevention*. This concentrates all the attention on the front end of any process – the inputs – and changes the emphasis to making sure the inputs are capable of meeting the requirements of the process. This is a managerial responsibility.

These ideas apply to every transformation process; they all must be subject to the same scrutiny of the methods, the people, skills, equipment and so on to make sure they are correct for the job. A person giving a lecture whose overhead projector equipment will not focus correctly, or whose teaching materials are not appropriate, will soon discover how difficult it is to provide a lecture that meets the requirements of the audience.

In every organization there are some very large processes – groups of smaller processes often called *core business processes* (see for example Figure 1.5). These are activities the organization must carry out especially well if its mission and objectives are to be achieved. The area will be dealt with in some detail in Chapter 13 on the implementation of TQM. It is crucial if the management of quality is to be integrated into the strategy for the organization.

The *control* of quality can only take place at the point of operation or production – where the letter is word-processed, the sales call made, the patient admitted, or the chemical manufactured. *The act of inspection is not quality control.* When the answer to, 'Have we done the job correctly?' is given indirectly by answering the questions of capability and control, then we have *assured* quality, and the activity of checking becomes one of *quality assurance* – making sure that the product or service represents the output from an effective *system* to ensure capability and control. It is frequently found that organizational barriers between functional or departmental empires encouraged the development of testing and checking of services or products in a vacuum, without interaction with other departments.

Quality control then is essentially the activities and techniques employed to achieve and maintain the quality of a product, process or service. It includes a monitoring activity, but is also concerned with finding and eliminating causes of quality problems so that the requirements of the customer are continually met.

Quality assurance is broadly the prevention of quality problems through planned and systematic activities (including documentation). These will include the establishment of a good-quality management system and the assessment of its adequacy, the audit of the operation of the system, and the review of the system itself.

Quality starts with 'marketing'

The author has been asked on more than one occasion if TQM applies to marketing. The answer to the question is not remarkable – its starts there!

The marketing function of an organization must take the lead in establishing the true requirements for the product or service. Having determined the need, marketing should define the market sector and demand, to determine such product or service features as grade, price, quality, timing, etc. For example, a major hotel chain thinking of opening a new hotel or refurbishing an old one will need to consider its location and accessibility before deciding whether it will be predominantly a budget, first-class, business or family hotel.

Marketing will also need to establish customer requirements by reviewing the market needs, particularly in terms of unclear or unstated expectations or preconceived ideas held by customers. Marketing is responsible for determining the key characteristics that determine the suitability of the product or service in the eyes of the customer. This may, of course, call for the use of market research techniques, data-gathering, and analysis of customer complaints. If necessary, quasi-quantitative methods may be employed, giving proxy variables that can be used to grade the characteristics in importance, and decide in which areas superiority over competitors exists. It is often useful to compare these findings with internal perceptions.

Excellent communication between customers and suppliers is the key to total quality; it will eradicate the 'demanding nuisance/idiot' view of customers, which still pervades some organizations. Poor communications often occur in the supply chain between organizations, when neither party realizes how poor they are. Feedback from both customers and suppliers needs to be improved where dissatisfied customers and suppliers do not communicate their problems. In such cases, non-conformance of purchased products or services is often due to customers' inability to communicate their requirements clearly. If these ideas are also used within an organization, then the internal supplier–customer interfaces will operate much more smoothly.

All the efforts devoted to finding the nature and timing of the demand will be pointless if marketing fails to communicate the requirements promptly, clearly and accurately to the remainder of the organization. The marketing processes should be capable of producing a formal statement or outline of the requirements for each product or service. This constitutes a preliminary set of *specifications*, which can be used as the basis for service or product design. The information requirements include:

1 Characteristics of performance and reliability – these must make reference to the conditions of use and any environmental factors that may be important.
2 Aesthetic characteristics, such as style, colour, smell, task, feel.
3 Any obligatory regulations or standards governing the nature of the product or service.

Marketing must also establish systems for feedback of customer information and reaction, and these systems should be designed on a continuous monitoring basis. Any information pertinent to the product or service should be collected and collated, interpreted, analysed and communicated, to improve the response to customer experience and expectations. These same principles must also be applied inside the organization if continuous improvement at every transformation process interface is to be achieved. If one function or department in a company has problems recruiting the correct sort of staff, and HR has not established mechanisms for gathering, analysing and responding to information on new employees, then frustration and conflict will replace communication and co-operation.

One aspect of the analysis of market demand that extends back into the organization is the review of market readiness of a new product or service. Items that require some attention include assessment of:

1 The suitability of the distribution and customer-service processes.
2 Training of personnel in the 'field'.
3 Availability of spare parts or support staff.
4 Evidence that the organization is capable of meeting customer requirements.

All organizations receive a wide range of information from customers through invoices, payments, requests for information, letters of complaint, responses to advertisements and promotion, etc. An essential component of a system for the analysis of market demand is that this data is channelled quickly into the appropriate areas for action and, if necessary, response.

There are various techniques of market research which are outside the scope of this book but have been well documented elsewhere. It is worth listing some of the most common and useful general methods that should be considered for use, both externally and internally:

● surveys – questionnaires, etc.
● panel or focus group techniques
● in-depth interviews
● brainstorming and discussions
● role rehearsal and reversal
● interrogation of trade associations.

The number of methods and techniques for researching the market is limited only by imagination and funds. The important point to stress is that the supplier, whether the internal individual or the external organization, keeps very close to the customer. Market research, coupled with analysis of complaints data, is an essential part of finding out what the requirements are, and breaking out from the obsession with inward scrutiny that bedevils quality.

Quality in all functions

For an organization to be truly effective, each part of it must work properly together. Each part, each activity, each person in the organization affects and is in turn affected by others. Errors have a way of multiplying, and failure to meet the requirements in one part or area creates problems elsewhere, leading to yet more errors, yet more problems, and so on. The benefits of getting it right first time everywhere are enormous.

Everyone experiences – almost accepts – problems in working life. This causes people to spend a large part of their time on useless activities – correcting errors, looking for things, finding out why things are late, checking suspect information, rectifying and reworking, apologizing to customers for mistakes, poor quality and lateness. The list is endless, and it is estimated that about one-third of our efforts are wasted in this way. In the service sector it can be much higher.

Quality, the way we have defined it as meeting the customer requirements, gives people in different functions of an organization a common language for improvement. It enables all the people, with different abilities and priorities, to communicate readily with one another, in pursuit of a common goal. When business and industry were local, the craftsman could manage more or less on his own. Business is now so complex and employs so many different specialist skills that everyone has to rely on the activities of others in doing their jobs.

Some of the most exciting applications of TQM have materialized from groups of people that could see little relevance when first introduced to its concepts. Following training, many different parts of organizations can show the usefulness of the techniques. Sales staff can monitor and increase successful sales calls, office staff have used TQM methods to prevent errors in word-processing and improve inputting to computers, customer-service people have monitored and reduced complaints, distribution has controlled lateness and disruption in deliveries.

It is worthy of mention that the first points of contact for some outside customers are the telephone operator, the security people at the gate, or the person in reception. Equally the paperwork and support services associated with the product, such as invoices and sales literature and their handlers, must match the needs of the customer. Clearly TQM cannot be restricted to the production or operational areas without losing great opportunities to gain maximum benefit.

Managements that rely heavily on exhortation of the workforce to 'do the right job right the first time', or 'accept that quality is your responsibility', will not only fail to achieve quality but may create division and conflict. These calls for improvement imply that faults are caused only by the workforce and that problems are departmental or functional when, in fact, the opposite is true – most problems are inter-departmental. The commitment of all members of an organization is a requirement of 'company-wide quality improvement'. Everyone must work together at every interface to achieve perfection. And that can only happen if the top management is really committed to quality improvement.

Chapter highlights

Quality, competitiveness and customers

- The reputation enjoyed by an organization is built by quality, reliability, delivery and price. Quality is the most important of these competitive weapons.
- Reputations for poor quality last for a long time, and good or bad reputations can become national. The management of quality can be learned and used to improve reputation.
- Quality is meeting the customer requirements, and this is not restricted to the functional characteristics of the product or service.
- Reliability is the ability of the product or service to continue to meet the customer requirements over time.
- Organizations 'delight' the customer by consistently meeting customer requirements, and then achieve a reputation of 'excellence' and gain customer loyalty.

Understanding and building the quality chains

- Throughout all organizations there are a series of internal suppliers and customers. These form the so-called 'quality chains', the core of 'company-wide quality improvement'.

- The internal customer–supplier relationships must be managed by interrogation, i.e. using a set of questions at every interface. Measurement of capability is vital.
- There are two distinct but interrelated aspects of quality, design and conformance to design. *Quality of design* is a measure of how well the product or service is designed to achieve the agreed requirements. *Quality of conformance to design* is the extent to which the product or service achieves the design. Organizations should assess how much time they spend doing the right things right.

Managing processes

- Asking the question, 'Have we done the job correctly?' should be replaced by asking, 'Are we capable of doing the job correctly?' and 'Do we continue to do the job correctly?'
- Asking the questions in the right order replaces a strategy of *detection* with one of *prevention.*
- Everything we do is a process, which is the transformation of a set of inputs into the desired outputs.
- In every organization there are some core business processes that must be performed especially well if the mission and objectives are to be achieved.
- Inspection is not *quality control*. The latter is the employment of activities and techniques to achieve and maintain the quality of a product, process or service.
- *Quality assurance* is the prevention of quality problems through planned and systematic activities.

Quality starts with 'marketing'

- Marketing establishes the true requirements for the product or service. These must be communicated properly throughout the organization in the form of specifications.

Quality in all functions

- All members of an organization need to work together on company-wide quality improvement. The co-operation of everyone at every interface is necessary to achieve perfection.

Chapter 2

Commitment and leadership

The total quality management approach

'What is quality management?' Something that is best left to the experts is often the answer to this question. But this is avoiding the issue, because it allows executives and managers to opt out. Quality is too important to leave to the so-called 'quality professionals'; it cannot be achieved on a company-wide basis if it is left to the experts. Equally dangerous, however, are the uninformed who try to follow their natural instincts because they 'know what quality is when they see it'. This type of intuitive approach can lead to serious attitude problems, which do no more than reflect the understanding and knowledge of quality that are present in an organization.

The organization which believes that the traditional quality control techniques, and the way they have always been used, will resolve their quality problems may be misguided. Employing more inspectors, tightening up standards, developing correction, repair and rework teams do not improve quality. Traditionally, quality has been regarded as the responsibility of the QA or QC department, and still it has not yet been recognized in some organizations that many quality problems originate in the service or administrative areas.

Total quality management is far more than shifting the responsibility of *detection* of problems from the customer to the producer. It requires a comprehensive approach that must first be recognized and then implemented if the rewards are to be realized. Today's business environment is such that managers must plan strategically to maintain a hold on market share, let alone increase it. We have known for years that consumers place a higher value on quality than on loyalty to home-based producers, and price is often not the major determining factor in consumer choice. Price has been replaced by quality, and this is true in industrial, service, hospitality, and many other markets.

TQM is an approach to improving the competitiveness, effectiveness and flexibility of a whole organization. It is essentially a way of planning, organizing and understanding each activity, and depends on each individual at each level. For an organization to be truly effective, each part of it must work properly together towards the same goals, recognizing that each person and each activity affects and in turn is affected by others. TQM is also a way of ridding people's lives of wasted effort by bringing everyone into the processes of improvement, so that results are achieved in less time. The methods and techniques used in TQM can be applied throughout any organization. They are equally useful in the manufacturing, public service, health care, education and hospitality industries.

The impact of TQM on an organization is, firstly, to ensure that the management adopts a strategic overview of quality. The approach must focus on developing a *problem-prevention* mentality; but it is easy to underestimate the effort that is required to change attitudes and approaches. Many people will need to undergo a complete change of 'mindset' to unscramble their intuition, which rushes into the detection/inspection mode to solve quality problems – 'We have a quality problem, we had better check every letter – take two samples out of each sack – check every widget twice', etc.

The correct mindset may be achieved by looking at the sort of barriers that exist in key areas. Staff may need to be trained and shown how to reallocate their time and energy to studying their processes in teams, searching for causes of problems, and correcting the causes, not the symptoms, once and for all. This often requires of management a positive, thrusting initiative to promote the right-first-time approach to work situations. Through *quality or process improvement teams*, these actions will reduce the inspection-rejection syndrome in due course. If things are done correctly first time round, the usual problems that create the need for inspection for failure should disappear.

The managements of many firms may think that their scale of operation is not sufficiently large, that their resources are too slim, or that the need for action is not important enough to justify implementing TQM. Before arriving at such a conclusion, however, they should examine their existing performance by asking the following questions:

1 Is any attempt made to asses the costs arising from errors, defects, waste, customer complaints, lost sales, etc.? If so, are these costs minimal or insignificant?
2 Is the standard of management adequate and are attempts being made to ensure that quality is given proper consideration at the design stage?
3 Are the organization's quality systems – documentation, procedures, operations, etc. – in good order?
4 Have personnel been trained in how to prevent errors and problems? Do they anticipate and correct potential causes of problems, or do they find and reject?
5 Do job instructions contain the necessary quality elements, are they kept up-to-date, and are employers doing their work in accordance with them?
6 What is being done to motivate and train employees to do work right first time?
7 How many errors and defects, and how much wastage, occurred last year? Is this more or less than the previous year?

If satisfactory answers can be given to most of these questions, an organization can be reassured that it is already well on the way to using adequate quality procedures and management. Even so, it may find that the introduction of TQM causes it to reappraise activities throughout. If answers to the above questions indicate problem areas, it will be beneficial to review the top management's attitude to quality. Time and money spent on quality-related activities are *not* limitations of profitability; they make significant contributions towards greater efficiency and enhanced profits.

Commitment and policy

To be successful in promoting business efficiency and effectiveness, TQM must be truly organization-wide, and it must start at the top with the Chief Executive or equivalent. The most senior directors and management must all demonstrate that they are serious about quality. The middle management have a particularly important role to play, since they must not only grasp the principles of TQM, they must go on to explain them to the people for whom they are responsible, and ensure that their own commitment is communicated. Only then will TQM spread effectively throughout the organization. This level of management also needs to ensure that the efforts and achievements of their subordinates obtain the recognition, attention and reward that they deserve.

The Chief Executive of an organization should accept the responsibility for and commitment to a quality policy in which he/she must really believe. This commitment is part of a broad approach extending well beyond the accepted formalities of the quality assurance function. It creates responsibilities for a chain of quality interactions between the marketing, design, production/operations, purchasing, distribution and service functions. Within each and every department of the organization at all levels, starting at the top, basic changes of attitude may be required to operate TQM. If the owners or directors of the organization do not recognize and accept their responsibilities for the initiation and operation of TQM, then these changes will not happen. Controls, systems and techniques are very important in TQM, but they are not the primary requirement. It is more an attitude of mind, based on pride in the job and teamwork, and it requires from the management total commitment, which must then be extended to all employees at all levels and in all departments.

Senior management commitment should be obsessional, not lip service. It is possible to detect real commitment; it shows on the shop floor, in the offices, in the hospital ward – at the point of operation. Going into organizations sporting poster-campaigning or quality instead of belief, one is quickly able to detect the falseness. The people are told not to worry if problems arise, 'just do the best you can', 'the customer will never notice'. The opposite is an organization where total quality means something, can be seen, heard, felt. Things happen at this operating interface as a result of *real* commitment. Material problems are corrected with suppliers, equipment difficulties are put right by improved maintenance programmes or replacement, people are trained, change takes place, partnerships are built, continuous improvement is achieved.

The quality policy

A sound quality policy, together with the organization and facilities to put it into effect, is a fundamental requirement, if a company is to begin to implement TQM. Every organization should develop and state its policy on quality, together with arrangements for its implementation. The content of the policy should be made known to all employees. The preparation and implementation of a properly thought out quality policy, together with continuous monitoring, make for smoother production or service operation, minimize errors and reduce waste.

Management must be dedicated to the regular improvement of quality, not simply a one-step improvement to an acceptable plateau. These ideas can be set out in a *quality policy* that requires top management to:

1 Identify the customer's needs (including perception).
2 Assess the ability of the organization to meet these needs economically.
3 Ensure that bought-in materials and services reliably meet the required standards of performance and efficiency.
4 Concentrate on the prevention rather than detection philosophy.
5 Educate and train for quality improvement.
6 Measure customer satisfaction.
7 Review the quality management systems to maintain progress.

The quality policy must be publicized and understood at all levels of the organization. An example of a good company quality policy is given below:

● Quality improvement is primarily the responsibility of management.
● In order to involve everyone in the organization in quality improvement, management will enable all employees to participate in the preparation, implementation and evaluation of improvement activities.
● Quality improvement will be tackled and followed up in a systematic and planned manner. This applies to every part of our organization.
● Quality improvement will be a continuous process.
● The organization will concentrate on its customers and suppliers, both external and internal.
● The performance of our competitors will be shown to all relevant units.
● Important suppliers will be closely involved in our quality policy. This relates to both external and internal suppliers of goods, resources and services.
● Widespread attention will be given to education and training activities, which will be assessed with regard to their contribution to the quality policy.
● Publicity will be given to the quality policy in every part of the organization so that everyone may understand it. All available methods and media will be used for its internal and external promotion and communication.
● Reporting on the progress of the implementation of the policy will be a permanent agenda item in management meetings.

The quality policy should be the concern of all employees, and the principles and objectives communicated as widely as possible. Practical assistance and training should be given, where necessary, to ensure that the relevant knowledge and experience are acquired for successful implementation of the policy.

Creating or changing the culture

The culture within an organization is formed by a number of components:

1 Behaviours based on people interactions.
2 Norms resulting from working groups.
3 Dominant values adopted by the organization.
4 Rules of the game for 'getting on'.
5 The climate.

Culture in any 'business' may be defined, then, as the beliefs that pervade the organization about how business should be conducted, and how employees should behave and should be treated. Any organization needs a vision framework that includes its *guiding philosophy, core values and beliefs* and a *purpose*. These should be combined into a *mission*, which provides a vivid description of what things will be like when it has been achieved (Figure 2.1).

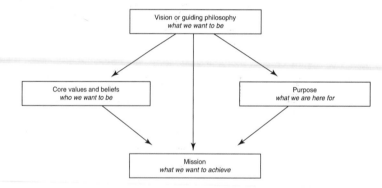

Figure 2.1 *Vision framework for an organization*

The *guiding philosophy* drives the organization and is shaped by the leaders through their thoughts and actions. It should reflect the vision of an organization rather than the vision of a single leader, and should evolve with time, although organizations must hold on to the *core* elements.

The *core values and beliefs* represent the organization's basic principles about what is important in business, its conduct, its social responsibility and its response to changes in the environment. They should act as a guiding force, with clear and authentic values, which are focused on employees, suppliers, customers, society at large, safety, shareholders, and generally stakeholders.

The *purpose* of the organization should be a development from the core values and beliefs and should quickly and clearly convey how the organization is to fulfil its role.

The *mission* will translate the abstractness of philosophy into tangible goals that will move the organization forward and make it perform to its optimum. It should not be limited by the constraints of strategic analysis, and should be proactive not reactive. Strategy is subservient to mission, the strategic analysis being done after, not during, the mission setting process.

Control

The effectiveness of an organization and its people depends on the extent to which each person and department performs their role and moves towards the common goals and objectives. Control is the process by which information or feedback is provided so as to keep all functions on track. It is the sum total of the activities that increase the probability of the planned results being achieved. Control mechanisms fall into three categories, depending upon their position in the managerial process:

Before the fact	*Operational*	*After the fact*
Strategic plan	Observation	Annual reports
Action plans	Inspection and correction	Variance reports
Budgets	Progress review	Audits
Job descriptions	Staff meetings	Surveys
Individual performance objectives	Internal information and data systems	Performance review
Training and development	Training programmes	Evaluation of training

Many organizations use after-the-fact controls, causing managers to take a reactive rather than a proactive position. Such 'crisis-orientation' needs to be replaced by a more anticipative one in which the focus is on preventive or before-the-fact controls.

Attempting to control performance through systems, procedures or techniques *external* to the individual is not an effective approach, since it relies on 'controlling' others; individuals should be responsible for their own actions. An externally based control system can result in a high degree of concentrated effort in a specific area if the system is overly structured, but it can also cause negative consequences to surface:

1 Since all rewards are based on external measures, which are imposed, the 'team members' often focus all their effort on the measure itself, e.g. to have it set lower (or higher) than possible, to manipulate the information which serves to monitor it, or to dismiss it as someone else's goal not theirs. In the budgeting process, for example, distorted figures are often submitted by those who have learned that their 'honest projections' will be automatically altered anyway.

2 When the rewards are dependent on only one or two limited targets, all efforts are directed at those, even at the expense of others. If short-term profitability is the sole criterion for bonus distribution or promotion, it is likely that investment for longer-term growth areas will be substantially reduced. Similarly, strong emphasis and reward for output or production may result in lowered quality.

3 The fear of not being rewarded, or even being criticized, for performance that is less than desirable may cause some to withhold information that is unfavourable but nevertheless should be flowing into the system.

4 When reward and punishment are used to motivate performance, the degree of risk-taking may lessen and be replaced by a more cautious and conservative approach. In essence, the fear of failure replaces the desire to achieve.

The following problem situations have been observed by the author and his colleagues within companies that have taken part in research and consultancy:

- The goals imposed are seen or known to be unrealistic. If the goals perceived by the subordinate are in fact accomplished, then the subordinate has proved himself wrong. This clearly has a negative effect on the effort expended, since few people are motivated to prove themselves wrong!
- Where individuals are stimulated to commit themselves to a goal, and where their personal pride and self-esteem are at stake, then the level of motivation is at a peak. For most people the toughest critic and the hardest taskmaster they confront is not their immediate boss but themselves.
- Directors and managers are often afraid of allowing subordinates to set the goals for fear of them being set too low, or loss of control over subordinate behaviour. It is also true that many do not wish to set their own targets, but prefer to be told what is to be accomplished.

TQM is concerned with moving the focus of control from outside the individual to within, the objective being to make everyone accountable for their own performance, and to get them committed to attaining quality in a highly motivated fashion. The assumptions which a director or manager must make in order to move in this direction are simply that people do not need to be coerced to perform well, and that people want to achieve, accomplish, influence activity, and challenge their abilities. If there is belief in this, then only the techniques remain to be discussed.

Total quality management is user-driven – it cannot be imposed from outside the organization, as perhaps can a quality standard or statistical process control. This means that the ideas for improvement must come from those with knowledge and experience of the processes, activities and tasks; this has massive implications for training and follow-up. TQM is not a cost-cutting or productivity improvement device in the traditional sense, and it must not be used as such. Although the effects of a successful programme will certainly reduce costs and improve productivity, TQM is concerned chiefly with changing attitudes and skills so that the culture of the organization becomes one of preventing failure – doing the right things, right first time, every time.

Effective leadership

Some management teams have broken away from the traditional style of management; they have made a 'managerial breakthrough'. Their new approach puts their organization head and shoulders above competitors in the fight for sales, profits, resources, funding and jobs. Many service organizations are beginning to move in the same way, and the successful quality-based strategy they are adopting depends very much on effective leadership.

Effective leadership starts with the Chief Executive's vision, capitalizing on market or service opportunities, continues through a strategy that will give the organization competitive advantage, and leads to business or service success. It goes on to embrace all the beliefs and values held, the decisions taken and the plans made by anyone anywhere in the organization, and the focusing of them into effective, value-adding action.

Together, effective leadership and total quality management result in the company or organization doing the right things, right first time.

The five requirements for effective leadership are the following:

I Developing and publishing clear documented corporate beliefs and purpose – a mission statement

Executives should express values and beliefs through a clear vision of what they want their company to be, and its purpose – what they specifically want to achieve in line with the basic beliefs. Together, they define what the company or organization is all about. The senior management team will need to spend some time away from the 'coal face' to do this and develop their programme for implementation.

Clearly defined and properly communicated beliefs and objectives, which can be summarized in the form of a mission statement, are essential if the directors, managers and other employees are to work together as a winning team. The beliefs and objectives should address:

- the definition of the business, e.g. the needs that are satisfied or the benefits provided.
- a commitment to effective leadership and quality
- target sectors and relationships with customers, and market or service position
- the role or contribution of the company, organization or unit, e.g. example, profit-generator, service department, opportunity-seeker
- the distinctive competence – a brief statement which applies only to that organization, company or unit
- indications for future direction – a brief statement of the principal plans which would be considered
- commitment to monitoring performance against customers' needs and expectations, and continuous improvement.

The mission statement and the broad beliefs and objective may then be used to communicate an inspiring vision of the organization's future. The top management must then show *TOTAL COMMITMENT* to it.

2 Developing clear and effective strategies and supporting plans for achieving the mission

The achievement of the company or service mission requires the development of business or service strategies, including the strategic positioning in the 'market place'. Plans can then be developed for implementing the strategies. Such strategies and plans can be developed by senior managers alone, but there is likely to be more commitment to them if employee participation in their development and implementation is encouraged.

3 Identifying the critical success factors and critical processes

The next step is the identification of the *critical success factors* (CSFs), a term used to mean the most important subgoals of a business or organization. CSFs are what must be accomplished for the mission to be achieved. The CSFs are followed by the key, *core business processes* for the organization – the activities that must be done particularly well for the CSFs to be achieved (Figure 2.2). This process is described in some detail in Chapter 13 on implementation.

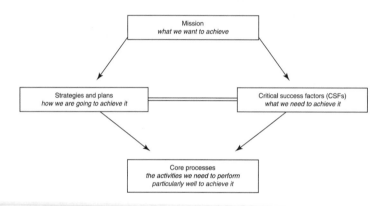

Figure 2.2 *Mission into action through CSFs and core processes*

4 Reviewing the management structure

Defining the corporate mission, strategies, CSFs and core processes might make it necessary to review the organizational structure. Directors, managers and other employees can be fully effective only if an effective structure based on process management exists. This includes both the definition of responsibilities for the organization's management and the operational procedures they will use. These must be the agreed best ways of carrying out the core processes.

The review of the management structure should also include the establishment of a process improvement team structure throughout the organization.

5 Empowerment – encouraging effective employee participation

For effective leadership it is necessary for management to get very close to the employees. They must develop effective communications – up, down and across the organization – and take action on what is communicated; and they should encourage good communications between all suppliers and customers.

Particular attention must be paid to the following:

Attitudes

The key attitude for managing any winning company or organization may be expressed as follows: 'I will personally understand who my customers are and what are their needs and expectations and I will take whatever action is necessary to satisfy them fully. I will also understand and communicate my requirements to my suppliers, inform them of changes and provide feedback on their performance.' This attitude should start at the top – with the Chairman or Chief Executive. It must then percolate down, to be adopted by each and every employee. That will happen only if managers lead by example. Words are cheap and will be meaningless if employees see from managers' actions that they do not actually believe or intend what they say.

Abilities

Every employee should be able to do what is needed and expected of him or her, but it is first necessary to decide what is really needed and expected. If it is not clear what the employees are required to do and what standards of performance are expected, how can managers expect them to do it?

Train, train, train and train again. Training is very important, but it can be expensive if the money is not spent wisely. The training should be related to needs, expectations and process improvement. It must be planned and its effectiveness *always* reviewed.

Participation

If all employees are to participate in making the company or organization successful (directors and managers included), then they must also be trained in the basics of disciplined management.

They must be trained to:

E	**Evaluate**	– the situation and define their *objectives*.
P	**Plan**	– to achieve those objectives fully.
D	**Do**	– i.e. implement the plans
C	**Check**	– that the objectives are being achieved.
A	**Amend**	– i.e. take corrective action if they are not.

The word 'disciplined' applied to people at all levels means that they will do what they say they will do. It also means that in whatever they do they will go through the full process of Evaluate, Plan, Do, Check and Amend, rather than the more traditional and easier option of starting by doing rather than evaluating. This will lead to a never-ending improvement helix (Figure 2.3).

This basic approach needs to be backed up with good project management, planning techniques and problem-solving methods, which can be taught to anyone in a relatively

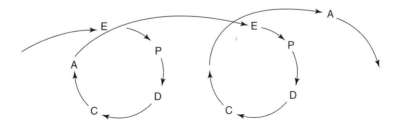

Figure 2.3 *The helix of never-ending improvement*

short period of time. The project management enables changes to be made successfully and the people to remove the obstacles in their way. Directors and managers need this training as much as other employees.

Ten points for senior management – the foundations of the TQM model

The vehicle for achieving effective leadership is total quality management. We have seen that it covers the entire organization, all the people and all the functions, including external organizations and suppliers. In the first two chapters, several facets of TQM have been reviewed, including:

- recognizing customers and discovering their needs
- setting standards that are consistent with customer requirements
- controlling processes, including systems, and improving their capability
- management's responsibility for setting the guiding philosophy, quality policy, etc., and providing motivation through leadership and equipping people to achieve quality
- empowerment of people at all levels in the organization to act for quality improvement.

The task of implementing TQM can be daunting, and the Chief Executive and directors faced with it may become confused and irritated by the proliferation of theories and packages. A simplification is required. The *core* of TQM must be the customer–supplier interfaces, both internally and externally, and the fact that at each interface there are processes to convert inputs to outputs. Clearly, there must be commitment to building-in quality through management of the inputs and processes.

How can senior managers and directors be helped in their understanding of what needs to be done to become committed to quality and implement the vision? Some American and Japanese quality 'gurus' have each set down a number of points or absolutes – words of wisdom in management and leadership – and many organizations are using these to establish a policy based on quality. These have been distilled down and modified here to ten points for senior management to adopt.

I The organization needs long-term COMMITMENT to constant improvement

There must be a constancy of purpose, and commitment to it must start from the top. The quality improvement process should be planned on a truly organization-wide basis, i.e. it must embrace all locations and departments and include customers, suppliers and subcontractors. It cannot start in 'one department' in the hope that the programme will spread from there.

The place to start the quality process is in the boardroom – leadership must be by example. Then the process should *progressively* expand to embrace all parts of the organization. It is wise to avoid the 'blitz' approach to TQM implementation, for it can lead to a lot of hype but no real changes in behaviour.

2 Adopt the philosophy of zero errors/defects to change the CULTURE to right first time

This should be based on a thorough understanding of the customer's needs and expectations, and on teamwork, developed through employee participation and rigorous application of the EPDCA helix.

3 Train the people to understand the CUSTOMER–SUPPLIER relationships

Again the commitment to customer needs must start from the top, from the Chairman or Chief Executive. Without that, time and effort will be wasted. Customer orientation should then be achieved for each and every employee, director and manager. The concept of internal customers and suppliers needs to be thoroughly understood and used.

4 Do not buy products or services on price alone – look at the TOTAL COST

Demand continuous improvement in everything, including suppliers. This will bring about improvements in product, service and failure rates. Continually improve the product or the service provided externally, so that the total cost of doing business is reduced.

5 Recognize that improvement of the SYSTEMS needs to be managed

Defining the performance standards expected and the systems to achieve them is a managerial responsibility. The rule has to be that the systems will be in line with the shared needs and expectations and will be part of the continuous improvement process.

6 Adopt modern methods of SUPERVISION and TRAINING – eliminate fear

It is all too easy to criticize mistakes, but it often seems difficult to praise efforts and achievements. Recognize and publicize efforts and achievements and provide the right sort of training, facilitation and supervision.

7 Eliminate barriers between departments by managing the PROCESS – improve COMMUNICATIONS and TEAMWORK

Barriers are often created by 'silo management' in which departments are treated like containers that are separate from one another. The customers are not interested in departments; they stand outside the organization and see slices through it – the *processes*. It is necessary to build teams and improve communications around the processes.

8 Eliminate the following:

- Arbitrary goals without methods.
- All standards based on numbers.
- Barriers to price of workmanship.
- Fiction. Get *FACTS* by using the correct *TOOLS*.

At all times it is essential to know how well you are doing in terms of satisfying the customers' needs and expectations. Help all employees to know *how* they will achieve their goals and how well they are doing.

Traditional piecework will not survive in a TQM environment, or vice versa, because it creates barriers and conflict. People should be proud of what they do and not be encouraged to behave like monkeys being thrown peanuts.

Train people to measure and report performance in language that the people doing the job can understand. Encourage each employee to measure his/her own performance. Do not stop with measuring performance in the organization – find out how well other organizations (competitive or otherwise) are performing against similar needs and expectations (*benchmark* against best practice).

The costs of quality mismanagement and the level of fire-fighting are excellent factual indicators of the internal health of an organization. They are relatively easily measured and simple for most people to understand.

9 Constantly educate and retrain – develop the 'EXPERTS' in the business

The experts in any business are the people who do the job every day of their lives. The 'energy' that lies within them can be released into the organization through education, training, encouragement and the chance to participate.

10 Develop a SYSTEMATIC approach to manage the implementation of TQM

TQM should not be regarded as a woolly-minded approach to running an organization. It requires a carefully planned and fully integrated strategy, derived from the mission. That way it will help any organization to realize its vision.

Summary
- Identify *customer–supplier* relationships.
- Manage *processes*.
- Change the *culture*.
- Improve *communication*.
- Show *commitment*.

The right culture, communication and commitment form the basis of the first part of a model for TQM – the 'soft' outcomes of TQM (Figure 2.4). The process core must be surrounded, however, by some 'hard' management necessities:

1 Systems (based on a good international standard; see Part 2 of this book).
2 Tools (for analysis, correlations and predictions for action for continuous improvement to be taken; see Part 3 of this book).
3 Teams (the councils, quality improvement teams, quality circles, corrective action teams, etc.; see Part 4 of this book).

The model now provides a multi-dimensional TQM 'vision' against which a particular organization's status can be examined, or against which a particular approach to TQM implementation may be compared and weaknesses highlighted. It is difficult

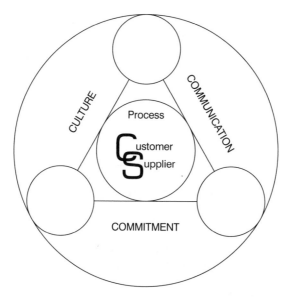

Figure 2.4 *Total quality management model – the 'soft' outcomes*

to draw in only two dimensions, but Figure 2.5 is an attempt to represent the major features of the model, the implementation of which is dealt with in Part 5.

One of the greatest tangible benefits of improved quality is the increased market share that results, rather than just the reduction in quality costs. The evidence for this can be seen already in some of the major consumer and industrial markets of the world.

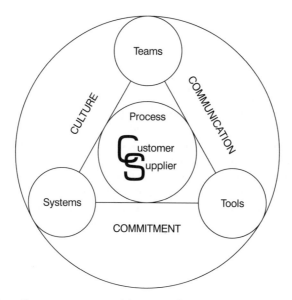

Figure 2.5 *Total quality management model – major features*

Superior quality can also be converted into premium prices and research now shows that quality clearly correlates with profit. The less tangible benefit of greater employee participation is equally, if not more, important in the longer term. The pursuit of continual improvement must become a way of life for everyone in an organization if it is to succeed in today's competitive environment.

Chapter highlights

The total quality management approach

- TQM is a comprehensive approach to improving competitiveness, effectiveness and flexibility through planning, organizing and understanding each activity, and involving each individual at each level. It is useful in all types of organization.
- TQM ensures that management adopts a strategic overview of quality and focuses on prevention, not detection, of problems.
- It often requires a mindset change to break down existing barriers. Managements that doubt the applicability of TQM should ask questions about the operation's costs, errors, wastes, standards, systems, training and job instructions.

Commitment and policy

- TQM starts at the top, where serious obsessional commitment to quality and leadership must be demonstrated. Middle management also has a key role to play in communicating the message.
- Every Chief Executive must accept the responsibility for commitment to a quality policy that deals with the organization for quality, the customer needs, the ability of the organization, supplied materials and services, education and training, and review of the management systems for never-ending improvement.

Creating or changing the culture

- The culture of an organization is formed by the beliefs, behaviours, norms, dominant values, rules and climate in the organization.
- Any organization needs a vision framework, comprising its guiding philosophy, core values and beliefs, purpose and mission.
- The effectiveness of an organization depends on the extent to which people perform their roles and move towards the common goals and objectives.
- TQM is concerned with moving the focus of control from the outside to the inside of individuals, so that everyone is accountable for his/her own performance.

Effective leadership

- Effective leadership starts with the Chief Executive's vision and develops into a strategy for implementation.

● Top management should develop the following for effective leadership: clear beliefs and objectives in the form of a mission statement; clear and effective strategies and supporting plans; the critical success factors and core processes; the appropriate management structure; employee participation through empowerment; and the EPDCA helix.

Ten points for senior management – the foundations of the TQM model

● Total quality is the key to effective leadership through commitment to constant improvement, a right first time philosophy, training people to understand customer–supplier relationships, not buying on price alone, managing systems improvement, modern supervision and training managing processes through teamwork and improved communications, elimination of barriers and fear, constant education and 'expert' development, a systematic approach to TQM implementation.
● The core of TQM is the customer–supplier relationship, where the processes must be managed. The 'soft' outcomes of TQM – the culture, communications and commitment – provide the foundation for the TQM model.
● The process core must be surrounded by the 'hard' management necessities of systems, tools and teams. The model provides a framework against which an organization's progress towards TQM can be examined.

Chapter 3

Design for quality

Design, innovation and improvement

Products, services and processes may be designed, both to add value to customers and to become more profitable. But leadership and management style is also designed, perhaps through internal communication methods and materials. Almost all areas of business have design issues inherent within them.

Design can be used to gain and hold on to competitive edge, save time and effort, deliver innovation, stimulate and motivate staff, simplify complex tasks, delight clients and stakeholders, dishearten competitors, achieve impact in a crowded market, and justify a premium price. Design can be used to take the drudgery out of the mundane and turn it into something inspiring, or simply make money. Design can be considered as a management function, a cultural phenomenon, an art form, a problem-solving process, a discrete activity, an end product or a service.

In the Collins Cobuild English Language Dictionary, design is defined as: 'the way in which something has been planned and made, including what it looks like and how well it works.' Using this definition, there is very little of an organization's activities that is not covered by 'planning' or 'making'. Clearly the consideration of what it looks like and how well it works in the eyes of the customer determines the success of products or services in the market place.

All organizations need to update their products, processes and services periodically. In markets such as electronics, audio and visual goods, and office automation, new variants of products are offered frequently – almost like fashion goods. While in other markets the pace of innovation may not be as fast and furious, there is no doubt that the rate of change for product, service and process design has accelerated on a broad front.

Innovation entails both the invention and design of radically new products and services, embodying novel ideas, discoveries and advanced technologies, *and* the continuous development and improvement of existing products, services and processes to enhance their performance and quality. It may also be directed at reducing costs of production or operations throughout the life cycle of the product or service system.

In many organizations innovation is predominantly either technology-led, e.g. in some chemical and engineering industries, or marketing-led, e.g. in some food companies. What is always striking about leading product or service innovators is that their developments are market-led, which is different from marketing-led. The latter means that the marketing function takes the lead in product and service developments. But most leading innovators identify and set out to meet the existing and potential demands profitably, and therefore are market-led, constantly striving to meet the requirements even more effectively through appropriate experimentation.

Everything we experience in or from an organization is the result of a design decision, or lack of one. This applies not just to the tangible things like products and services, but the intangibles too: the systems and processes which affect the generation of products and delivery of systems. Design is about combining function and form to achieve fitness for purpose, be it an improvement to a supersonic aircraft, the synthesis of a new drug, a staff incentive scheme or this book.

Once fitness for purpose has been achieved, of course, the goalposts change. Events force a reassessment of needs and expectations and customers want something different. In such a changing world, design is an ongoing activity, dynamic not static, a 'verb' not a noun – *design is a process*.

The design process

Commitment in the most senior management helps to build quality throughout the *design process* and to ensure good relationships and communication between various groups and functional areas. Designing customer satisfaction and loyalty into products and services contributes greatly to competitive success. Clearly, it does not guarantee it, because the conformance aspect of quality must be present and the operational processes must be capable of producing to the design. As in the marketing/operations interfaces, it is never acceptable to design a product, service, system or process that the customer wants but the organization is incapable of achieving.

The design process often concerns technological innovation in response to, or in anticipation of, changing market requirements and trends in technology. Those companies with impressive records of product- or service-led growth have demonstrated a state-of-the-art approach to innovation based on three principles:

- *Strategic balance* to ensure that both old and new product service developments are important. Updating old products, services and processes ensures continuing cash generation from which completely new products may be funded.
- *Top management approach* to design to set the tone and ensure that commitment is the common objective by visibly supporting the design effort. Direct control should be concentrated on critical decision points, since over-meddling by very senior people in day-to-day project management can delay and demotivate staff.
- *Teamwork*, to ensure that once projects are under way, specialist inputs, e.g. from marketing and technical experts, are fused and problems are tackled simultaneously.

The teamwork should be urgent yet informal, for too much formality will stifle initiative, flair and the fun of design.

The extent of the design process should not be underestimated, but it often is. Many people associate design with *styling* of products, and this is certainly an important aspect. But for certain products and many service operations the *secondary design* considerations are vital. Anyone who has bought an 'assemble-it-yourself' kitchen unit will know the importance of the design of the assembly instructions, for example. Aspects of design that affect quality in this way are packaging, customer-service arrangements, maintenance routines, warranty details and their fulfilment, spare-part availability, etc.

An industry that has learned much about the secondary design features of its products is personal computers. Many of the problems of customer dissatisfaction experienced in this market have not been product design features but problems with user manuals, availability and loading of software, and applications. For technically complex products or service systems, the design and marketing of after-sales arrangements are an essential component of the design activity. The design of production equipment and its layout to allow ease of access for repair and essential maintenance, or simple use as intended, widens the management of design quality into suppliers and contractors and requires their total commitment.

Proper design of plant and equipment plays a major role in the elimination of errors, defectives, and waste. Correct initial design also obviates the need for costly and wasteful modifications to be carried out after the plant or equipment has been constructed. It is at the plant design stage that such important matters as variability, reproducibility, ease of use in operation, maintainability, etc. should receive detailed consideration.

Designing

If design quality is taking care of all aspects of the customer's requirements, including cost, production, safe and easy use, and maintainability of products and services, then *designing* must take place in all aspects of:

- identifying the need (including need for change)
- developing that which satisfies the need
- checking the conformance to the need
- ensuring that the need is satisfied.

Designing covers every aspect, from the identification of a problem to be solved, usually a market need, through the development of design concepts and prototypes to the generation of detailed specifications or instructions required to produce the artefact or provide the service. It is the process of presenting needs in some physical form, initially as a solution, and then as a specific configuration or arrangement of materials resources, equipment and people. Design permeates strategically and operationally many areas of an organization and, while design professionals may control detailed product styling, decisions on design involve many people from other functions. Total quality management supports such cross-functional interpretation of design.

Design, like any other activity, must be carefully managed. A flowchart of the various stages and activities involved in the design and development process appears in Figure 3.1.

By structuring the design process in this way, it is possible to:

● Control the various stages.
● Check that they have been completed.

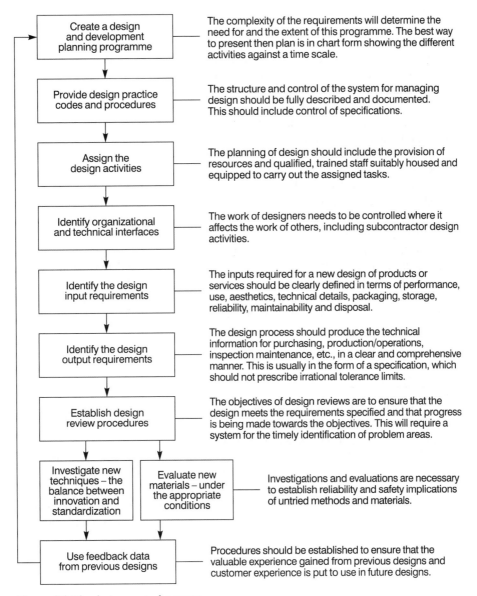

The complexity of the requirements will determine the need for and the extent of this programme. The best way to present then plan is in chart form showing the different activities against a time scale.

The structure and control of the system for managing design should be fully described and documented. This should include control of specifications.

The planning of design should include the provision of resources and qualified, trained staff suitably housed and equipped to carry out the assigned tasks.

The work of designers needs to be controlled where it affects the work of others, including subcontractor design activities.

The inputs required for a new design of products or services should be clearly defined in terms of performance, use, aesthetics, technical details, packaging, storage, reliability, maintainability and disposal.

The design process should produce the technical information for purchasing, production/operations, inspection maintenance, etc., in a clear and comprehensive manner. This is usually in the form of a specification, which should not prescribe irrational tolerance limits.

The objectives of design reviews are to ensure that the design meets the requirements specified and that progress is being made towards the objectives. This will require a system for the timely identification of problem areas.

Investigations and evaluations are necessary to establish reliability and safety implications of untried methods and materials.

Procedures should be established to ensure that the valuable experience gained from previous designs and customer experience is put to use in future designs.

Figure 3.1 *The design control process*

- Decide which management functions need to be brought in and at what stage.
- Estimate the level of resources needed.

The control of the design process must be carefully handled to avoid stifling the creativity of the designer(s), which is crucial in making design solutions a reality. It is clear that the design process requires a range of specialized skills, and the way in which these skills are managed, the way they interact, and the amount of effort devoted to the different stages of the design and development process are fundamental to the quality, producibility and price of the service or final product. A team approach to the management of design can play a major role in the success of a project.

It is never possible to exert the same tight control on the design effort as on other operational efforts, yet the cost and the time used are often substantial, and both must appear somewhere within the organization's budget.

Certain features make control of the design process difficult:

1 No design will ever be 'complete' in the sense that, with effort, some modification or improvement cannot be made.
2 Few designs are entirely novel. An examination of most 'new' products, services or processes will show that they employ existing techniques, components or systems to which have been added novel elements.
3 The longer the time spent on a design, the less the increase in the value of the design, unless a technological breakthrough is achieved. This diminishing return from the design effort must be carefully managed.
4 External and/or internal customers will impose limitations on design time and cost. It is as difficult to imagine a design project whose completion date is not implicitly fixed, either by a promise to a customer, the opening of a trade show or exhibition, a seasonal 'deadline', a production schedule, or some other constraint, as it is to imagine an organization whose funds are unlimited, or a product whose price has no ceiling.

Total design processes

Quality of design, then, concerns far more than the product or service design and its ability to meet the customer requirements. It is also about the activities of design and development. The appropriateness of the actual *design process* has a profound influence on the performance of any organization, and much can be learned by examining successful companies and how their strategies for research, design and development are linked to the efforts of marketing and operations. In some quarters this is referred to as 'total design', and the term 'simultaneous engineering' has been used. This is an integrated approach to a new product or service introduction, similar in many ways to Quality Function Deployment (QFD – see the next section) in using multifunction teams or task forces to ensure that research, design, development, manufacturing, purchasing, supply and marketing all work in parallel from concept through to the final launch of the product or service into the market place, including servicing and maintenance.

Quality function deployment (QFD) – the house of quality

The 'house of quality' is the framework of the approach to design management known as quality function deployment (QFD). It originated in Japan in 1972 at Mitsubishi's Kobe shipyard, but it has been developed in numerous ways by Toyota and its suppliers, and many other organizations. The house of quality (HOQ) concept, initially referred to as quality tables, has been used successfully by manufacturers of integrated circuits, synthetic rubber, construction equipment, engines, home appliances, clothing and electronics, mostly Japanese. Ford and General Motors use it, and other organizations, including AT&T, Bell Laboratories, Digital Equipment, Hewlett-Packard, Procter & Gamble, ITT, Rank Xerox and Jaguar have applications. In Japan its design applications include public services, retail outlets and apartment layout.

Quality function deployment is a 'system' for designing a product or service, based on customer demands, with the participation of members of all functions of the supplier organization. It translates the customer's requirements into the appropriate technical requirements for each stage. The activities included in QFD are:

1 Market research
2 Basic research
3 Innovation
4 Concept design
5 Prototype testing
6 Final-product or service testing
7 After-sales service and trouble-shooting.

These are performed by people with different skills in a team whose composition depends on many factors, including the products or services being developed and the size of the operation. In many industries, such as cars, video equipment, electronics and computers, 'engineering designers' are seen to be heavily into designing. But in other industries and service operations designing is carried out by people who do not carry the word 'designer' in their job title. The failure to recognize the design inputs they make, and to provide appropriate training and support, will limit the success of the design activities and result in some offering that does not satisfy the customer. This is particularly true of internal customers.

The QFD team in operation

The first step of a QFD exercise is to form a cross-functional QFD team. Its purpose is to take the needs of the market and translate them into such a form that they can be satisfied within the operating unit and delivered to the customers.

As with all organizational problems, the structure of the QFD team must be decided on the basis of the detailed requirements of each organization. One thing, however, is clear – close liaison must be maintained at all times between the design, marketing and operational functions represented in the team.

The QFD team must answer three questions – *WHO*, *WHAT* and *HOW*. That is:

- *WHO* are the customers?
- *WHAT* does the customer need?
- *HOW* will the needs be satisfied?

WHO may be decided by asking, 'Who will benefit from the successful introduction of this product, service, or process?' Once the customers have been identified, *WHAT* can be ascertained through interview/questionnaire/focus group processes, or from the knowledge and judgement of the QFD team members. *HOW* is more difficult to determine, and will consist of the attributes of the product, service or process under development. This will constitute many of the action steps in a 'QFD strategic plan'.

WHO, *WHAT* and *HOW* are entered into a QFD matrix or grid of 'house of quality', which is a simple 'quality table'. The *WHAT*s are recorded in rows and the *HOW*s are placed in the columns.

The HOQ provides structure to the design and development cycle, often likened to the construction of a house, because of the shape of the matrices when they are fitted together. The key to building the house is the focus on the customer requirements, so that the design and development processes are driven more by what the customer needs than by innovations in technology. This ensures that more effort is used to obtain vital customer information. It may increase the initial planning time in a particular development project, but the overall time, including design and redesign, taken to bringing a product of service to the market will be reduced.

This requires that marketing people, design staff (including engineers) and production/operations personnel work closely together from the time the new service, process or product is conceived. It will need to replace in many organizations the 'throwing it over the wall' approach, where a solid wall exists between each pair of functions (Figure 3.2).

The HOQ provides an organization with the means for inter-departmental or inter-functional planning and communications, starting with the so-called customer

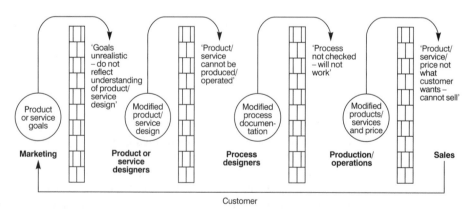

Figure 3.2 *'Throw it over the wall.' The design and development process is sequential and walled into separate functions*

attributes (CAs). These are phrases customers use to describe product, process and service characteristics.

A complete QFD project will lead to the construction of a sequence of HOQ diagrams, which translate the customer requirements into specific operational process steps. For example, the 'feel' that customers like on the steering wheel of a motor car may translate into a specification for 45 standard degrees of synthetic polymer hardness, which in turn translates into specific manufacturing process steps, including the use of certain catalysts, temperatures, processes and additives.

The first steps in QFD lead to a consideration of the product as a whole, and subsequent steps to consideration of the individual components. For example, a complete hotel service would be considered at the first level, but subsequent QFD exercises would tackle the restaurant, bedrooms and reception. Each of the sub-services would have customer requirements, but they all would need to be compatible with the general service concept.

The QFD or house of quality tables

Figure 3.3 shows the essential components of the quality table or HOQ diagram. The construction begins with the *customer requirements*, which are determined through the

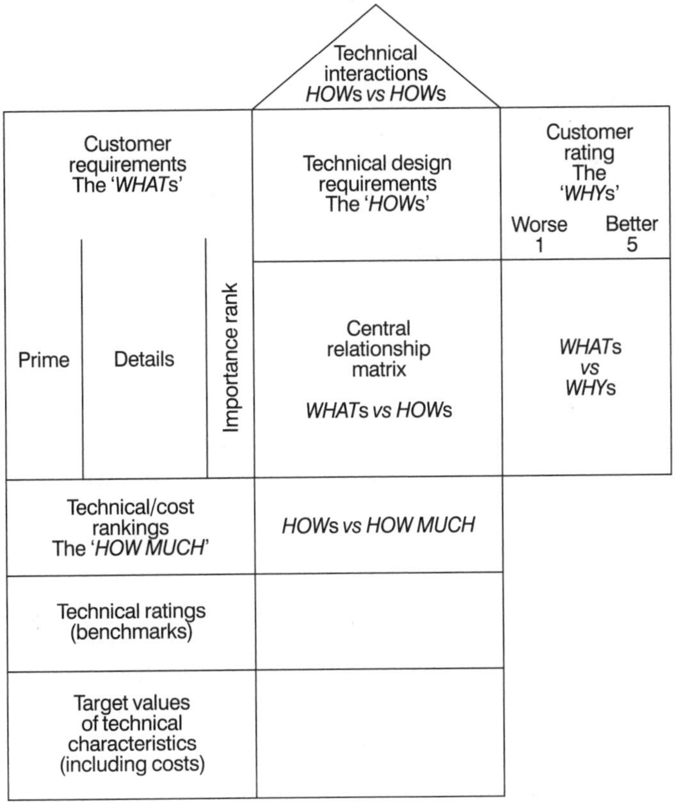

Figure 3.3 *The house of quality*

'voice of the customer' – the marketing and market research activities. These are entered into the blocks to the left of the central relationship matrix. Understanding and prioritizing the customer requirements by the QFD team may require the use of competitive and compliant analysis, focus groups, and the analysis of market potential. The prime or broad requirements should lead to the detailed *WHATs*.

Once the customer requirements have been determined and entered into the table, the *importance* of each is rated and rankings are added. The use of the 'emphasis technique' or paired comparison may be helpful here (see Chapter 8).

Each customer requirement should then be examined in terms of customer rating; a group of customers may be asked how they perceive the performance of the organization's product or service versus those of competitors'. These results are placed to the right of the central matrix. Hence the customer requirements' importance rankings and competition ratings appear from left to right across the house.

The *WHATs* must now be converted into the *HOWs*. These are called the *technical design requirements* and appear on the diagram from top to bottom in terms of requirements, rankings (or costs) and ratings against competition (technical benchmarking, see Chapter 7). These will provide the 'voice of the process'.

The technical design requirements themselves are placed immediately above the central matrix and may also be given a hierarchy of prime and detailed requirements. Immediately below the customer requirements appear the rankings of technical difficulty, development time or costs. These will enable the QFD team to discuss the efficiency of the various technical solutions. Below the technical rankings on the diagram comes the benchmark data, which compares the technical processes of the organization against its competitors'.

The *central relationship matrix* is the working core of the HOQ diagram. Here the *WHATs* are matched with the *HOWs*, and each customer requirement is systematically assessed against each technical design requirement. The nature of any relationship – strong positive, positive, neutral, negative, strong negative – is shown by symbols in the matrix. The QFD team carries out the relationship estimation, using experience and judgement, the aim being to identify *HOW* the *WHATs* may be achieved. All the *HOWs* listed must be necessary and together sufficient to achieve the *WHATs*. Blank rows (customer requirements not met) and columns (redundant technical characteristics) should not exist.

The roof of the house shows the interactions between the technical design requirements. Each characteristic is matched against the others, and the diagonal format allows the nature of relationships to be displayed. The symbols used are the same as those in the central matrix.

The complete QFD process is time-consuming, because each cell in the central and roof matrices must be examined by the whole team. The team must examine the matrix to determine which technical requirement will need design attention, and the costs of that attention will be given in the bottom row. If certain technical costs become a major issue, the priorities may then be changed. It will be clear from the central matrix if there is more than one way to achieve a particular customer requirement, and the roof matrix wiil show if the technical requirements to achieve one customer requirement will have a negative effect on another technical issue.

The very bottom of the HOQ diagram shows the *target* values of the *technical characteristics*, which are expressed in physical terms. They can only be decided by the team after discussion of the complete house contents. While these targets are the physical output of the QFD exercise, the whole process of information-gathering, structuring and ranking generates a tremendous improvement in the team's cross-functional understanding of the product/service design delivery system. The target technical characteristics may be used to generate the next level HOQ diagram, where they become the *WHATs*, and the QFD process determines the further details of *HOW* they are to be achieved. In this way the process 'deploys' the customer requirements all the way to the final operational stages. Figure 3.4 shows how the target technical characteristics at each level become the inputs to the next level matrix.

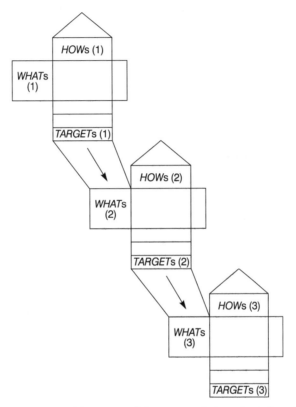

Figure 3.4 *The 'deployment' of the 'voice of the customer' through quality tables*

QFD progresses now through the use of the 'seven new planning tools'[1] and other standard techniques such as value analysis,[2] experimental design,[3] statistical process control,[4] and so on.

The benefits of QFD

The aim of the HOQ is to co-ordinate the inter-functional activities and skills within an organization. This should lead to products and services designed, produced/operated and marketed so that customers will want to purchase them and continue doing so.

The use of competitive information in QFD should help to prioritize resources and to structure the existing experience and information. This allows the identification of items that can be acted upon.

There should be reductions in the number of midstream design changes, and these reductions in turn will limit post-introduction problems and reduce implementation time. Because QFD is consensus-based, it promotes teamwork and creates communications at functional interfaces, while also identifying required actions. It should lead to a 'global view' of the development process, from a consideration of all the details.

If QFD is introduced systematically, it should add structure to the information, generate a framework for sensitivity analysis, and provide documentation, which must be 'living' and adaptable to change. In order to understand the full impact of QFD it is necessary to examine the changes that take place in the team and the organization during the design and development process.

The main benefit of QFD is of course the increase in customer satisfaction and loyalty, which may be measured in terms of, for example, repeat business and reductions in warranty claims.

Specifications and standards

There is a strong relationship between standardization and specification. To ensure that a product or a service is *standardized* and may be repeated a large number of times in exactly the manner required, *specifications* must be written so that they are open to only one interpretation. The requirements, and therefore the quality, must be built into the design specification. There are national and international standards which, if used, help to ensure that specifications will meet certain accepted criteria of technical or managerial performance, safety, etc.

Standardization does not guarantee that the best design or specification is selected. It may be argued that the whole process of standardization slows down the rate and direction of technological development, and affects what is produced. If standards are used correctly, however, the process of drawing up specifications should provide opportunities to learn more about particular innovations and to change the standards accordingly.

It is possible to strike a balance between innovation and standardization. Clearly, it is desirable for designers to adhere where possible to past-proven materials and methods, in the interests of reliability, maintainability and variety control. Hindering designers from using recently developed materials, components or techniques, however, can cause the design process to stagnate technologically. A balance must be achieved by analysis of materials, products and processes proposed in the design, against the background of their known reproducibility and reliability. If breakthrough innovations are proposed, then analysis or testing should be indicated objectively, justifying their adoption in preference to the established alternatives.

It is useful to define a specification. The International Standards Organization (ISO) defines it in ISO 8402 (1986) as 'The document that prescribes the requirements with which the product or service has to conform'. A document not giving a detailed statement or description of the requirements to which the product, service or process must comply cannot be regarded as a specification, and this is true of much sales literature.

The specification conveys the customer requirements to the supplier to allow the product or service to be designed, engineered, produced or operated by means of conventional or stipulated equipment, techniques and technology. The basic requirements of a specification are that it gives the:

- performance requirements of the product or service
- parameters – such as dimensions, concentration, turn-round time – which describe the product or service adequately (these should be quantified and include the units of measurement)
- materials to be used by stipulating properties or referring to other specifications
- method of production or delivery of the service
- inspection/testing/checking requirements
- references to other applicable specifications or documents.

To fulfil its purpose the specification must be written in terminology that is readily understood, and in a manner that is unambiguous and so cannot be subject to differing interpretation. This is not an easy task, and is one which requires all the expertise and knowledge available. Good specifications are usually the product of much discussion, deliberation and sifting of information and data, and represent tangible output from a QFD team.

Design in the service sector

The emergence of the services sector has been suggested by economists to be part of the natural progression in which economic dominance changes first from agriculture to manufacturing and then to services. It is argued that if income elasticity of demand is higher for services than it is for goods, then as incomes rise, resources will shift toward services. The continuing growth of services verifies this, and is further explained by changes in culture, fitness, safety, demography and lifestyles.

In considering the design of a service it is important to consider the differences between goods and services. Some authors argue that the marketing and design of goods and services should conform to the same fundamental rules, whereas others claim that there is a need for a different approach to services because of the recognizable differences between the goods and services themselves.

In terms of design, it is possible to recognize three distinct elements in the service package – the physical elements or facilitating goods, the explicit service or sensual benefits, and the implicit service or psychological benefits. In addition, the particular characteristics of service delivery systems may be itemized:

- Intangibility
- Perishability
- Simultaneity
- Heterogeneity.

It is difficult, if not impossible, to design the intangible aspects of a service, since consumers often must use experience or the reputation of a service organization and its representatives to judge quality.

Perishability is often an important issue in services, since it is often impossible or undesirable to hold stocks of the explicit service element of the service package. This aspect often requires that service operation and service delivery must exist simultaneously.

Simultaneity occurs because the consumer must be present before many services can take place. Hence, services are often formed in small and dispersed units, and it is difficult to take advantage of economies of scale. The rapid developments in computing and communications technologies are changing this in sectors such as banking, but contact continues to be necessary for many service sectors. Design considerations here include the environment and the systems used. Service facilities, procedures and systems should be designed with the customer in mind, as well as the 'product' and the human resources. Managers need a picture of the total span of the operation, so that factors which are crucial to success are not neglected. This clearly means that the functions of marketing, design and operations cannot be separated in services, and this must be taken into account in the design of the operational controls, such as the diagnosing of individual customer expectations. A QFD approach here is most appropriate.

Heterogeneity of services occurs in consequence of explicit and implicit service elements relying on individual preferences and perceptions. Differences exist in the outputs of organizations generating the same service, within the same organization, and even the same employee on different occasions. Clearly, unnecessary variation needs to be controlled, but the variation attributed to estimating, and then matching, the consumers' requirements is essential to customer satisfaction and loyalty and must be designed into the systems. This inherent variability does, however, make it difficult to set precise quantifiable standards for all the elements of the service.

In the design of services it is useful to classify them in some way. Several sources from the literature on the subject help us to place services in one of five categories:

- Service factory
- Service shop
- Mass service
- Professional service
- Personal services.

Several service attributes have particular significance for the design of service operations:

1 *Labour intensity* – the ratio of labour costs incurred to the value of assets and equipment used (people versus equipment-based services).
2 *Contact* – the proportion of the total time required to provide the service for which the consumer is present in the system.
3 *Interaction* – the extent to which the consumer actively intervenes in the service process to change the content of the service; this includes customer participation to provide information from which needs can be assessed, and customer feedback from which satisfaction levels can be inferred.

4 *Customization* – which includes *choice* (providing one or more selections from a range of options, which can be single or fixed) and *adaptation* (the interaction process in which the requirement is decided, designed and delivered to match the need).
5 *Nature of service act* – either tangible, i.e. perceptible to touch and can be owned, or intangible, i.e. insubstantial.
6 *Recipient of service* – either people or things.

Table 3.1 gives a list of some services with their assigned attribute types and Table 3.2 shows how these may be used to group the services under the various classifications.

Table 3.1 *A classification of selected services*

Service	Labour intensity	Contact	Inter- action	Custom- ization	Nature of act	Recipient of service
Accountant	High	Low	High	Adapt	Intangible	Things
Architect	High	Low	High	Adapt	Intangible	Things
Bank	Low	Low	Low	Fixed	Intangible	Things
Beautician	High	High	High	Adapt	Tangible	People
Bus/coach service	Low	High	High	Choice	Tangible	People
Cafeteria	Low	High	High	Choice	Tangible	People
Cleaning firm	High	Low	Low	Fixed	Tangible	People
Clinic	Low	High	High	Adapt	Tangible	People
Sports coaching	High	High	High	Adapt	Intangible	People
College	High	High	Low	Fixed	Intangible	People
Courier firm	High	Low	Low	Adapt	Tangible	Things
Dental practice	High	High	High	Adapt	Tangible	Things
Driving school	High	High	High	Adapt	Intangible	People
Equip. hire	Low	Low	Low	Choice	Tangible	Things
Finance consult.	High	Low	High	Adapt	Intangible	People
Hairdresser	High	High	High	Adapt	Tangible	People
Hotel	High	High	Low	Choice	Tangible	People
Leisure centre	Low	High	High	Choice	Tangible	People
Maintenance	Low	Low	Low	Choice	Tangible	Things
Manage. consult.	High	High	High	Adapt	Intangible	People
Nursery	High	Low	Low	Fixed	Tangible	People
Optician	High	Low	High	Adapt	Tangible	People
Postal service	Low	Low	Low	Adapt	Tangible	Things
Rail service	Low	High	Low	Choice	Tangible	People
Repair firm	Low	Low	Low	Adapt	Tangible	Things
Restaurant	High	High	Low	Choice	Tangible	People
Service station	Low	High	High	Choice	Tangible	People
Solicitors	High	Low	High	Adapt	Intangible	Things
Take away	High	Low	Low	Choice	Tangible	People
Veterinary	High	Low	High	Adapt	Tangible	Things

Table 3.2 *Grouping of similar services*

PERSONAL SERVICES

Driving school	Sports coaching
Beautician	Dental practice
Hairdresser	Optician

SERVICE SHOP

Clinic	Cafeteria
Leisure centre	Service station

PROFESSIONAL SERVICES

Accountant	Architect
Finance consultant	Management consultant
Solicitor	Veterinary

MASS SERVICES

Hotel	Restaurant
College	Bus service
Coach service	Rail service
Take away	Nursery
Courier firm	

SERVICE FACTORY

Cleaning firm	Postal service
Repair firm	Equipment hire
Maintenance	Bank

It is apparent that services are part of almost all organizations and not confined to the service sector. What is clear is that the service classifications and different attributes must be considered in any service design process.

(The author is grateful to the contribution made by John Dotchin to this section of Chapter 3.)

The links between good design and managing the business

Recent research carried out by the European Centre for Business Excellence[5] has led to a series of specific aspects that should be addressed to integrate design into the business or organization. These are presented under various business criteria below:

Leadership and management style
- 'Listening' is designed into the organization.
- Management communicates the importance of good design in good partnerships and vice versa.

- A management style is adopted that fosters innovation and creativity, and that motivates employees to work together effectively.

Customers, strategy and planning

- The customer is designed into the organization as a focus to shape policy and strategy decisions.
- Designers and customers communicate directly.
- Customers are included in the design process.
- Customers are helped to articulate and participate in the understanding of their own requirements.
- Systems are in place to ensure that the changing needs of the customers inform changes to policy and strategy.
- Design and innovation performance measures are incorporated into policy and strategy reviews.
- The design process responds quickly to customers.

People – their management and satisfaction

- People are encouraged to gain a holistic view of design within the organization.
- There is commitment to design teams and their motivation, particularly in cross-functional teamwork (e.g. quality function deployment teams).
- The training programme is designed, with respect to design, in terms of people skills training (e.g. interpersonal, management teamwork) and technical training (e.g. resources, software).
- Training helps integrate design activities into the business.
- Training impacts on design (e.g. honing creativity and keeping people up to date with design concepts and activity).
- Design activities are communicated (including new product or service concepts).
- Job satisfaction is harnessed to foster good design.
- The results of employee surveys are fed back into the design process.

Resource management

- Knowledge is managed proactively, including investment in technology.
- Information is shared in the organization.
- Past experience and learning is captured from design projects and staff.
- Information resources are available for planning design projects.
- Suppliers contribute to innovation, creativity and design concepts.
- Concurrent engineering and design is integrated through the supply chains.

Process management

- Design is placed at the centre of process planning to integrate different functions within the organization and form partnerships outside the organization.
- 'Process thinking' is used to resolve design problems and foster teamwork within the organization and with external partners.

Impact on society and business performance

- Consideration is given to how the design of a product or service impacts or.
  - the environment
  - the recyclability and disposal of materials

- packaging and wastage of resources
- the (local) economy (e.g. reduction of labour requirements)
- the business results, both financial and non-financial

This same research showed that strong links exist between good design and proactive flexible deployment of business policies and strategies. These can be used to further improve design by encouraging the sharing of best practice within and across industries, by allowing designers and customers to communicate directly, by instigating new product/service introduction policies, project audits and design/innovation measurement policies and by communicating the strategy to employees. The findings of this work may be summarized by thinking in terms of the 'value chain', as shown in Figure 3.5.

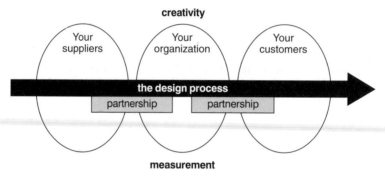

Figure 3.5 *The value chain*

Effective people management skills are essential for good design – these include the ability to listen and communicate, to motivate employees and encourage teamwork, as well as the ability to create an organizational climate which is conducive to creativity and continuous innovation.

The only way to ensure that design actively contributes to business performance is to make sure it happens 'by design', rather than by accident. In short, it needs co-ordinating and managing right across the organization.

Chapter highlights

Design, innovation and improvement

- Design is a multifaceted activity which covers many aspects of an organization.
- All businesses need to update their products, processes and services.
- Innovation entails both invention and design, *and* continuous improvement of existing products, services and processes.

- Leading product/service innovations are market-led, not marketing-led.
- Everything in or from an organization results from design decisions.
- Design is an ongoing activity, dynamic not static, a 'verb' not a noun – design is a process.

The design process

- Commitment at the top is required to building-in quality throughout the design process. Moreover, the operational processes must be capable of achieving the design.
- State-of-the-art approach to innovation is based on a strategic balance of old and new, top management approach to design, and teamwork.
- The 'styling' of products must also be matched by secondary design considerations, such as operating instructions and software support.
- Designing takes in all aspects of identifying the need, developing something to satisfy the need, checking conformance to the need and ensuring the need is satisfied.
- The design process must be carefully managed and can be flowcharted, like any other process, into: planning, practice codes, procedures, activities assignments, identification of organizational and technical interfaces and design input requirements, review investigation and evaluation of new techniques and materials, and use of feedback data from previous designs.
- Total design or 'simultaneous engineering' is similar to quality function deployment and uses multifunction teams to provide an integrated approach to product or service introduction.

Quality function deployment (QDF) – the house of quality

- The 'house of quality' (HOQ) is the framework of the approach to design management known as quality function deployment (QFD). It provides structure to the design and development cycle, which is driven by customer needs rather than innovation in technology.
- QFD is a system for designing a product or service, based on customer demands, and bringing in all members of the supplier organization.
- A QFD team's purpose is to take the needs of the market and translate them into such a form that they can be satisfied within the operating unit.
- The QFD team answers the following question. *WHO* are the customers? *WHAT* do the customers need? *HOW* will the needs be satisfied?
- The answers to the *WHO*, *WHAT* and *HOW* questions are entered into the QFD matrix or quality table, one of the seven new tools of planning and design.
- The foundations of the HOQ are the customer requirements; the framework is the central planning matrix, which matches the 'voice of the customer' with the 'voice of the processes' (the technical descriptions and capabilities); and the roof is the interrelationships matrix between the technical design requirements.
- The benefits of QFD include customer-driven design, prioritizing of resources, reductions in design change and implementation time, and improvements in teamwork, communications, functional interfaces and customer satisfaction.

Specifications and standards

- There is a strong relation between standardization and specifications. If standards are used correctly, the process of drawing up specifications should provide opportunities to learn more about innovations and change standards accordingly.
- The aim of specifications should be to reflect the true requirements of the product/service that are capable of being achieved.

Design in the service sector

- In the design of services, three distinct elements may be recognized in the service package: physical (facilitating goods), explicit service (sensual benefits) and implicit service (psychological benefits). Moreover, the characteristics of service delivery may be itemized as intangibility, perishability, simultaneity and heterogeneity.
- Services may be classified generally as service factory, service shop, mass service, professional service and personal service. The service attributes that are important in designing services include labour intensity, contact interaction, customerization, nature of service act and the direct recipient of the act.
- Use of this framework allows services to be grouped under the five classifications.

The links between good design and managing the business

- Recent research[5] has led to a series of specific aspects to address in order to integrate design into an organization.
- The aspects may be summarized under the headings of: leadership and management style; customers, strategy and planning; people – their management and satisfaction; resource management; process management; impact on society and business performance.
- The research shows that strong links exist between good design and proactive flexible deployment of business policies and strategies – design needs co-ordinating and managing right across the organization.

References

1. Oakland, J.S., *Total Quality Management* (2nd edition), Butterworth-Heinemann, 1993.
2. Lockyer, K.G., Muhlemann, A.P. and Oakland, J.S., *Production and Operations Management* (6th edition), Pitman, 1992.
3. Caulcutt, R., *Statistics in Research and Development* (2nd edition), Chapman and Hall, 1991.
4. Oakland, J.S., *Statistical Process Control* (4th edition), Butterworth-Heinemann, 1999.
5. *Designing Business Excellence,* European Centre for Business Excellence (the Research and Education Division of Oakland Consulting plc, 33 Park Square, Leeds LS1 2PF) / British Quality Foundation / Design Council, 1998.

Discussion questions

1 You are planning to open a wine bar, and have secured the necessary capital. Your aim is to attract both regular customers and passing trade.

 Discuss the key implications of this for the management of the business.

2 Discuss the following:

 a) the difference between quality and reliability
 b) total quality related costs (Part 3)
 c) 100% inspection.

3 Discuss the various facets of the 'quality control' function, paying particular attention to its interfaces with the other functional areas within the organization.

4 Explain what you understand by the term 'Total Quality Management', paying particular attention to the following terms: quality, supplier–customer interfaces, and process.

5 Present a 'model' for total quality management, describing briefly the various elements of the model.

6 You are a management consultant with particular expertise in the area of product design and development. You are at present working on projects for four firms:

 a) a chain of hotels
 b) a mail order goods firm
 c) a furniture manufacture
 d) a road construction contractor.

 What factors do you consider are important generally in your area of specialization? Compare and contrast how these factors apply to your four current projects.

7 Select one of the so-called 'gurus' of quality management, such as Juran, Deming, Crosby or Ishikawa, and explain his approach, with respect to the 'Oakland Model' of TQM. Discuss the strengths and weaknesses of the approach using this framework.

8 Discuss the application of the TQM concept in the service sector, paying particular attention to the nature of services and the customer–supplier interfaces.

9 In your new role as quality manager of the high-tech unit of a large national company, you identify a problem which is typified by the two internal memos shown below. Discuss in some detail the problems illustrated by this conflict, explaining how you would set about trying to make improvements.

From: Marketing Director
To: Managing Director
c.c.
Production Director
Works Manager

Date: 4th August

We have recently carried out a customer survey to examine how well we are doing in the market. With regard to our product range, the reactions were generally good, but the 24 byte microwinkle thrystor is a problem. Without exception everyone we interviewed said that its quality is not good enough. Although it is not yet apparent, we will inevitably lose our market share.

As a matter of urgency, therefore, will you please authorize a complete redesign of this product?

From: Works Manager
To: Production Director
Date: 6th August

This really is ridiculous!

I have all the QC records for the past ten years on this product. How can there be anything seriously wrong with the quality when we only get 0.1% rejects at final inspection and less than 0.01% returns from customers?

10 Discuss the application of quality function deployment (QFD) and the 'house of quality' in:

a) a fast-moving consumer goods (fmcg) company, such as one which designs, produces and sells/distributes cosmetic products
b) an industrial company, such as one producing plastic material
c) a commercial service organization such as a bank or insurance company.

TQM – The Role of the Quality System

I must Create a System, or be enslav'd by another Man's.

William Blake, 1757–1827, from 'Jerusalem'

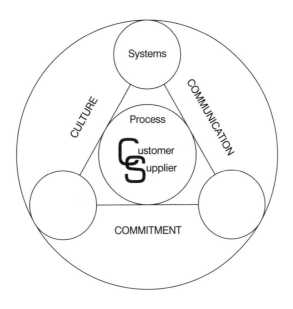

Chapter 4

Planning and processes for quality

Quality planning

Systematic planning is a basic requirement for effective quality management in all organizations. For quality planning to be useful, however, it must be part of a continuous review process that has as its objective zero errors or defectives, through a strategy of never-ending improvement. Before an appropriate quality management system can be developed, it is necessary to carry out a preliminary analysis to ensure that a quality organization structure exists, that the resources required will be made available, and that the various assignments will be carried out. This analysis has been outlined in the flowchart of Figure 4.1. The answers to the questions will generate the appropriate action plans.

In quality planning it is always necessary to review existing programmes within the organization's functional areas, and these may be compared with the results of the preliminary analysis to appraise the strengths and areas for improvement throughout the business or operation. When this has been done, the required systems and programmes may be defined in terms of detailed operating plans, procedures and techniques. This may proceed through the flowchart of Figure 4.2, which provides a logical approach to developing a multifunctional total quality management system.

A quality plan

A quality plan is a document which is specific to each product, activity or service (or group) that sets out the necessary quality-related activities. The plan should include references to any:

- Purchased material or service specifications
- Quality system procedures
- Product formulation or service type

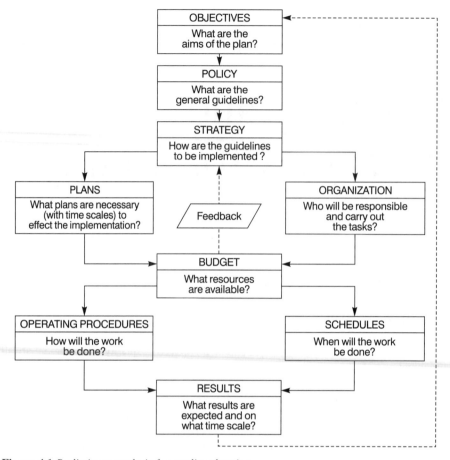

Figure 4.1 *Preliminary analysis for quality planning*

- Process control
- Sampling and inspection procedures
- Packaging or distribution specifications
- Miscellaneous, relevant procedures.

Such a quality plan might form part of a detailed operating procedure.

For projects relating to new products or services, or to new processes, written quality plans should be prepared to define:

1 Specific allocation of responsibility and authority during the different stages of the project.
2 Specific procedures, methods and instructions to be applied throughout the project.
3 Appropriate inspection, testing, checking or audit programmes required at various defined stages.
4 Methods of changes or modifications in the plan as the project proceeds.

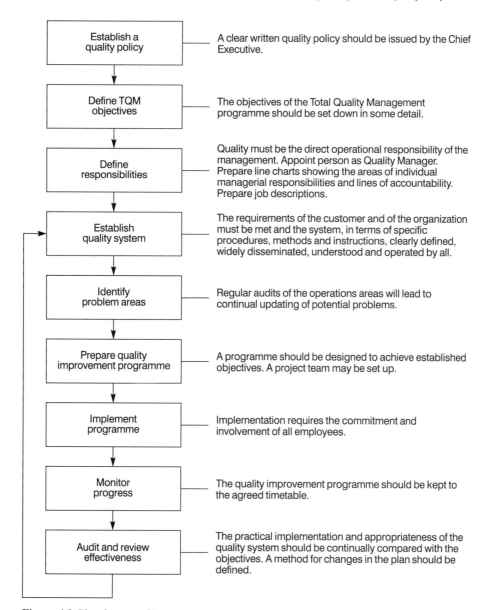

Figure 4.2 *Plan for a quality system*

Some of the main points in the planning of quality relate very much to the *inputs* of processes:

- *Plant/equipment* – the design, layout and inspection of plant and equipment, including heating, lighting, storage, disposal of waste, etc.
- *Processes* – the design, and monitoring of processes to reduce to a minimum the possibility of malfunction and/or failure.

- *Workplace* – the establishment and maintenance of suitable, clean and orderly places of work.
- *Facilities* – the provision and maintenance of adequate facilities.
- *Procedures* – the preparation of procedures for all operations. These may be in the form of general plans and guides rather than tremendous detail, but they should include specific operational duties and responsibilities.
- *Training* – the provision of effective training in quality, technology, process and plant operation.
- *Information* – the lifeblood of all quality management systems. All processes should be accompanied by good data collection, recording and analysis, followed by appropriate action.

The quality plan should focus on providing action to prevent cash leaking away through waste. If the quality management system does not achieve this, then there is something wrong with the plan and the way it has been set up or operated – not with the principle. The whole approach should be methodical and systematic, and designed to function irrespective of changes in management or personnel.

The principles and practice of setting up a good quality management system are set out in Chapter 5. The quality system must be planned and developed to take into account all other functions, such as design, development, production or operations, subcontracting, installation, maintenance, and so on. The remainder of this chapter is devoted to certain aspects of quality planning and processes that require specific attention or techniques.

The Process Classification Framework

The Process Classification Framework was developed and copyrighted by the American Productivity and Quality Center (APQC) International Benchmarking Clearinghouse, with the assistance of several major international corporations, and is in close partnership with Arthur Andersen & Co.

The intent was to create a high-level generic enterprise model that encourages businesses and other organizations to see their activities from a cross-industry, process viewpoint rather than from a narrow, functional viewpoint.

The Process Classification Framework supplies a generic view of business processes often found in multiple industries and sectors – manufacturing and service companies, health care, government, education, and others. Many organizations now seek to understand their inner workings from a horizontal, process viewpoint, rather than from a vertical, functional viewpoint.

The Process Classification Framework seeks to represent major processes and subprocesses, not functions, through its structure (Figure 4.3) and vocabulary. The framework does not list all processes within any specific organization. Likewise, not every process listed in the framework is present in every organization.

About the framework

The Process Classification Framework was originally envisioned as a 'taxonomy' of business processes during the design of the American Productivity & Quality Center's

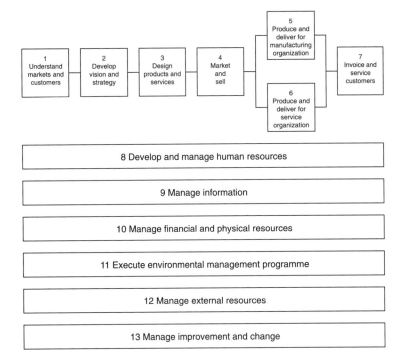

Figure 4.3 *Process Classification Framework: overview*

International Benchmarking Clearinghouse. That design process involved more than 80 organizations with a strong interest in advancing the use of benchmarking in the USA and around the world. The Process Classification Framework can be a useful tool in understanding and mapping business processes. In particular, a number of organizations have used the framework to classify both internal and external information for the purpose of cross-functional and cross-divisional communication.

The Process Classification Framework is an evolving document and the Center will continue to enhance and improve it on a regular basis. To that end, the Center welcomes your comments, suggestions for improvement, and any insights you gain from applying it within your organization. The Center would like to see the Process Classification Framework receive wide distribution, discussion and use. Therefore, it grants permission for copying the framework, as long as acknowledgement is made to the American Productivity & Quality Center.*

*Please direct your comments, suggestions and questions to:

APAC International Benchmarking Clearinghouse Information Services Dept.
123 North Post Oak Lane, 3rd Floor, Houston, Texas 77024.

713–681–4020 (phone)
713–681–8578 (fax)
Internet: apqcinfo@apqc.org

For updates, visit the Web site at http://www.apqc.org.

Process modelling

More than 25 years ago the US Air Force adopted Integration Definition Function Modelling (IDEF0), as part of its Integrated Computer-Aided Manufacturing (ICAM) architecture. The IDEF0 modelling language, now described in a Federal Information Processing Standards Publication (FIPS PUBS), provides a useful structured graphical framework for describing and improving business processes. The associated Integration Definition for Information Modelling (IDEFIX) language allows the development of a logical model of data associated with processes, such as measurement.

These techniques are widely used in business process re-engineering (BPR) and business process improvement (BPI) projects, and to integrate process information. A range of specialist software (including Windows/PC based) is also available to support the applications. IDEF0 may be used to model a wide variety of new and existing processes, define the requirements, and design an implementation to meet the requirements.

An IDEF0 model consists of a hierarchical series of diagrams, text and glossary, cross-referenced to each other through boxes (process components) and arrows (data and objects). The method is expressive and comprehensive and is capable of representing a wide variety of business, service and manufacturing processes. The relatively simple language allows coherent, rigorous and precise process expression, and promotes consistency (Figure 4.4).

For a full description of the IDEF0 methodology it is necessary to consult the FIPS PUBS standard (Federal Information Processing Standard Publication 183 (December 1993), National Institute of Standards and Technology (NIST)). It should be possible, however, from the simple description given here, to begin process modelling (or mapping) using the technique.

Processes can be any combination of things, including people, information, software, equipment, systems, products or materials. The IDEF0 model describes what a process

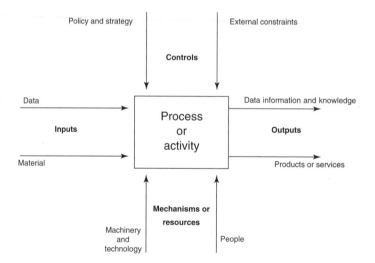

Figure 4.4 *IDEF0 process language. Federal Information Processing Standard Publication 183 (December 1993), National Institute of Standards and Technology (NIST)*

does, what controls it, what things it works on, what means it uses to perform its functions, and what it produces. The combined graphics and text are comprised of:

- **Boxes**, which provide a description of what happens in the form of an active verb or verb phrase.
- **Arrows**, which convey data or objects related to the processes to be performed (they do not represent flow or sequence as in the traditional process flow model).

Each side of the process box has a standard meaning in terms of box/arrow relationships. Arrows on the left side of the box are **inputs**, which are transformed or consumed by the process to produce **output** arrows on the right side. Arrows entering the top of the box are **controls** which specify the conditions required for the process to generate the correct outputs. Arrows connected to the bottom of the box represent '**mechanisms**' or **resources**. The abbreviation ICOR (inputs, controls, outputs, resources) is sometimes used.

Using these relationships, process diagrams are broken down or decomposed into more detailed diagrams, the top-level diagram providing a description of the highest level process. This is followed by a series of child diagrams providing details of the subprocesses (Figure 4.5).

Each process model has a top-level diagram on which the process is represented by a single box with its surrounding arrows (e.g. Figure 4.6). Each subprocess is modelled individually by a box, with parent boxes detailed by child diagrams at the next lower level (e.g. Figure 4.7).

Text and glossary

An IDEFO diagram may have associated structured text to give an overview of the process model. This may also be used to highlight features, flows and inter-box connections and to clarify significant patterns. A glossary may be used to define acronyms, key words and phrases used in the diagrams.

Arrows

Arrows on high-level IDEF0 diagrams represent data or objects as constraints. Only at low levels of detail can arrows represent flow or sequence. These high-level arrows may usefully be thought of as pipelines or conduits with general labels. An arrow may branch, fork or join, indicating that the same kind of data or object may be needed or produced by more than one process or subprocess.

IDEF0 process modelling, improvement and teamwork

The IDEF0 methodology includes procedures for developing and critiquing process models by a group or team of people. The creation of an IDEF0 process model provides a disciplined teamwork procedure for process understanding and improvement. As the group works on the process following the discipline, the diagrams are changed to reflect corrections and improvements. More detail can be added by creating more diagrams, which in turn can be reviewed and altered. The final model represents an agreement on the process for a given purpose and from a given viewpoint, and can be the basis of new process or system improvement projects.

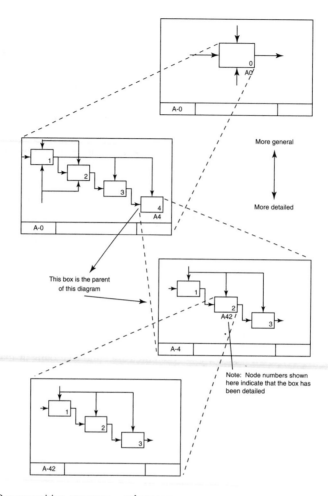

Figure 4.5 *Decomposition structure – subprocesses*

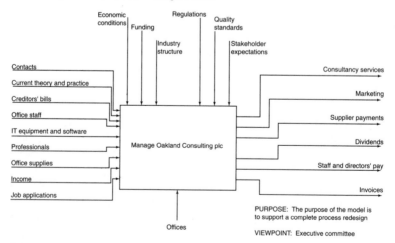

Figure 4.6 *A top-level process diagram*

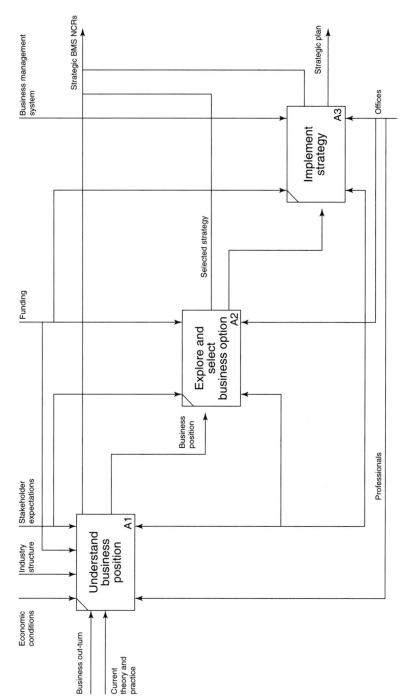

Figure 4.7 *Process mapping at sub-subprocess level*

IDEFIX

This is used to produce structural graphical information models for processes, which may support the management of data, the integration of information systems, and the building of computer databases. It is described in detail in the FIPS PUB 184 (December 1993, NIST). Its use is facilitated by the introduction of IDEF0 modelling for process understanding and improvement.

A number of commercial software packages are available which support IDEF0 and IDEFIX implementation.

Process flowcharting

In the systematic planning or detailed examination of any process, whether that be a clerical, manufacturing or managerial activity, it is necessary to record the series of events and activities, stages and decisions in a form that can be easily understood and communicated to all. If improvements are to be made, the facts relating to the existing method must be recorded first. The statements defining the process should lead to its understanding and will provide the basis of any critical examination necessary for the development of improvements. It is essential therefore that the descriptions of processes are accurate, clear and concise.

The usual method of recording facts is to write them down, but this is not suitable for recording the complicated processes that exist in any organization, particularly when an exact record is required of a long process, and its written description would cover several pages requiring careful study to elicit every detail. To overcome this difficulty, certain methods of recording have been developed, and the most powerful of these is flowcharting. This method of describing a process owes much to computer programming, where the technique is used to arrange the sequence of steps required for the operation of the program. It has a much wider application, however, than computing.

Certain standard symbols are used on the chart, as shown in Figure 4.8. The starting point of the process is indicated by a circle. Each processing step, indicated by a rectangle, contains a description of the relevant operation, and where the process ends is indicated by an oval. A point where the process branches because of a decision is

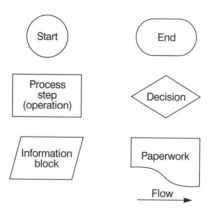

Figure 4.8 *Flowcharting symbols*

shown by a diamond. A parallelogram relates to process information but is not a processing step. The arrowed lines are used to connect symbols and to indicate direction of flow. For a complete description of the process, all operation steps (rectangles) and decisions (diamonds) should be connected by pathways to the start circle and end oval. If the flowchart cannot be drawn in this way, the process is not fully understood.

It is a salutary experience for most people to sit down and try to draw the flowchart for a process in which they take part every working day. It is often found that:

● The process flow is not fully understood.
● A single person is unable to complete the flowchart without help from others.

The very act of flowcharting will improve knowledge of the process, and will begin to develop the teamwork necessary to find improvements. In many cases the convoluted flow and octopus-like appearance of the chart will highlight unnecessary movements of people and materials and lead to commonsense suggestions for waste elimination.

Example of flowcharting in use – improving a travel procedure

We start by describing the original process for a male employee, though clearly it applies equally to females.

The process starts with the employee explaining his travel plans to his secretary. The secretary then calls the travel agent to enquire about the possibilities and gives feedback to the employee. The employee decides if the travel arrangements, e.g. flight numbers and dates, are acceptable and informs his secretary, who calls the agent to make the necessary bookings or examine alternatives. The administrative procedure, which starts as soon as the bookings have been made, is as follows:

1 The employee's secretary prepares the travel request (which is in four parts, A, B, C and D), and gives it to the employee. The request is then sent to the employee's manager, who approves it. The manager's secretary sends it back to the employee's secretary.
2 The employee's secretary sends copies A, B and C to the agent and gives copy D to the employee. The travel agent delivers the ticket to the employee's secretary, together with copy B of the travel request. The secretary endorses copy B for receipt of the ticket, sends it to Accounting, and gives the ticket to the employee.
3 The travel agent bills the credit card company, and sends Accounting a pro-forma invoice with copy C of the travel request. Accounting matches copies B and C, and charges the employee's 181 account.
4 Accounting receives the monthly bill from the credit card company, matches it against the travel request, then books and pays the credit card company.
5 The employee reports the travel request on his expense statement. Accounting matches and books to balance the employee's 181 account.

The total time taken for the administrative procedure, excluding the correction of errors and the preparation of overview reports, is 23 minutes per travel request.

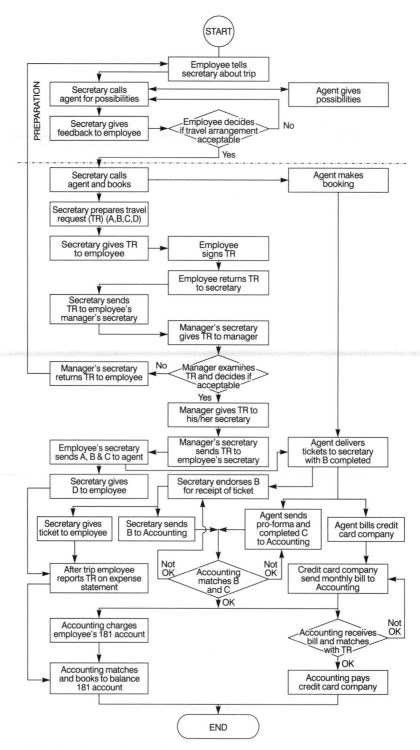

Figure 4.9 *Original process for travel procedure*

The flowchart for the process is drawn in Figure 4.9. A quality-improvement team was set up to analyse the process and make recommendations for improvement, using brainstorming and questioning techniques. They made the following proposal to change the procedure. The preparation for the trip remained the same but the administrative steps following the bookings being made became:

1 The travel agent sends the ticket to the secretary, along with a receipt document, which is returned to the agent with the secretary's signature.
2 The agent sends the receipt to the credit card company, which bills the company on a monthly basis with a copy of all the receipts. Accounting pays the credit-card company and charges the employee's 181 account.
3 The employee reports the travel on his expense statement, and Accounting books to balance the employee's 181 account.

The flowchart for the improved process is shown in Figure 4.10. The proposal reduced the total administrative effort per travel request (or per travel arrangement, because the travel request was eliminated) from 23 minutes to 5 minutes.

The details that appear on a flowchart for an existing process must be obtained from direct observation of the process, not by imagining what is done or what should be

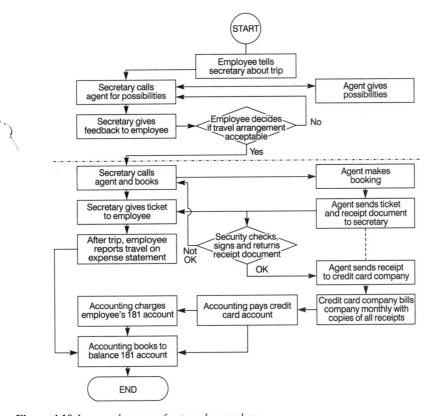

Figure 4.10 *Improved process for travel procedure*

done. The latter may be useful, however, in the planning phase, or for outlining the stages in the introduction of a new concept. Such an application is illustrated in Figure 4.11 for the installation of statistical process control charting systems (see Chapter 8). Similar charts may be used in the planning of quality management systems.

It is surprisingly difficult to draw flowcharts for even the simplest processes, particularly managerial ones, and following the first attempt it is useful to ask whether:

- the facts have been correctly recorded
- any over-simplifying assumptions have been made
- all the factors concerning the process have been recorded.

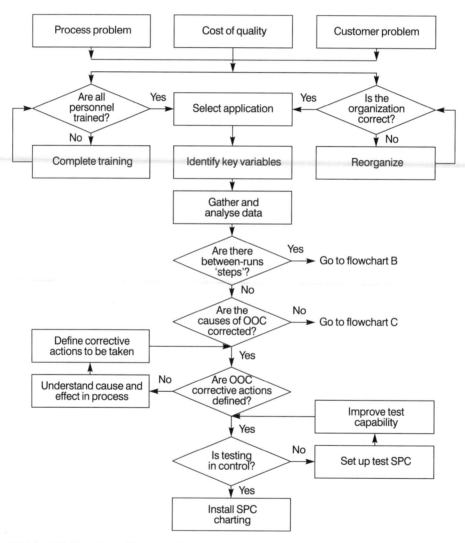

Figure 4.11 *Flowchart (A) for installation of SPC charting systems. (The author is grateful to Exxon Chemical International for permission to use and modify this chart)*

The author has seen too many process flowcharts that are so incomplete as to be grossly inaccurate.

Summarizing, then, a flowchart is a picture of the steps used in performing an activity or task. Lines connect the steps to show the flow of the various tasks or steps. Flowcharts provide excellent documentation and are useful trouble-shooting tools to determine how each step is related to the others. By reviewing the flowchart, it is often possible to discover inconsistencies and determine potential sources of variation and problems. For this reason, flowcharts are very useful in process improvement when examining an existing process to highlight the problem areas. A group of people, with the knowledge about the process, should take the following simple steps:

1 Draw a flowchart of the existing process.
2 Draw a second chart of the flow the process could or should follow.
3 Compare the two to highlight the changes necessary.

A number of commercial software packages which support process flowcharting are available.

Planning for purchasing

Very few organizations are self-contained to the extent that their products and services are all generated at one location, from basic materials. Some materials or services are usually purchased from outside organizations, and the primary objective of purchasing is to obtain the correct equipment, materials and services in the right quantity, of the right quality, from the right origin, at the right time and cost. Purchasing also plays a vital role as the organization's 'window-on-the-world', providing information on any new products, processes, materials and services. It should also advise on probable prices, deliveries and performance of products under consideration by the research design and development functions.

Although purchasing is clearly an important area of managerial activity it is often neglected by both manufacturing and service industries. The separation of purchasing from selling has, however, been removed in many large retail organizations, which have recognized that the purchaser must be responsible for the whole 'product line' – its selection, quality, specification, delivery, price, acceptability and reliability. If any part of this chain is wrong, the purchasing function must resolve the problem. This concept is clearly very appropriate in retailing, where transformation activities on the product itself, between purchase and sale, are small or zero, but it shows the need to include market information in the buying decision processes in all organizations.

The purchasing system should be set out in a written manual which:

1 Assigns responsibilities for and within the purchasing function.
2 Defines the manner in which suppliers are selected, to ensure that they are continually capable of supplying the requirements in terms of material and services.
3 Indicates the purchasing documentation – written orders, specifications, etc. – required in any modern purchasing activity.

So what does an organization require from its suppliers? The goals are easy to state, but less easy to reach:

- Consistency – low variability.
- Centring – on target.
- Process evolution and development to continually reduce variability.
- Correct delivery performance.
- Speed of response.
- A *systematic* quality management approach to achieve the above.

Historically many organizations, particularly in the manufacturing industries, have operated an inspection-oriented quality system for bought-in parts and materials. Such an approach has many disadvantages. It is expensive, imprecise and impossible to apply evenly across all material and parts, which all lead to variability in the degree of appraisal. Many organizations, such as Ford, have found that survival and future growth in both volume and variety demand that changes be made to this approach.

The prohibitive cost of holding large stocks of components and raw materials also pushed forward the 'just-in-time' (JIT) concept. As this requires that suppliers make frequent, on-time, deliveries of small quantities of material, parts, components, etc., often straight to the point of use, in order that stocks can be kept to a minimum, the approach requires an effective supplier network – one producing goods and services that can be trusted to conform to the real requirements with a high degree of confidence.

Commitment and involvement

The process of improving suppliers' performance is complex and clearly relies very heavily on securing real commitment from the senior management of the supplier organizations. This may be aided by presentations made to groups of directors of the suppliers brought together to share the realization of the importance of their organizations' performance in the quality chains. The synergy derived from different suppliers meeting together, being educated, and discussing mutual problems, will be tremendous. If this can be achieved, within the constraints of business and technical confidentiality, it is always a better approach than separate meetings and presentations on the suppliers' premises.

The author recalls the benefits that accrued from bringing together suppliers of a photocopier, paper and ring binders to explain to them the way their inputs were used to generate training-course materials and how they in turn were used during the courses themselves. The suppliers were able to understand the business in which their customers were engaged, and play their part in the whole process. A supplier of goods *or* services that has received such attention, education and training, and understands the role its inputs play, is less likely to offer non-conforming materials and services, and more likely to alert customers to potential problems.

Policy

One of the first things to communicate to any external supplier is the purchasing organization's policy on quality of incoming goods and services. This can include such statements as:

- It is the policy of this company to ensure that the quality of all purchased materials and services meets its requirements.
- Suppliers who incorporate a quality management system into their operations will be selected. This system should be designed, implemented and operated according to the International Standards Organization (ISO) 9000 series (see Chapter 5).
- Suppliers who incorporate statistical process control (SPC) methods into their operations (see Chapter 8) will be selected.
- Routine inspection, checking, measurement and testing of incoming goods and services will *not* be carried out by this company on receipt.
- Suppliers will be audited and their operating procedures, systems and SPC methods will be reviewed periodically to ensure a never-ending improvement approach.
- It is the policy of this company to pursue uniformity of supply, and to encourage suppliers to strive for continual reduction in variability. (This may well lead to the narrowing of specification ranges.)

Quality system assessment certification

Many customers examine their suppliers' quality management systems themselves, operating a second-party assessment scheme (see Chapter 6). Inevitably this leads to high costs and duplication of activity, for both the customer and supplier. If a qualified, independent third party is used instead to carry out the assessment, attention may be focused by the customer on any special needs and in developing closer partnerships with suppliers. Visits and dialogue across the customer–supplier interface are a necessity for the true requirements to be met, and for future growth of the whole business chain. Visits should be concentrated, however, on improving understanding and capability, rather than on close scrutiny of operating procedures, which is best left to experts, including those within the supplier organizations charged with carrying out internal system audits and reviews.

Planning for just-in-time (JIT) management

There are so many organizations throughout the world that are practising just-in-time (JIT) management principles that the probability of encountering it is very high. JIT, like many modern management concepts, is credited to the Japanese, who developed and began to use it in the late 1950s. It took approximately 20 years for JIT methods to reach Western hard goods industries and a further 10 years before business realized the generality of the concepts.

Basically JIT is a programme directed towards ensuring that the right quantities are purchased or produced at the right time, and that there is no waste. Anyone who perceives it purely as a material-control system, however, is bound to fail with JIT. JIT fits well under the TQM umbrella, for many of the ideas and techniques are very similar and, moreover, JIT will not work without TQM in operation.

The Kanban system

Kanban is a Japanese word meaning 'visible record', but in the West it is generally taken to mean a 'card' that signals the need to deliver or produce more parts or components. In manufacturing, various types of records, e.g. job orders or route information, are used for ordering more parts in a *push* type, schedule-based system. In a push system a multi-period master production schedule of future demands is prepared, and a computer explodes this into detailed schedules for producing or purchasing the appropriate parts or materials. The schedules then *push* the production of the parts or components, out and onward. These systems, when computer-based, are usually called Material Requirements Planning (MRP) or more recently Manufacturing Resource Planning (MRPII).

The main feature of the Kanban system is that it *pulls* parts and components through the production processes when they are needed. Each material, component or part has its own special container designed to hold a precise, preferably small, quantity. The number of containers for each part is a carefully considered management decision. Only standard containers are used, and they are always filled with the prescribed quantity.

A Kanban system provides parts when they are needed but without guesswork, and therefore without the excess inventory that results from bad guesses. The system will only work well, however, within the context of a JIT system in general, and the reduction of set-up times and lot sizes in particular. A JIT programme can succeed without a Kanban-based operation, but Kanban will not function effectively independently of JIT.

Just-in-time purchasing

Purchasing is an important feature of JIT. The development of long-term partnerships with a few suppliers, rather than short-term ones with many, leads to the concept of *co-producers* in networks of trust providing dependable quality and delivery of goods and services. Each organization in the chain of supply is encouraged to extend JIT methods to its suppliers. The requirements of JIT mean that suppliers are usually located near the purchaser's premises, delivering small quantities, often several times per day, to match the usage rate. Paperwork is kept to a minimum and standard quantities in standard containers are usual. The requirement for suppliers to be located near the buying organization, which places those at some distance at a competitive disadvantage, causes lead times to be shorter and deliveries to be more reliable.

It can be argued that JIT purchasing and delivery are suitable mainly for assembly line operations, and less so for certain process and service industries, but the reduction in the inventory and transport costs that it brings should encourage innovations to lead to is widespread adoption. Those committed to open competition and finding the lowest price will find most difficulty. Nevertheless, there must be a recognition of the need to develop closer relationships and to begin the dialogue – the sharing of information and problems – that leads to the product or service of the right quality, being delivered in the right quantity, at the right time.

Chapter highlights

Quality planning

- Systematic planning is a basic requirement for TQM.
- A quality plan sets out details for systems, procedures, purchased materials or services, products/services, plant/equipment, process control, sampling/inspection, training, packaging and distribution.

The Process Classification Framework

- The APQC's Process Classification Framework creates a high-level generic, cross-functional process view of an enterprise – a taxonomy of business processes.
- The IDEF (Integrated Definition Function Modelling) language provides a useful structured graphical framework for describing and improving business processes. It consists of a hierarchical series of diagrams and text, cross-referenced to each other through boxes. The processes are described in terms of inputs, controls, outputs and resources (ICOR).

Process modelling

- The IDEF (Integrated Definition Function) modelling language provides a useful structured graphical framework for describing and improving business processes.
- The IDEF0 and IDEF1X techniques are widely used in business process re-engineering (BPR) and business process improvement (BPI) projects. A specialist range of software is available to support the techniques.
- An IDEF0 model uses boxes and arrows to describe process inputs, controls, outputs and resources (ICOR). Using these, high level processes may be decomposed into more detailed subprocesses and activities.

Process flowcharting

- Flowcharting is a method of describing a process in pictures, using symbols – rectangles for operation steps, diamonds for decisions, parallelograms for information, and circles/ovals for the start/end points. Arrow lines connect the symbols to show the 'flow'.
- Flowcharting improves knowledge of the process and helps to develop the team of people involved.
- Flowcharts document processes and are useful as trouble-shooting tools and in process improvement. An improvement team would flowchart the existing process and the improved or desired process, comparing the two to highlight the changes necessary.

Planning for purchasing

- The prime objective of purchasing is to obtain the correct equipment, materials and services in the right quantity, of the right quality, from the right origin, at the right time and cost. Purchasing also acts as a 'window-on-the-world'.
- The separation of purchasing from selling has been eliminated in many retail organizations, to give responsibility for a whole 'product line'. Market information must be included in *any* buying decision.
- The purchasing system should be documented in a form which gives responsibilities, the means of selecting suppliers, and any documentation to be used.
- An organization requires from its suppliers consistency, on target, process evolution, good delivery performance, speed of response and systematic quality management.
- Improving supplier performance requires from the suppliers' senior management commitment, education, a policy, an assessed quality system and supplier approval.

Planning for just-in-time (JIT) management

- JIT fits well under the TQM umbrella and is essentially a programme which ensures the right quantities are purchased or produced at the right time without waste.
- Kanbans signal the need to deliver or produce more parts or components. The system of Kanbans will work well only in the context of JIT.
- Purchasing is an important feature of JIT. Long-term partnerships with a few suppliers, or 'co-producers', are developed in networks of trust to provide quality goods and services.

Chapter 5

System design and contents

Why a quality management system?

In earlier chapters we have seen how the keystone of quality management is the concept of customer and supplier working together for their mutual advantage. For any particular organization this becomes 'total' quality management if the supplier–customer interfaces extend beyond the immediate customers, back inside the organization, and beyond the immediate suppliers. In order to achieve this, a company must organize itself in such a way that the human, administrative and technical factors affecting quality will be under control. This leads to the requirement for the development and implementation of a quality management system that enables the objectives set out in the quality policy to be accomplished. Clearly, for maximum effectiveness and to meet individual customer requirements, the management system in use must be appropriate to the type of activity and product or service being offered.

It may be useful to reflect on why such a device is necessary to achieve control of processes. The author remembers being at a table in a restaurant with eight people who all ordered the 'Chef's Special Individual Soufflé'. All eight soufflés arrived together at the table, magnificent in their appearance and consistency, each one exhibiting an almost identical size and shape – a truly remarkable demonstration of culinary skill. How had this been achieved? The chef had *managed* such consistency by making sure that, for each soufflé, he used the same ingredients (materials), the same equipment (plant), the same method (procedure) in exactly the same way every time. The process was under control. This is the aim of a good quality management system, to provide the 'operator' of the process with consistency and satisfaction in terms of methods, materials, equipment, etc. (Figure 5.1). Two feedback loops are also required: the 'voice' of the customer (marketing activities) and the 'voice' of the process (measurement activities).

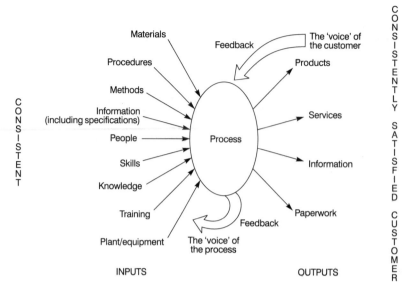

Figure 5.1 *The systematic approach to process management*

The chef's soufflés were not British Standard, NIST Standard, Australian Standard, or ISO Standard soufflés – they were the chef's special soufflés. It is not conceivable that the chef sat down with a blank piece of paper to invent a soufflé recipe. Why reinvent wheels? He probably used a standard formula and changed it slightly to make it his own. This is exactly the way in which organizations must use the international standards on quality management systems that are available. The 'wheel' has been invented but it must be built in a way that meets the specific organizational and product or service requirements. The International Organization for Standardization (ISO) Standard 9000: 2000 Series (1998) sets out the methods by which a management system can be implemented in an organization to ensure that all the specified performance requirements and needs of the customer are fully met.

Let us return to the chef in the restaurant and propose that his success leads to a desire to open eight restaurants in which are served his special soufflés. Clearly he cannot rush from each one of these establishments to another every evening making soufflés. The only course open to him to ensure consistency of output, in all eight restaurants, is for him to write down in some detail the system he uses, and then make sure that it is used on all sites, every time a soufflé is produced. Moreover, he must periodically visit the different sites to ensure that:

1 The people involved are operating according to the documented system (a system audit).
2 The soufflé system still meets the requirements (a system review).

If in his system audits and reviews he discovers that an even better product or less waste can be achieved by changing the method or one of the materials, then he may wish to effect a change. To maintain consistency, he must ensure that the appropriate changes are made to the management system, *and* that everyone concerned is issued with the revision and begins to operate accordingly.

A fully documented quality management system will ensure that two important requirements are met:

- *The customer's requirements* – for confidence in the ability of the organization to deliver the desired product or service consistently.
- *The organization's requirements* – both internally and externally, and at an optimum cost, with efficient utilization of the resources available – material, human, technological and informational.

The requirements can be truly met only if objective evidence is provided, in the form of information and data, which supports the system activities, from the ultimate supplier through to the ultimate customer.

A *quality management system* may be defined, then, as an assembly of components, such as the organizational structure, responsibilities, processes and resources for implementing total quality management. These components interact and are affected by being in the system, so the isolation and study of each one in detail will not necessarily lead to an understanding of the system as a whole. Often the interactions between the components – such as materials and processes, procedures and responsibilities – are just as important as the components themselves, and problems can arise from these interactions as much as from the components. Clearly, if one of the components is removed from the system, the whole thing will change.

Quality management system design

The quality management system should apply to and interact with all processes in the organization. It begins with the identification of the customer requirements and ends with their satisfaction, at every transaction interface. The activities may be classified in several ways – generally as processing, communicating and controlling, but more usefully and specifically as shown in the quality management process model described in ISO 9001: 2000 (1999), Figure 5.2.

This process model is as presented in ISO 9001: 2000, and reflects graphically the integration of four major areas:

- Management responsibility
- Resource management
- Process management
- Measurement, analysis and improvement.

The management system requirements under these headings are specified in the International Standard.

It is interesting to bring together the concept of Deming's cycle of continuous improvement – *PLAN DO CHECK ACT* – and quality management systems. A simplification of what a good management system is trying to do is given in Figure 5.3, which follows the improvement cycle.

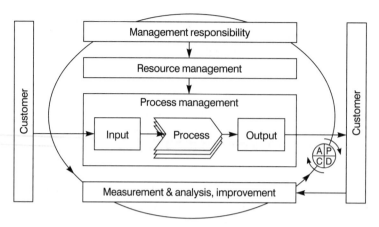

Figure 5.2 *Quality management process model. (Source: ISO/SCI 9001: 2000 Quality Management Systems, 1999)*

In many organizations established methods of working already exist around identified processes, and all that is required is the *writing down of what is currently done*. In some instances companies may not have procedures to satisfy the requirements of a good standard, and they may have to begin to devise them. Alternatively, it may be found that two people, supposedly performing the same task, are working in different ways, and there is a need to standardize the procedure. Some organizations use the effective slogan, 'If it isn't written down, it doesn't exist.' This can be a useful discipline, provided it doesn't lead to bureaucracy.

Justify that the *system* as it is designed *meets the requirements of a good international standard*, such as ISO 9001. There are other excellent standards that are used, and these provide similar checklists of things to consider in the establishment of the quality system.

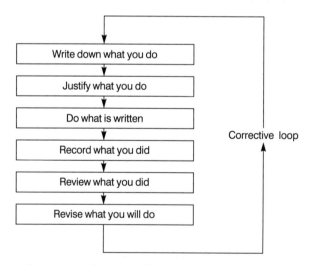

Figure 5.3 *The quality system and never-ending improvement*

University of Chester, Queen's Park Library

Title: Pocket guide to TQM : a pictorial guide for managers / John Oakland and Peter Morris.
ID: 01063471
Due: 23-03-18

Title: Total quality management : text with cases / John S. Oakland.
ID: 01063474
Due: 23-03-18

Total items: 2
02/03/2018 14:06

Renew online at:
http://libcat.chester.ac.uk/patroninfo

Thank you for using Self Check

248

The system must be a working one with the documents 'well fingered' in use. One person alone cannot document a quality management system; the task is the job of all personnel who have responsibility for any part of it. The quality manual must be a *practical working document* – that way it ensures that consistency of operation is maintained and it may be used as a training aid.

In the operation of any process, a useful guide is:

- No process without data collection.
- No data collection without analysis.
- No analysis without decisions.
- No decisions without actions, which can include doing nothing.

This excellent discipline is built into any good-quality management system, primarily through the audit and review mechanism. The requirement to *audit or 'check'* that the system is functioning according to plan, and to *review* possible system improvements, utilizing audit results, should ensure that the *improvement* cycle is engaged through the *corrective action* procedures. The overriding requirement is that the systems must reflect the established practices of the organization, improved where necessary to bring them into line with current and future requirements.

Quality management system requirements

The quality management system that needs to be documented and implemented will be determined by the nature of the process carried out to ensure that the product or service conforms to customer requirement. Certain fundamental principles are applicable, however, throughout industry, commerce and the services. These fall into generally well-defined categories which are detailed in ISO 9001: 2000 (1999).

1 Management responsibilities

Customer needs/requirements (see Chapter 1)
The organization must determine customer needs and specify them as defined requirements for the organization. The aim of this is to achieve customer confidence in the products and/or services provided. It is also necessary to ensure that the defined requirements are understood and fully met.

Quality policy (see Chapter 2)
The organization should define and publish its quality policy, which forms one element of the corporate policy. Full commitment is required from the most senior management to ensure that the policy is communicated, understood, implemented and maintained at all levels in the organization. It should, therefore, be authorized by top management and signed by the Chief Executive, or equivalent, who must also ensure that it:

- is suitable for the needs/requirements of the customers
- includes commitment to meeting requirements and continual improvement for all levels of the organization

- provides a framework for establishing and reviewing quality objectives
- is regularly reviewed for its suitability and objectiveness.

Quality objectives and planning

Organizations should establish written quality objectives and define the responsibilities of each function and level in the organization.

One manager reporting to top management, with the necessary authority, resources, support and ability, should be given the responsibility to co-ordinate, implement and maintain the quality management system, resolve any problems and ensure prompt and effective corrective action. This includes responsibility for ensuring proper handling of the system and reporting on needs for improvement. Those who control sales, service operations, warehousing, delivery and reworking of non-conforming product or service processes should also be identified.

Management review

Management reviews of the system must be carried out by top management at defined intervals, with records to indicate the actions decided upon. The effectiveness of these actions should be considered during subsequent reviews. Reviews typically include data on the internal quality audits, customer satisfaction and complaints, non-conformance analysis, process reports, and the status of preventive, corrective and improvement actions.

Quality manual

The organization should prepare a quality manual that is appropriate. It should include, but not necessarily be limited to:

a) the quality policy
b) defining the quality management system
c) the organizational structure
d) inclusion or reference to the system procedures to be used.

In the quality manual for a large organization it may be convenient to indicate simply the existence and contents of other manuals, those containing the details of procedures and practices in operation in specific areas of the system.

Before an organization can agree to supply to a specification, it must ensure that:

a) the processes and equipment (including any that are subcontracted) are capable of meeting the requirements
b) the operators have the necessary skills and training
c) the operating procedures are documented and not simply passed on verbally
d) the plant and equipment instrumentation is capable (e.g. measuring the process variables with the appropriate accuracy and precision)
e) the quality control procedures, and any inspection, check or test methods available, provide results to the required accuracy and precision, and are documented
f) any subjective phrases in the specification, such as 'finely ground', 'low moisture content', 'in good time', are understood, and procedures to establish the exact customer requirement exist.

Control of documents

The organization needs to establish procedures for controlling the new and revised documents required for the operation of the quality management system. Documents of external origin must also be controlled. These procedures should be designed to ensure that:

a) documents are approved
b) documents are periodically reviewed, and revised as necessary
c) the current versions of relevant documents are available at all locations where activities essential to the effective functioning of the processes are performed
d) obsolete documents are promptly removed from all points of issue and use, or otherwise controlled to prevent unplanned use
e) any obsolete documents retained for legal or knowledge-preservation purposes are suitably identified.

Documentation needs to be legible, revision controlled, readily identifiable and maintained in an orderly manner. Of course, the documentation may be in any form or any type of medium.

Control of quality records

Quality records are needed to demonstrate conformance to requirements and effective operation of the quality management system. Quality records from suppliers also need to be controlled. This aspect includes record identification, collection, indexing, access, filing, storage and disposition. In addition, the retention time of quality records needs to be established.

2 Resource management

The organization should determine and provide the necessary resources to establish and improve the quality management system, including all processes and projects.

Human resources

The organization needs to select and assign people who are competent, on the basis of applicable education, training and experience, to those activities which impact the conformity of product and/or service.
    The organization also needs to:

a) determine the training needed to achieve conformity of product and/or service
b) provide the necessary training to address these needs
c) evaluate the effectiveness of the training on a continual basis.

Individuals clearly need to be educated and trained to qualify them for the activities they perform. Competence, including qualification levels achieved, needs to be demonstrated and documented.
    Information is ever increasingly a vital resource and any organization needs to define and maintain the current information and the infrastructure necessary to achieve

conformity of products and/or services. The management of information, including access and protection of information to ensure integrity and availability, needs also to be considered.

3 Process management

As we have seen in Figure 5.2, any organization needs to determine the processes required to convert customer requirements into customer satisfaction, by providing the required product and/or service. In determining such processes the organization needs to consider the outputs from the quality planning process.

The sequence and interaction of these processes need to be determined, planned and controlled to ensure they operate effectively, and there is a need to assign responsibilities for the operation and monitoring of the product/service generating processes.

These processes clearly need to be operated under controlled conditions and produce outputs which are consistent with the organization's quality policy and objective and it is necessary to:

a) determine how each process influences the ability to meet product and/or service requirements
b) establish methods and practices relevant to process activities, to the extent necessary to achieve consistent operation of the process
c) verify that processes can be operated to achieve product and/or service conformity
d) determine and implement the criteria and methods to control processes related to the achievement of product and/or service conformity
e) determine and implement arrangements for measurement, monitoring and follow-up actions, to ensure processes operate effectively and the resultant product/service meets the requirements
f) ensure availability of process documentation and records which provide operating criteria and information, to support the effective operation and monitoring of the processes. (This documentation needs to be in a format to suit the operating practices, including written quality plans)
g) provide the necessary resources for the effective operation of the processes.

Customer-related processes

One of the first processes to be established is the one for identifying customer requirements. This needs to consider:

a) the extent to which customers have specified the product/service requirements
b) the requirements not specified by the customer but necessary for fitness for purpose
c) the obligations related to the product/service, including regulatory and legal requirements
d) the customer requirements for availability, delivery and support of product and/or service.

The identified customer requirements need also to be reviewed before a commitment to supply a product/service is given to the customer (e.g. submission of a tender, acceptance of a contract or order). This should determine that:

a) identified customer requirements are clearly defined for the product and/or service
b) the order requirements are confirmed before acceptance, particularly where the customer provides no written statement of requirements
c) the contract or order requirements differing from those in the tender or quotation are resolved.

This should also apply to amended customer contracts or orders. Moreover, each commitment to supply a product/service, including amendment to a contract or order, needs to be reviewed to ensure the organization will have the ability to meet the requirements.

Any successful organization needs to implement effective liaison with customers, particularly regarding:

a) product and/or service information
b) enquiry and order handling, including amendments
c) customer complaints and other reports relating to non-conformities
d) recall processes, where applicable
e) customer responses relating to conformity of product/service.

Where an organization is supervising or using customer property, care needs to be exercised to ensure verification, storage and maintenance. Any customer product or property that is lost, damaged or otherwise found to be unsuitable for use should, of course, be recorded and reported to the customer. Customer property may, of course, include intellectual property, e.g. information provided in confidence.

Design and development

The organization needs to plan and control design and development of products and/or services, including:

a) stages of the design and development process
b) required review, verification and validation activities
c) responsibilities for design and development activities.

Interfaces between different groups involved in design and development need to be managed to ensure effective communication and clarity of responsibilities, and any plans and associated documentation should be:

a) made available to personnel that need them to perform their work
b) reviewed and updated as design and development evolves.

The requirements to be met by the product/service need to be defined and recorded, including identified customer or market requirements, applicable regulatory and legal requirements, requirements derived from previous similar designs, and any other requirements essential for design and development. Incomplete, ambiguous or conflicting requirements must be resolved.

The outputs of the design and development process need to be recorded in a format that allows verification against the input requirements. So, the design and development output should:

a) meet the design and development input requirements
b) contain or make reference to design and development acceptance criteria
c) determine characteristics of the design essential to safe and proper use, and application of the product or service.

Design and development output documents should also be reviewed and approved before release.

Validation needs to be performed to confirm that the resultant product/service is capable of meeting the needs of the customers or users under the planned conditions. Wherever possible, validation should be defined, planned and completed prior to the delivery or implementation of the product or service. Partial validation of the design or development output may be necessary at various stages to provide confidence in their correctness, using such methods as:

a) reviews involving other interested parties
b) modelling and simulation studies
c) pilot production, construction or delivery trials of key aspects of the product and/or service.

Design and development changes or modifications need to be determined as early as possible, recorded, reviewed and approved before implementation. At this stage, the effect of changes on compatibility requirements and the usability of the product or service throughout its planned life need to be considered.

Purchasing

Purchasing processes need to be controlled to ensure purchased products/services conform to the organization's requirements. The type and extent of methods for doing this are dependent on the effect of the purchased product/service on the final product/service. Clearly suppliers need to be evaluated and selected on their ability to supply the product or service in accordance with the organization's requirements. Supplier evaluations, supplier audit records and evidence of previously demonstrated ability should be considered when selecting suppliers and when determining the type and extent of supervision applicable to the purchased materials/services.

The purchasing documentation should contain information clearly describing the product/service ordered, including:

a) requirements for approval or qualification of product and/or service, procedures, processes, equipment and personnel
b) any management system requirements.

Review and approval of purchasing documents, for adequacy of the specification of requirements prior to release, is also necessary.

Any purchased products/services need some form of verification. Where this is to be carried out at the supplier's premises, the organization needs to specify the arrangements and methods for product/service release in the purchasing documentation.

Production and service delivery processes

The organization needs to control production and service delivery processes through:

a) clearly understandable work standards or instructions
b) suitable production, installation and service provision equipment
c) suitable working environments
d) suitable inspection, measuring and test equipment, capable of the necessary accuracy and precision
e) implementation of suitable monitoring, inspection or testing activities
f) provision for identifying the status of the product/service, with respect to required measurement and verification activities
g) suitable methods for release and delivery of products and/or services.

Where applicable, the organization needs to identify the product/service by suitable means throughout all processes. Where traceability is a requirement for the organization, there is a need to control the identification of product/service. There is also a need to ensure that, during internal processing and final delivery of the product/ service, the identification, packaging, storage, preservation and handling do not adversely affect conformity with the requirements. This applies equally to parts or components of a product and elements of a service.

Where the resulting output cannot be easily or economically verified by monitoring, inspection or testing, including where processing deficiencies may become apparent only after the product is in use or the service has been delivered, the organization needs to validate the production and service delivery processes to demonstrate their effectiveness and acceptability.

The arrangements for validation might include:

a) processes being qualified prior to use
b) qualification of equipment or personnel
c) use of specific procedures or records.

Evidence of validated processes, equipment and personnel needs to be recorded and maintained, of course.

Control of non-conformities

Product and services which do not conform to requirements need to be controlled to prevent unplanned use, application or installation, and the organization needs to identify, record and review the nature and extent of the problem encountered, and determine the action to be taken. This needs to include how non-conforming service will be:

a) corrected or adjusted to conform to requirements, or
b) accepted under concession, with or without correction, or
c) reassigned for an alternative, valid application, or
d) rejected as unsuitable.

The responsibility and authority for the review and resolving of non-conformities needs to be defined, of course.

When required by the contract, the proposed use or repair of non-conforming product or a modified service needs to be reported for concession to the customer. The descriptions of any corrections or adjustments, accepted non-conformities, product repairs or service modifications also need to be recorded. Where it is necessary to repair or rework a product or modify a service, verification requirements need to be determined and implemented.

Post-delivery services

Where there is a requirement for the organization to provide support services, after delivery of the product or service, this needs to be planned and in line with the customer requirement.

4 Measurement, analysis and improvement

Any organization needs to define and implement measurement, analysis and improvement processes to demonstrate that the products or services conform to the specified requirements. The type, location and timing of these measurements needs to be determined and the results recorded based on their importance. The results of data analysis and improvement activities should be an input to the management review process, of course.

Measurement

There is a need to determine and establish processes for measurement of the quality management system performance. Customer satisfaction must be a primary measure of system output and the internal audits should be used as a primary tool for evaluating ongoing system compliance.

The organization needs to establish a process for obtaining and monitoring information and data on customer satisfaction. The methods and measures for obtaining customer satisfaction information and data and the nature and frequency of reviews need to be defined to demonstrate the level of customer confidence in the delivery of conforming product and/or service supplied by the organization. Suitable measures for establishing internal improvement need to be implemented and the effectiveness of the measures periodically evaluated.

The organization must establish a process for performing internal audits of the quality management system and related processes. The purpose of the internal audit is to determine whether:

● the quality management system established by the organization conforms to the requirements of the International Standard, and
● the quality management system has been effectively implemented and maintained.

The internal audit process should be based on the status and importance of the activities, areas or items to be audited, and the results of previous audits.

The internal audit process should include:

- planning and scheduling the specific activities, areas or items to be audited
- assigning trained personnel independent of those performing the work being audited
- assuring that a consistent basis for conducting audits is defined.

The results of internal audits should be recorded, including:

- activities, areas and processes audited
- non-conformities or deficiencies found
- status of commitments made as the result of previous audit, such as corrective actions or product audits
- recommendations for improvement.

The results of the internal audits should be communicated to the area audited and the management personnel responsible need to take timely corrective action on the non-conformities recorded.

Suitable methods for the measurement of processes necessary to meet customer requirements need to be applied, including monitoring the output of the processes that control conformity of the product or service provided to customers. The measurement results then need to be used to determine opportunities for improvements.

The organization needs also to apply suitable methods for the measurement of the product or service to verify that the requirements have been met. Evidence from any inspection and testing activities and the acceptance criteria used need to be recorded. If there is an authority responsible for release of the product and/or service, this should also be recorded.

Products or services should not be dispatched until all the specified activities have been satisfactorily completed and the related documentation is available and authorized. The only exception to this is when the product or service is released under positive recall procedures.

There is a need to control, calibrate, maintain, handle and store the applicable measuring, inspection and test equipment to specified requirements. Measuring, inspection and test equipment should be used in a way which ensures that any measurement uncertainty, including accuracy and precision (see Chapter 8), is known and is consistent with the required measurement capability. Any test equipment software should meet the applicable requirements for the design and development of the product (see Section 3 above).

The organization certainly needs to:

a) calibrate and adjust measuring, inspection and test equipment at specified intervals, or prior to use, against equipment traceable to international or national standards. Where no standards exist, the basis used for calibration needs to be recorded
b) identify measuring, inspection and test equipment with a suitable indicator or approved identification record to show its calibration status

c) record the process for calibration of measuring, inspection and test equipment

d) ensure the environmental conditions are suitable for any calibrations, measurements, inspections and tests

e) safeguard measuring, inspection and test equipment from adjustments which would invalidate the calibration

f) verify the validity of previous inspection and test results when equipment is found to be out of calibration

g) establish the action to be initiated when calibration verification results are unsatisfactory.

Analysis of data

Analysis of data needs to be established as a means of determining where system improvements can be made. Data needs to be collected from relevant sources, including internal audits, corrective and preventive action, non-conforming product service, customer complaints and customer satisfaction results.

The organization should then analyse the data to provide information on:

a) the effectiveness of the quality management system

b) process operation trends

c) customer satisfaction, and

d) conformance to customer requirements.

There is also a need to determine the statistical techniques to be used for analysing data, including verifying process operations and product service characteristics. Of course, the statistical techniques selected should be suitable and their use controlled and monitored.

Improvement

The organization needs to establish a process for eliminating the causes of non-conformity and preventing recurrence. Non-conformity reports, customer complaints and other suitable quality management system records are useful as inputs to the corrective action process. Responsibilities for corrective action need to be established, together with the procedures for the corrective action process, which should include:

a) identification of non-conformities of the products, services, processes, the quality management system, and customer complaints

b) investigation of causes of non-conformities, and recording results of investigations

c) determination of corrective actions needed to eliminate causes of non-conformities

d) implementation of corrective action

e) follow-up to ensure corrective action taken is effective and is recorded.

Corrective actions also need to be implemented for products or services already delivered but subsequently discovered to be non-conforming, and customers need to be notified where possible.

The organization needs to establish a process for eliminating the causes of potential non-conformities to prevent their occurrence. Quality management system records and results from the analysis of data should be used as inputs for this and responsibilities for preventive action established. The process should include:

a) identification of potential product, service and process non-conformities
b) investigation of the causes of potential non-conformities of products/services, process and the quality management system, and recording the results
c) determination of preventive action needed to eliminate causes of potential non-conformities
d) implementation of preventive action needed
e) follow-up to ensure preventive action taken is effective, recorded and submitted for management review.

Processes for the continual improvement of the quality management system need to be established, including methods and measures suitable for the products/services.

Environmental management systems

Organizations of all kinds are increasingly concerned to achieve and demonstrate sound environmental performance. Many have undertaken environmental audits and reviews to assess this. To be effective these need to be conducted within a structured management system, which in turn is integrated with the overall management activities dealing with all aspects of desired environmental performance.

Such a system should establish processes for setting environmental policy and objectives, and achieving compliance to them. It should be designed to place emphasis on the prevention of adverse environmental effects, rather than on detection after occurrence. It should also identify and assess the environmental effects arising from the organization's existing or proposed activities, products or services and from incidents, accidents and potential emergency situations. The system must identify the relevant regulatory requirements, the priorities, and pertinent environmental objectives and targets. It needs also to facilitate planning, control, monitoring, auditing and review activities to ensure that the policy is complied with, that it remains relevant, and is capable of evolution to suit changing circumstances.

The international standard ISO 14001 contains a specification for environmental management systems for ensuring and demonstrating compliance with stated policies and objectives. The standard is designed to enable any organization to establish an effective management system, as a foundation for both sound environmental performance and participation and environmental auditing schemes.

ISO 14001 shares common management system principles with the ISO 9001: 2000 standard and organizations may elect to use an existing management system, developed in conformity with that standard, as a basis for environmental management. The ISO 14001 standard defines environmental policy, objectives, targets, effect, management, systems, manuals, evaluation, audits and reviews. It mirrors the ISO 9001 standard in many of its own requirements, and it includes a guide to these in an informative annex.

The rings of confidence

Management systems are needed in all areas of activity, whether large or small businesses, manufacturing, service or public sector. The advantages of systems in manufacturing are obvious, but they are just as applicable in areas such as marketing, sales, personnel, finance, research and development, as well as in the service industries and public sectors.

No matter where it is implemented, a good management system will improve process control, reduce wastage, lower costs, increase market share (or funding), facilitate training, involve staff and raise morale.

The processes which must be addressed in the design and implementation of a good management system may be considered to be attached to a 'ring of confidence', which starts and ends with the customer (Figure 5.4).

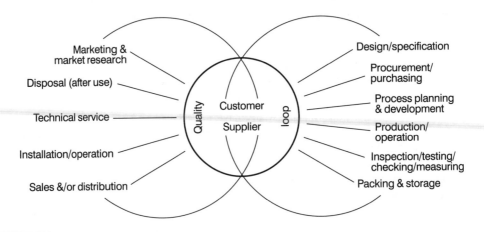

Figure 5.4 *The rings of confidence*

It is possible to group these into two spheres of activities:

- those involving direct interaction with the customer
- those concerning primarily the internal activities of the supplier.

The overlap necessary between customer and supplier is clearly illustrated by this model. Equally obvious is that separation will lead to dysfunction and dissatisfaction.

It cannot be stated too often that the customer–supplier interactions, which generate satisfaction of needs, are just as necessary internally. The principles of management system design, documentation and implementation set out in this chapter must apply to every single person, every department, every process transaction, and every type of organization. The vocabulary in the engineering factory system may be different from that used in the hotel, the hospital system will be set out differently to that of the drug manufacturer, but the underlying concepts will be the same.

It is not acceptable for the managers in industries, or parts of organizations, less often associated with standards on management systems to find 'technological' reasons for avoiding the requirement to manage. The author and his colleagues have heard the excuse that 'our industry (or organization) differs from any other industry (or organization)', in almost every industry and organization with which they have been involved. Clearly, there are technological differences between all industries and nearly all organizations, but in terms of management processes there are hardly any at all.

Senior managers in every type and size of organization must take the responsibility for the adoption of the appropriate documented management system based on process understandings. If this requires translation from 'engineering language', so be it – get someone from inside or outside the organization to do it. Do not wait for the message to be translated into different forms – customer dissatisfaction, inefficiencies, waste, high costs, crippling competition, loss of market.

Chapter highlights

Why a quality management sytem?

- An appropriate quality management system will enable the objectives set out in the quality policy to be accomplished.
- The International Organization for Standardization (ISO) 9000: 2000 series set out methods by which a system can be implemented to ensure that the specified customer requirements are met.
- A quality system may be defined as an assembly of components, such as the organizational structure responsibilities, process and resources.

Quality management system design

- Quality management systems should apply to and interact with processes in the organization. The activities are generally processing, communicating and controlling. These should be documented in the form of a quality manual.
- The system should follow the *PLAN DO CHECK ACT* cycle, through documentation, implementation, audit and review.

Quality management system requirements

- The general categories of the ISO 9001: 2000 standard on quality management systems include: management responsibilities, resource management, process management, measurement analysis and improvement.

Environmental management systems

- The International Standard ISO 14001 contains specifications for environmental management systems for ensuring and demonstrating compliance with the stated policies and objectives, and acting as a base for auditing and review schemes. It shares common principles with the ISO 9001 standard on quality management systems.

The rings of confidence

● The activities needed in the design and implementation of a good-quality management system start and end with the customer, in two spheres – a customer sphere and a supplier sphere.
● Senior management in all types of industry must take responsibility for the adoption and documentation of the appropriate management systems in their organization.

Chapter 6

Quality management system audit/review and self-assessment

Securing prevention by audit and review of the system

Error or defect prevention is the process of removing or controlling error/defect causes in the system. There are two major elements of this:

- Checking the system.
- Error/defect investigation and follow-up.

These have the same objectives – to find, record and report *possible* causes of error, and to recommend future corrective action.

Checking the system

There are six methods in general use:

a) *Quality audits and reviews*, which subject each area of an organization's activity to a systematic critical examination. Every component of the total system is included, i.e. quality policy, attitudes, training, processes, decision features, operating procedures, documentation. Audits and reviews, as in the field of accountancy, aim to disclose the strengths and the main areas of vulnerability or risk – the areas for improvement.

b) *Quality survey*, a detailed, in-depth examination of a narrower field of activity, i.e. major key areas revealed by quality audits, individual plants, procedures or specific problems common to an organization as a whole.

c) *Quality inspection*, which takes the form of a routine scheduled inspection of a unit or department. The inspection should check standards, employee involvement and working practices, and that work is carried out in accordance with the procedures, etc.

d) *Quality tour*, which is an unscheduled examination of a work area to ensure that, for example, the standards of operation are acceptable, obvious causes of errors are removed, and in general quality standards are maintained.

e) *Quality sampling*, which measures by random sampling, similar to activity sampling, the error potential. Trained observers perform short tours of specific locations by prescribed routes and record the number of potential errors or defects seen. The results may be used to portray trends in the general quality situation.

f) *Quality scrutinies*, which are the application of a formal, critical examination of the process and technological intentions for new or existing facilities, or to assess the potential for mal-operation or malfunction of equipment and the consequential effects of quality. There are similarities between quality scrutinies and FMECA studies (see Chapter 8).

The design of a prevention programme, combining all these elements, is represented in Figure 6.1.

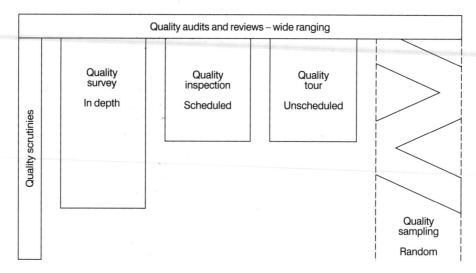

Figure 6.1 *A prevention programme combining various elements of 'checking' the system*

Error or defect investigations and follow-up

The investigation of errors and defects can provide valuable error prevention information. The general method is based on:

- *Collecting* data and information relating to the error or defect.
- *Checking* the validity of the evidence.
- *Selecting* the evidence without making assumptions or jumping to conclusions.

The results of the analysis are then used to:

- *Decide* the most likely cause(s) of the error or defect.
- *Notify* immediately the person(s) able to take corrective action.
- *Record* the findings and outcomes.
- *Report* them to everyone concerned, to prevent a recurrence.

The investigation should not become an inquisition to apportion blame, but should focus on the positive preventive aspects. The types of follow-up to errors and their effects are shown in Table 6.1.

Table 6.1 *Following up errors*

System type	Aim	General effects
Investigation	To prevent a similar error or defect	*Positive:* identification, notification, correction
Inquisition	To identify responsibility	*Negative:* blame, claims, defence

It is hoped that errors or defects are not normally investigated so frequently that the required skills are developed by experience, nor are these skills easily learned in a classroom. One suggested way to overcome this problem is the development of a programmed sequence of questions to form the skeleton of an error or defect investigation questionnaire. This can be set out with the following structure:

a) *Plant equipment* – description, condition, controls, maintenance, suitability, etc.
b) *Environment* – climatic, space, humidity, noise, etc.
c) *People* – duties, information, supervision, instruction, training, attitudes, etc.
d) *Systems* – procedures, instructions, monitoring, control methods, etc.

Internal and external quality management system audits and reviews

A good management system will not function without adequate audits and reviews. The system reviews, which need to be carried out periodically and systematically, are conducted to ensure that the system achieves the required effect, whilst audits are carried out to make sure that actual methods are adhering to the documented procedures. The reviews should use the findings of the audits, for failure to operate according to the plan often signifies difficulties in doing so. A re-examination of the procedures actually being used may lead to system improvements unobtainable by other means.

A schedule for carrying out the *audits* should be drawn up, with different activities perhaps requiring different frequencies. All procedures and systems should be audited at least once during a specified cycle, but not necessarily all at the same audit. For example, every 3 months a selected random sample of the processes could be audited, with the selection designed so that each process is audited at least once per year. There must be, however, a facility to adjust this on the basis of the audit results.

A quality management system *review* should be instituted, perhaps every 12 months, with the aims of:

- ensuring that the system is achieving the desired results
- revealing defects or irregularities in the system
- indicating any necessary improvements and/or corrective actions to eliminate waste or loss
- checking on all levels of management
- uncovering potential danger areas
- verifying that improvements or corrective action procedures are effective.

Clearly, the procedures for carrying out the audits and reviews and the results from them should be documented, and themselves be subject to review. Useful guidance on quality management system audits is given in the international standard ISO 10011.

The assessment of a quality system against a particular standard or set of requirements by internal audit and review is known as a *first-party* assessment or approval scheme. If an *external* customer makes the assessment of a supplier against either its own or a national or international standard, a *second-party* scheme is in operation. The assessment by an independent organization, not connected with any contract between customer and supplier, but acceptable to them both, is known as an *independent third-party* assessment scheme. The latter usually results in some form of certification or registration by the assessment body.

One advantage of the third-party schemes is that they obviate the need for customers to make their own detailed checks, potentially saving both suppliers and customers time and money, and avoiding issues of commercial confidentiality. Just one knowledgeable organization has to be satisfied, rather than a multitude with varying levels of competence. This method often certifies suppliers for contracts without further checking.

Each certification body usually has its own recognized mark, which may be used by registered organizations of assessed capability in their literature, letter headings and marketing activities. There are also publications containing lists of organizations whose quality management systems and/or products and services have been assessed. To be of value, the certification body must itself be recognized and, usually, assessed and registered with a national or international accreditation scheme.

Many organizations have found that the effort of designing and implementing a quality management system good enough to stand up to external independent third-party assessment has been extremely rewarding in:

- involving staff and improving morale
- better process control and improvement
- reduced wastage
- reduced customer service costs.

This is also true of those organizations that have obtained third-party registrations and supply companies which still insist on their own second-party assessment. The reason for this is that most of the standards on management systems, whether national, international, or company-specific, are now very similar indeed. A system that meets the requirements of the ISO 9001 standard, for example, should meet the requirements of most other standards, with only the slight modifications and small emphases here and there required for specific customers. It is the author's experience, and that of his colleagues, that an assessment carried out by one of the independent certified assessment bodies is at least as rigorous and delving as any carried out by a second-party representative.

Internal system audits and reviews should be positive and conducted as part of the preventive strategy and not as a matter of expediency resulting from problems. They should not be carried out only prior to external audits, nor should they be left to the external auditor – whether second or third party. An external auditor discovering discrepancies between actual and documented systems will be inclined to ask why the internal review methods did not discover and correct them, as this type of behaviour in financial control and auditing is commonplace.

Managements need to be fully committed to operating an effective quality management system for all the people within the organization, not just the staff in the 'quality department'. The system must be planned to be effective and achieve its objectives in an uncomplicated way. Having established and documented the processes it is necessary to ensure that they are working and that everyone is operating in accordance with them. The system once established is not static; it should be flexible, to enable the constant seeking of improvements or streamlining.

Quality auditing standard

The growing use of standards internationally emphasizes the importance of auditing as a management tool for this purpose. There are available several guides to management systems auditing (e.g ISO 10011) and the guidance provided in these can be applied equally to any one of the three specific and yet different auditing activities:

● *First-party or internal audits*, carried out by an organization on its own systems, either by staff who are independent of the systems being audited, or by an outside agency.
● *Second-party audits*, carried out by one organization (a purchaser or its outside agent) on another with which it either has contracts to purchase goods or services or intends to do so.
● *Third-party audits*, carried out by independent agencies, to provide assurance to existing and prospective customers for the product or service.

Audit objectives and responsibilities, including the roles of auditors and their independence, and those of the 'client' or auditee, should be understood. The generic steps involved then are as follows:

● *Initiation*, including its scope and frequency.
● *Preparation*, including review of documentation, the programme and working documents.

- *Execution*, including the opening meeting, examination and evaluation, collecting evidence, observations, and closing the meeting with the auditee.
- *Report*, including its preparation, content and distribution.
- *Completion*, including report submission and retention.

Attention should be given at the end of the audit to corrective action and follow-up and the improvement process should be continued by the auditee after the publication of the audit report. This may include a call by the client for a verification audit of the implementation of any corrective actions specified.

Frameworks for self-assessment

Organizations everywhere are under constant pressure to improve their business performance, measure themselves against world-class standards and focus their efforts on the customer. To help in this process, many are turning to total quality models such as the European Foundation for Quality Management's Excellence Model.

Total quality management is the goal of many organizations but it has been difficult until relatively recently to find a universally accepted definition of what this actually means. For some people TQM means statistical process control (SPC) or quality management systems; for others, teamwork and involvement of the workforce.

Clearly there are many different views on what constitutes the 'excellent' organization and, even with an understanding of a framework, there exists the difficulty of calibrating the performance or progress of any organization towards it.

The so-called excellence models now available recognize that customer satisfaction, business objectives, safety and environmental considerations are mutually dependent and are applicable in any organization. Clearly, the application of the ideas involves investment, primarily in people and time – time to implement new concepts, time to train, time for people to recognize the benefits and move forward into new or different organizational cultures. But how will organizations know when they are getting close to excellence or whether they are even on the right road? How will they measure their progress and performance?

There have been many recent developments, and there will continue to be many more, in the search for a standard or framework against which organizations may be assessed or measure themselves, and carry out the so-called 'gap analysis'. To many organizations the ability to judge progress against an accepted set of criteria would be most valuable and informative.

The Malcolm Baldrige National Quality Award (USA)

Most TQM approaches strongly emphasize measurement. Some insist on the use of cost of quality. The recognition that total quality management is a broad culture change vehicle with internal and external focus embracing behavioural and service issues, as well as quality assurance and process control, prompted the United States to develop one of the most famous and now widely used frameworks, the Malcolm Baldrige National Quality Award (MBNQA). The award itself, which is composed of two solid crystal forms 14 inches high, is presented annually to recognize companies in the USA that have 'excelled in quality management and quality achievement'. But it is not the award itself, or even the fact that it is presented each year by the President of the USA, which has attracted the attention of most organizations; it is the excellent framework, which is one of the closest things we have to an international standard for TQM.

The value of a structured discipline using a points system has been well established in quality and safety assurance systems (for example, ISO 9000 and vendor auditing). The extension of this approach to a total quality auditing process has been long established in the Japanese Deming Prize, which is perhaps the most demanding and intrusive auditing process, and there are other excellent models and standards used throughout the world.

In 1987 the MBNQA was introduced for US-based organizations. Many companies have realized the necessity to assess themselves against the Baldrige criteria, if not to enter for the Baldrige Award then certainly as an excellent basis for self-audit and review, to highlight areas for priority attention and provide internal and external benchmarking.

The MBNQA aims to promote:

- Understanding of the requirements for performance excellence and competitiveness improvement.
- Sharing of information of successful performance strategies and the benefits to be derived from using these strategies.

The award criteria are built upon a set of core values and concepts:

- Customer-driven quality
- Leadership
- Continuous improvement and learning
- Valuing employees
- Fast response
- Design quality and prevention
- Long-range view of the future
- Management by fact
- Partnership development
- Company responsibility and citizenship
- Results focus.

These are embodied in a framework of seven first-level categories which are used to assess organizations:

1 Leadership
2 Strategic Planning
3 Customer and Market Focus
4 Information and Analysis
5 Human Resource Focus
6 Process Management
7 Business Results.

Figure 6.2 shows how the framework's system connects and integrates the categories. This has three basic elements: strategy and action plans (customer and market focused), system, and information and analyses. The main driver is the senior executive leadership which creates the values, goals and systems, and guides the sustained pursuit of quality and performance objectives. The system includes a set of well-defined and well-designed processes for meeting the organization's direction and performance requirements. Measures of progress provide a results-oriented basis for channelling actions to deliver ever-improving customer values and organization

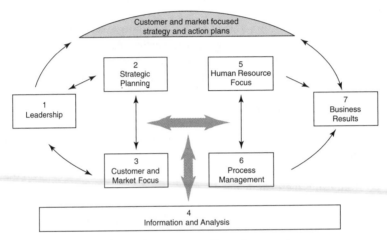

Figure 6.2 *Baldrige criteria for performance excellence framework – a systems perspective. (Source: Malcolm Baldrige National Quality Award, 'Criteria for Performance Excellence', 1999, US National Institute of Standards and Technology, Gaithesburg, USA)*

performance. The overall goal is the delivery of customer satisfaction and market success leading, in turn, to excellent business results. The seven criteria categories are further subdivided into items and areas to address. These are described in some detail in the 'Criteria for Performance Excellence' available from the US National Institute of Standards and Technology, in Gaithesburg, USA.

The European Award for Excellence

In Europe it has also been recognized that the technique of self-assessment is very useful for any organization wishing to monitor and improve its performance. In 1992 the European Foundation for Quality Management (EFQM) launched a European Quality Award which is now widely used for systematic review and measurement of operations. The EFQM model recognized that processes are the means by which a company or organization harnesses and releases the talents of its people to produce results performance. Moreover, improvement in the performance can be achieved only by improving the processes by involving the people. This simple model is shown in Figure 6.3.

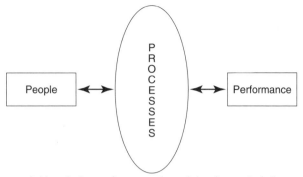

Figure 6.3 *The simple model for improved performance*

Figure 6.4 displays graphically the principle of the full excellence model. Essentially customer satisfaction (results), employee satisfaction (results) and a favourable impact on society (results) are achieved through leadership driving policy and strategy, people partnerships, resources and processes, which lead ultimately to excellence in business results (key performance results) – the enablers deliver the results which in turn drive innovation and learning. The EFQM have provided a weighting for each of the criteria which may be used in scoring self-assessments and making awards. The weightings are not rigid and may be modified to suit specific organizational needs.

The EFQM have thus built a model of criteria and a review framework against which an organization may face and measure itself, to examine any 'gaps'. Such a process is known as self-assessment. Several organizations publish guidelines for self-assessment, including specific ones directed at public sector organizations.

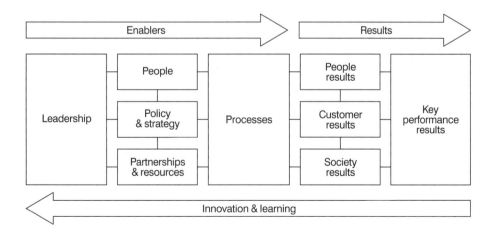

Figure 6.4 *The EQFM excellence model*

Many managers feel the need for a rational basis on which to measure progress in their organization, especially in those companies a few years 'into TQM' which would like the answers to questions such as: 'Where are we now?', 'Where do we need/want to be?' and 'What have we got to do to get there?' These questions need to be answered from internal employees' views, the customers' views and the views of suppliers.

Gap analyses using self-assessment to the European model

Self-assessment promotes business excellence by involving a regular and systematic review of processes and results. It highlights strengths and improvement opportunities, and drives continuous improvement.

Enablers

In the European model, the enabler criteria of: leadership, policy and strategy, people, partnerships, resources and processes focus on what is needed to be done to achieve results. The structure of the enabler criteria is shown in Figure 6.5.

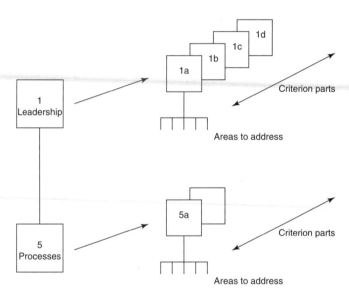

Figure 6.5 *Structure of the criteria – enablers*

The detailed criterion parts are as follows:

1 *Leadership*

How leaders develop and facilitate the achievement of the mission and vision, develop values required for long-term success and implement these via appropriate actions and behaviours, and are personally involved in ensuring that the organization's management system is developed and implemented.

Self-assessment should demonstrate how:

a) leaders develop the mission, vision and values and are role models of a culture of excellence

b) leaders are personally involved in ensuring that the organization's management system is developed, implemented and continuously improved

c) leaders are involved with customers, partners and representatives of society

d) leaders motivate, support and recognize the organization's people.

2 *Policy and strategy*

How the organization implements its mission and vision via a clear stakeholder-focused strategy, supported by relevant policies, plans, objectives, targets and processes.

Self-assessment should demonstrate how:

a) p&s are based on the present and future needs and expectations of stakeholders

b) p&s are based on information from performance measurement, research, learning and creativity-related activities

c) p&s are developed, reviewed and updated

d) p&s are deployed through a framework of key processes

e) p&s are communicated and implemented.

3 *People*

How the organization manages, develops and releases the knowledge and full potential of its people at an individual, team-based and organization-wide level, and plans these activities in order to support its policy and strategy and the effective operation of its processes.

Self-assessment should demonstrate how:

a) people resources are planned, managed and improved

b) people's knowledge and competencies are identified, developed and sustained

c) people are involved and empowered

d) people and the organization have a dialogue

e) people are rewarded, recognized and cared for.

4 *Partnerships and resources*

How the organization plans and manages its external partnerships and internal resources in order to support its policy and strategy and the effective operation of its processes.

Self-assessment should demonstrate how:

a) external partnerships are managed

b) finances are managed

c) buildings, equipment and materials are managed

d) technology is managed

e) information and knowledge are managed.

5 *Processes*

How the organization designs, manages and improves its processes in order to support its policy and strategy and fully satisfy, and generate increasing value for, its customers and stakeholders.

Self-assessment should demonstrate how:

a) processes are systematically designed and managed

b) processes are improved, as needed, using innovation in order to fully satisfy and generate increasing value for customers and other stakeholders

c) products and services are designed and developed based on customer needs and expectations

d) products and services are produced, delivered and serviced
e) customer relationships are managed and enhanced.

Results

The European model's result criteria of: customer results, people results, society results and key performance results focus on what the organization has achieved and is achieving in relation to its:

- external customers
- people
- local, national, and international society, as appropriate
- planned performance.

These can be expressed as discrete results, but ideally as trends over a period of years. The structure of the results criteria is shown in Figure 6.6. Key performance outcomes may include financial and non-financial outcomes. Key performance indicators may include those related to processes, external resources (including partnerships), buildings, equipment, materials, technology, information, knowledge and financial indicators.

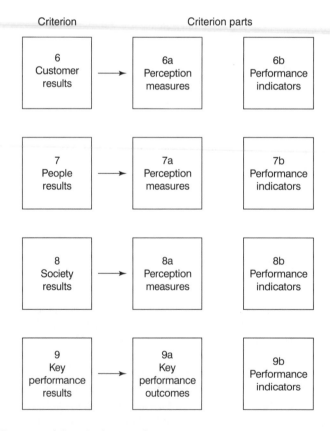

Criterion   Criterion parts

6 Customer results	→	6a Perception measures	6b Performance indicators
7 People results	→	7a Perception measures	7b Performance indicators
8 Society results	→	8a Perception measures	8b Performance indicators
9 Key performance results	→	9a Key performance outcomes	9b Performance indicators

Figure 6.6 *Structure of the criteria – results*

'Performance excellence' is assessed relative to the organization's business environment and circumstances, based on information which sets out:

● the organization's actual performance
● the organization's own targets

and wherever possible:

● the performance of competitors or similar organizations
● the performance of 'best in class' organizations.

Assessing the criteria

The model criteria are concerned with *what* an organization or business unit has achieved, and is achieving and *how* it achieves it. Assessment against the framework is performed using the so-called RADAR system:

Results
Approach
Deployment
Assessment
Review

The RADAR 'screen' with the next level of detail is shown in Figure 6.7

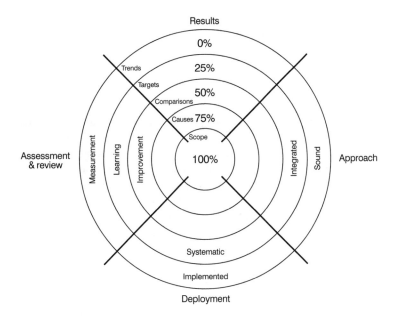

Figure 6.7 *The RADAR 'screen'*

Methodologies for self-assessment

The EFQM provide a flow diagram of the general steps involved in undertaking self-assessment. A simplified version of this is shown in Figure 6.8.

There are a number of approaches to carrying out self-assessment, including:

- discussion group/workshop methods
- surveys, questionnaires and interviews (peer involvement)
- pro formas
- organizational self-analysis matrices
- an award simulation
- activity or process audits
- hybrid approaches.

Whichever method is used, the emphasis should be on understanding the organization's strengths and areas for improvement, rather than the score. The scoring charts provide a consistent basis for establishing a quantitative measure of performance

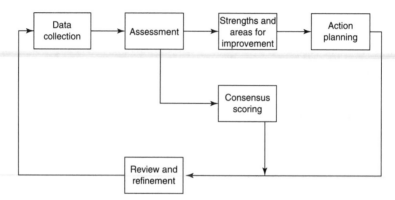

Figure 6.8 *The key steps in self-assessment*

against the model, and gaining consensus promotes discussion and development of the issues facing the organization. It should also gain the involvement, interest and commitment of the senior management, but the scores should not become an end in themselves. Tito Conti, often called 'the father of self-assessment', following the contribution he made to its establishment and development through the EFQM, when he was head of Fiat, has expressed concern that organizations can become obsessed with self-assessment scores rather than focusing on the improvement opportunities identified.

A few last words on self-assessment

There is great overlap between the criteria used by the various awards and it may be necessary for an organization to rationalize them. The main components, however, must be the organization's processes, management systems, people management and results, customer results and key 'business' performance results. Self-assessment provides an organization with vital information in monitoring its progress towards its goals and 'excellence'. The external assessments used in the processes of making awards must be based on these self-assessments that are performed as prerequisites for improvement.

Management jargon is increasingly confused by a vast literature, spiced with acronyms, the generation of which often bend the meaning of words. There is also often in the leadership of large organizations an ego-driven or publicity-seeking wish to invent new buzz words. It may be necessary to assess the status of the language to be used before launching a self-assessment process. If recipients are not familiar with certain language, many propositions will be meaningless. A preliminary teach-in or awareness process may even be necessary.

Whatever are the main 'motors' for driving an organization towards its *vision* or *mission*, they must be linked to the five stakeholders embraced by the values of any organization, namely:

Customers		Shareholders
Employees	and	Community
Suppliers		

In any normal business or organization, measurements are continuously being made, often in retrospect, by the leaders of the organization to reflect the value put on the organization by its five stakeholders. Too often, these continuous readings are made by internal biased agents with short-term priorities, not always in the best long-term interests of the organization or its customers, i.e. narrow fire-fighting scenarios which can blind the organization's strategic eye. Third-party agents, however, can carry out or facilitate periodic audits and reviews from the perspective of one or more of the key stakeholders, with particular emphasis on forward priorities and needs. These reviews will allow realignment of the principal driving motors to focus on the critical success factors and continuous improvement, to maintain a balanced and powerful general thrust which moves the whole organization towards its mission.

The relative importance of the five stakeholders may vary in time but all are important. The first group, customers, employees and suppliers, which comprise the core value chain, are the *determinant* elements. The application of total quality principles in these areas will provide satisfaction as a *resultant* to the shareholders and the community. Thus, added value will benefit the community and the environment. The ideal is a long way off in most organizations, however, and active attention to the needs of the shareholders and/or community remains a priority for one major reason – they are the 'customers' of most organizational activities and are vital stakeholders.

Any instrument which is developed for self-assessment may be used at several stages in an organization's history:

- *before* starting an improvement programme to identify 'strengths' and 'areas for improvement', and focus attention. At this stage a parallel cost of quality exercise may be a powerful way to overcome scepticism and get 'buy-in'
- as part of a programme launch, especially using a 'survey' instrument
- every one or two years after the launch to steer and benchmark.

The systematic measurement and review of operations is one of the most important management activities of any organization. Self-assessment leads to clearly discerned strengths and areas for improvement by focusing on the relationship between the people, processes and performance. Within any successful organization it will be a regular activity.

Adding the systems to the TQM model

In Chapters 1 and 2 the foundations for TQM were set down. The core of total quality was established as the customer–supplier chains that extend through and out from an organization. It was recognized that if the chains are 'cut' anywhere, processes that must be managed will be found. Within the TQM framework were identified the 'soft' outcomes of total quality, namely culture change, communication improvements and commitment.

To this foundation must be added the first hard management necessity – a quality system, based on any good international standard. This is shown in Figure 6.9.

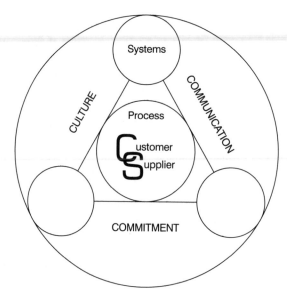

Figure 6.9 *Total quality management model – the quality management system*

Chapter highlights

Securing prevention by audit and review of the system

- There are two major elements of error or defect prevention: checking the system, and error/defect investigations and follow-up. Six methods of checking the quality systems are in general use: audits and reviews, surveys, inspections, tours, sampling and scrutinies.

Error or defect investigations and follow-up

- Investigations proceed by collecting, checking and selecting data, and analysing it by deciding causes, notifying people, recording and reporting findings and outcomes.

Internal and external quality management system audits and reviews

- A good-quality management system will not function without adequate audits and reviews. Audits make sure the actual methods are adhering to documented procedures. Reviews ensure the system achieves the desired effect.
- System assessment by internal audit and review is known as first-party, by external customer as second-party, and by an independent organization as third-party certification. For the latter to be of real value the certification body must itself be recognized.

Frameworks for self-assessment

- One of the most widely used frameworks for TQM self-assessment in the USA is the Malcolm Baldrige National Quality Award (MBNQA).
- The MBNQA criteria are built on ten core values and concepts, which are embodied on a framework of seven first-level categories: leadership (driver), information and analyses, strategic process planning, human resource development and management, management business (system), business results (measures of progress) and customer focus and satisfaction (goal). These are comparable with the categories of the Japanese Deming Prize, and the nine components of the European Quality Award: leadership, policy and strategy partnerships, people, resources, and processes (ENABLERS), people results, customer results, society results, and key performance results (RESULTS).
- The various award criteria provide rational bases against which to measure progress towards TQM in organizations. Self-assessment against, for example, the EFQM Excellence model should be a regular activity, as it identifies opportunities for improvement in performance through processes and people.

Adding the systems to the TQM model

- To the foundation framework of the customer–supplier chain, processes and the 'soft' outcomes of TQM must be added the first hard management necessity – a quality system based on a good international standard.

Discussion questions

1 Discuss the preparations required for the negotiation of a one-year contract with a major material supplier.

2 Imagine that you are the chief executive or equivalent in an organization of your own choice, and that you plan to introduce the concept of just-in-time (JIT) into the organization:

   a) Prepare a briefing of your senior managers, which should include your assessment of the aims, objectives and benefits to be gained from the implementation.
   b) Outline the steps you would take to implement JIT, and explain how you would attempt to ensure its success.

3 You are the manager of a busy insurance office. Last year's abnormal winter gales led to an exceptionally high level of insurance claims for house damage caused by strong winds, and you had considerable problems in coping with the greatly increased workload. The result was excessively long delays in both acknowledging and settling customers' claims.

   Your area manager has asked you to outline a plan for dealing with such a situation should it arise again. The plan should identify what actions you would take to deal with the work, and what, if anything, should be done now to enable you to take those actions should the need arise.

   What proposals would you make, and why?

4 Explain the basic philosophy behind quality management systems such as those specified in the ISO 9000 series. How can an effective quality management system contribute to continuous improvement in an international banking operation?

5 What role does a quality management system based on ISO 9001 have in TQM? How should an organization such as British Aerospace view such a standard?

6 Explain what is meant by independent third-party certification to a standard such as ISO 9000^{AQ}, and discuss the merits of such a scheme for an organization.

7 Compare and contrast the role of quality management systems in the following organizations:

a) a private hospital
b) a medium-sized engineering company
c) a branch of a clearing bank.

8 List the nine main categories of the EFQM Excellence Model. How may such criteria be used as the basis for a self-assessment process?

9 Self-assessment using the EFQM Excellence Model criteria enables an organization to systematically review its business processes and results. Briefly describe the criteria and discuss the main aspects of self-assessment.

10 Self-appraisal or assessment against the EFQM Excellence Model can be used by organizations to monitor the progress of their TQM programmes:

a) Briefly describe the criteria and explain the steps that an organization would have to follow to carry out a self-assessment.
b) How could self-assessment against the model be used in a large multi-site organization to drive continuous improvement?

TQM – The Tools and the Improvement Cycle

How doth the little busy bee
Improve each shining hour,
And gather honey all the day
From every opening flower!

Isaac Watts, 1674–1748, from 'Against Idleness and Mischief'

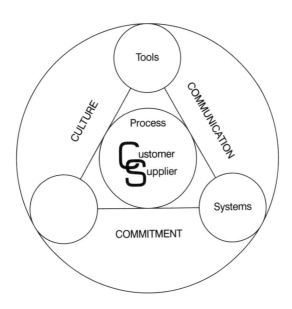

Chapter 7

Measurement of quality

Performance measurement and the improvement cycle

Traditionally, performance measures and indicators have been derived from cost-accounting information, often based on outdated and arbitrary principles. These provide little motivation to support attempts to introduce TQM and, in some cases, actually inhibit continuous improvement because they are unable to map process performance. In the organization that is to succeed over the long term, performance must begin to be measured by the improvements seen by the customer.

In the cycle of never-ending improvement, measurement plays an important role in:

- tracking progress against organizational goals
- identifying opportunities for improvement.
- comparing performance against internal standards.
- comparing performance against external standards.

Measures are used in *process control*, e.g. control charts (see Chapter 8), and in *performance improvement,* e.g. quality improvement teams (see Chapters 10 and 11), so they should give information about how well processes and people are doing and motivate them to perform better in the future.

The author has seen many examples of so-called performance measurement systems that frustrated improvement efforts. Various problems include systems that:

1 Produce irrelevant or misleading information.
2 Track performance in single, isolated dimensions.
3 Generate financial measures too late, e.g. quarterly, for mid-course corrections or remedial action.

4 Do not take account of the customer perspective, both internal and external.
5 Distort management's understanding of how effective the organization has been in implementing its strategy.
6 Promote behaviour and *undermine* the achievement of the strategic objectives.

Typical harmful summary measures of local performance are purchase price, machine or plan efficiencies, direct labour costs, and ratios of direct to indirect labour. These are incompatible with quality-improvement measures such as process and throughput times, delivery performance, inventory reductions and increases in flexibility, which are first and foremost *non-financial*. Financial summaries provide valuable information of course, but they should not be used for control. Effective decision-making requires direct physical measures for operational feedback and improvement.

One example of a 'measure' with these shortcomings is return on investment (ROI). ROI can be computed only after profits have been totalled for a given period. It was designed therefore as a single-period, long-term measure, but it is often used as a short-term one. Perhaps this is because most executive bonus 'packages' in the West are based on short-term measures. ROI tells us what happened, not what is happening or what will happen, and, for complex and detailed projects, ROI is inaccurate and irrelevant.

Many managers have a poor or incomplete understanding of their processes and products or services, and, looking for an alternative stimulus, become interested in financial indicators. The use of ROI, for example, for evaluating strategic requirements and performance can lead to a discriminatory allocation of resources. In many ways the financial indicators used in many businesses have remained static while the environment in which they operate has changed dramatically.

Traditionally, the measures used have not been linked to the processes where the value-adding activities take place. What has been missing is improvement measures that provide feedback to people in all areas of business operations. Of course, TQM stresses the need to start with the process for fulfilling customer needs.

The critical elements of a good performance measurement and management effort look like any other list associated with total quality management:

- Leadership and commitment
- Full employee involvement
- Good planning
- Sound implementation strategy
- Measurement and evaluation
- Control and improvement
- Achieving and maintaining standards of excellence.

The Deming cycle of continuous improvement – *PLAN DO CHECK ACT* – clearly requires measurement to drive it, and yet it is a useful design aid for the measurement system itself:

PLAN   – establish performance objectives and standards.
DO   – measure actual performance.

CHECK – compare actual performance with the objectives and standards – determine the gap.

ACT   – take the necessary actions to close the gap and make the necessary improvements.

Before we use performance measurement in the improvement cycle, however, we should attempt to answer four basic questions:

1 Why measure?
2 What to measure?
3 Where to measure?
4 How to measure?

Why measure?

It has been said often that it is not possible to manage what cannot be measured.

Whether this is strictly true or not there are clear arguments for measuring. In a quality-driven, never-ending improvement environment, the following are some of the main reasons *why measurement is needed* and why it plays a key role in quality and productivity improvement:

- To ensure customer requirements *have* been met.
- To be able to set sensible *objectives* and comply with them.
- To provide *standards* for establishing comparisons.
- To provide *visibility* and provide a 'scoreboard' for people to *monitor* their own performance levels.
- To highlight *quality problems* and determine which areas require *priority attention*.
- To give an indication of the *costs of poor quality.*
- To justify the *use of resources.*
- To provide *feedback* for driving the improvement effort.

It is also important to know the impact of TQM on improvements in business performance, on sustaining current performance, and perhaps on reducing any decline in performance.

What to measure?

In the business of process improvement, process understanding, definition, measurement and management are tied inextricably together. In order to assess and evaluate performance accurately, appropriate measurement must be designed, developed and maintained by people who *own* the processes concerned. They may find it necessary to measure effectiveness, efficiency, quality, impact and productivity. In these areas there are many types of measurement, including direct output or input figures, the cost of poor quality, economic data, comments and complaints from customers, information from customer or employee surveys, etc., generally continuous variable measures (such as time) or discrete attribute measures (such as absentees).

No one can provide a generic list of what should be measured but, once it has been decided what measures are appropriate, they may be converted into indicators. These include ratios, scales, rankings, and financial and time-based indicators. Whichever measures and indicators are used by the process owners, they must reflect the true performance of the process in customer–supplier terms, and emphasize continuous improvement. Time-related measures and indicators have great value.

Where to measure?

If true measures of the effectiveness of TQM are to be obtained, there are three components that must be examined – the human, technical and business components.

The human component is clearly of major importance and the key tests are that, wherever measures are used, they must be:

1 Understood by all the people being measured.
2 Accepted by the individuals concerned.
3 Compatible with the rewards and recognition systems.
4 Designed to offer minimal opportunity for manipulation.

Technically, the measures must be the ones that truly represent the controllable aspects of the processes, rather than simple output measures that cannot be related to process management. They must also be correct, precise and accurate.

The business component requires that the measures are objective, timely and result-oriented, and above all they must mean something to those working in and around the process, *including the customers.*

How to measure?

Measurement, as any other management system, requires the stages of design, analysis, development, evaluation, implementation and review. The system must be designed to measure *progress*, otherwise it will not engage the improvement cycle. Progress is important in five main areas: effectiveness, efficiency, productivity, quality and impact.

Effectiveness

Effectiveness may be defined as the percentage actual output over the expected output:

$$\text{Effectiveness} = \frac{\text{Actual output}}{\text{Expected output}} \times 100 \text{ per cent}$$

Hence effectiveness looks at the *output* side of the process and is about the implementation of the objectives – doing what you said you would do. Effectiveness measures should reflect whether the organization, group or process owner(s) are achieving the desired results, accomplishing the right things. Measures of this may include:

- Quality, e.g. a grade of product, or a level of service.
- Quantity, e.g. tonnes, lots, bedrooms cleaned, accounts opened.
- Timeliness, e.g. speed of response, product lead times, cycle time.
- Cost/price, e.g. unit costs.

Efficiency

Efficiency is concerned with the percentage resource actually over the resources that were planned to be used:

$$\text{Efficiency} = \frac{\text{Resources actually used}}{\text{Resources planned to be used}} \times 100 \text{ per cent}$$

Clearly, this is a process *input* issue and measures performance of the process system management. It is, of course, possible to use resources 'efficiently' while being *ineffective*, so performance efficiency improvement must be related to certain output objectives.

All process inputs may be subjected to efficiency measurement, so we may use labour/staff efficiency, equipment efficiency (or utilization), materials efficiency, information efficiency, etc. Inventory data and throughput times are often used in efficiency and productivity ratios.

Productivity

Productivity measures should be designed to relate the process outputs to its inputs:

$$\text{Productivity} = \frac{\text{Outputs}}{\text{Inputs}}$$

and this may be quoted as expected or actual productivity:

$$\text{Expected productivity} = \frac{\text{Expected output}}{\text{Resources expected to be consumed}}$$

$$\text{Actual productivity} = \frac{\text{Actual output}}{\text{Resources actually consumed}}$$

There is a vast literature on productivity and its measurement, but simple ratios such as tonnes per man-hour (expected and actual), computer output per operator-day, and many others like this are in use. Productivity measures may be developed for each combination of inputs, e.g. sales/all employee costs.

Quality

This has been defined elsewhere, of course (see Chapter 1). The *non-quality* related measures include the simple counts of defect or error rates (perhaps in parts per million), percentage outside specification or Cp/Cpk values, deliveries not on time, or more generally as the costs of poor quality. When the positive costs of prevention of poor quality are included, these provide a balanced measure of the costs of quality.

The quality measures should also indicate positively whether we are doing a good job in terms of customer satisfaction, implementing the objectives, and whether the designs, systems and solutions to problems are meeting the requirements. These really are voice-of-the-customer measures.

Impact

Impact measures should lead to key performance indicators for the business or organization, including monitoring improvement over time. Value-added management (VAM) requires the identification and elimination of all non-value-adding wastes, including time. Value added is simply the volume of sales (or other measure of 'turnover') minus the total input costs, and provides a good direct measure of the impact of the improvement process on the performance of the business. A related ratio, percentage return on value added (ROVA) is another financial indicator that may be used:

$$\text{ROVA} = \frac{\text{Net profits before tax}}{\text{Value added}} \times 100 \text{ per cent}$$

Other measures or indicators of impact on the business are *growth* in sales, assets, numbers of passengers/students, etc., and *asset-utilization* measures such as return on investment (ROI) or capital employed (ROCE), earnings per share, etc.

Some of the impact measures may be converted to people productivity ratios, e.g.:

$$\frac{\text{Value added}}{\text{Number of employees (or employee costs)}}$$

Activity-based costing (ABC) is an information system that maintains and processes data on an organization's activities and cost objectives. It is based on the activities performed being identified and the costs being traced to them. ABC uses various 'cost drivers' to trace the cost of activities to the cost of the products or services. The activity and cost-driver concepts are the heart of ABC. Cost drivers reflect the demands placed on activities by products, services or other cost targets. Activities are processes or procedures that cause work and thereby consume resources. This clearly measures impact, both on and by the organization.

The implementation of performance measurement systems

It has already been established that a good measurement system will start with the customer and measure the right things. The value of any measure clearly needs to be compared with the cost of producing it. There will be appropriate measures for different parts of the organization, but everywhere they must relate process performance to the needs of the process customer. All critical parts of the process must be measured, and it is often better to start with simple measures and improve them.

There must be a recognition of the need to distinguish between different measures for different purposes. For example, an operator may measure time, various process parameters and amounts, while at the management level measuring costs and delivery timeliness may be more appropriate.

Participation in the development of measures enhances their understanding and acceptance. Process-owners can assist in defining the required performance measures, provided that senior managers have communicated their mission clearly, determined the critical success factors, and identified the critical processes (see Chapter 13).

If all employees participate, and own the measurement processes, there will be lower resistance to the system, and a positive commitment towards future changes will be engaged. This will derive from the 'volunteered accountability', which will in turn make the individual contribution more visible. Involvement in measurement also strengthens the links in the customer–supplier chains and gives quality improvement teams much clearer objectives. This should lead to greater short-term and long-term productivity gains.

There are a number of possible reasons why measurement systems fail:

1 They do not define performance operationally.
2 They do not relate performance to the process.
3 The boundaries of the process are not defined.
4 The measures are misunderstood or misused or measure the wrong things.
5 There is no distinction between control and improvement.
6 There is a fear of exposing poor and good performance.
7 They are seen as an extra burden in terms of time and reporting.
8 There is a perception of reduced autonomy.
9 Too many measurements are focused internally and too few are focused externally.
10 There is a fear of the introduction of tighter management controls.

These and other problems are frequently due to poor planning at the implementation stage or a failure to assess current systems of measurement. Before the introduction of a total quality-based performance measurement system, an audit of the existing systems should be carried out. Its purpose is to establish the effectiveness of existing measures, their compatibility with the quality drive, their relationship with the processes concerned, and their closeness to the objectives of meeting customer requirements. The audit should also highlight areas where performance has not been measured previously, and indicate the degree of understanding and participation of the employees in the existing systems and the actions that result.

Generic questions that may be asked during the audit include:

● Is there a performance measurement system in use?
● Has it been effectively communicated throughout the organization?
● Is it systematic?
● Is it efficient?
● Is it well understood?
● Is it applied?
● Is it linked to the mission and objectives of the organization?
● Is there a regular review and update?

- Is action taken to improve performance following the measurement?
- Are the people who own the processes engaged in measuring their own performance?
- Have employees been properly trained to conduct the measurement?

Following such an audit, there are twelve basic steps for the introduction of TQM-based performance measurement. Half of these are planning steps and the other half implementation.

Planning
1 Identify the purpose of conducting measurement, i.e. is it for:
   a) Reporting, e.g. ROI reported to shareholders.
   b) Controlling, e.g. using process data on control charts.
   c) Improving, e.g. monitoring the results of a quality improvement team project.
2 Choose the right balance between individual measures (activity- or task-related) and group measures (process- and subprocess-related) and make sure they reflect process performance.
3 Plan to measure all the key elements of performance, not just one, e.g. time, cost and product quality variables may all be important.
4 Ensure that the measures will reflect the voice of the internal/external customers.
5 Carefully select measures that will be used to establish standards of performance.
6 Allow time for the learning process during the introduction of a new measurement system.

Implementation
7 Ensure full participation during the introductory period and allow the system to mould through participation.
8 Carry out cost/benefit analysis on the data generation, and ensure measures that have high 'leverage' are selected.
9 Make the effort to spread the measurement system as widely as possible, since effective decision-making will be based on measures from *all* areas of the business operation.
10 Use *surrogate* measures for subjective areas where quantification is difficult, e.g. improvements in morale may be 'measured' by reductions in absenteeism or staff turnover rates.
11 Design the measurement systems to be as flexible as possible, to allow for changes in strategic direction and continual review.
12 Ensure that the measures reflect the quality drive by showing small incremental achievements that match the never-ending improvement approach.

In summary, the measurement system must be designed, planned and implemented to reflect customer requirements, give visibility to the processes and the progress made, communicate the total quality effort and engage the never-ending improvement cycle. So it must itself be periodically reviewed. A performance measurement framework related to strategy development and goal deployment is provided in Chapter 13.

Benchmarking

Product, service and process improvements can only take place in relation to established standards, and the improvements then being incorporated into the new standards. *Benchmarking*, one of the most transferable aspects of Rank Xerox's approach to total quality management, and thought to have originated in Japan, measures an organization's operations, products and services against those of its competitors in a ruthless fashion. It is a means by which targets, priorities and operations that will lead to competitive advantage can be established.

Benchmarking is the continuous process of measuring products, services and processes against those of industry leaders or the toughest competitors. This results in a search for best practices, those that will lead to superior performance, through measuring performance, continuously implementing change and emulating the best.

There may be many reasons for carrying out benchmarking. Some of them are set against various objectives in Table 7.1. The links between benchmarking and TQM are clear – establishing objectives based on industry best practice should directly contribute to better meeting of the internal and external customer requirements.

Table 7.1 *Reasons for benchmarking*

Objectives	Without benchmarking	With benchmarking
Becoming competitive	● Internally focused ● Evolutionary change	● Understanding of competitiveness ● Ideas from proven practices
Industry best practices	● Few solutions ● Frantic catch-up activity	● Many options ● Superior performance
Defining customer requirements	● Based on history or gut feeling ● Perception	● Market reality ● Objective evaluation
Establishing effective goals and objectives	● Lacking external focus ● Reactive	● Credible, unarguable ● Proactive
Developing true measures of productivity	● Pursuing pet projects ● Strength and weaknesses not understood ● Route of least resistance	● Solving real problems ● Understanding outputs ● Based on industry best practices

There are four basic types of benchmarking:

Internal – a comparison of internal operations.
Competitive – specific competitor-to-competitor comparisons for a product or function of interest
Functional – comparisons to similar functions within the same broad industry or to industry leaders

Generic   – comparisons of business processes that are very similar regardless of the industry.

The evolution of benchmarking in an organization is likely to progress through four focuses. Initially attention may be concentrated on competitive products or services, including, for example, design, development and operational features. This should develop into a focus on industry best practices and may include, for example, aspects of distribution or service. The real breakthrough is when the organization focuses on all aspects of the total business performance, across all functions and aspects, and addresses current *and projected* performance gaps. This should lead to the focus on true continuous improvement.

At its simplest, competitive benchmarking, the most common form, requires every department to examine itself against the counterpart in the best competing companies. This includes a scrutiny of all aspects of their activities. Benchmarks which may be important for *customer satisfaction*, for example, might include:

● Product or service consistency
● Correct and on-time delivery
● Speed of response or new product development
● Correct billing.

For *impact* the benchmarks may include:

● Waste, rejects or errors
● Inventory levels/work in progress
● Costs of operation
● Staff turnover.

The task is to work out what has to be done to improve on the competition's performance in each of the chosen areas.

At regular (say, monthly) meetings, managers discuss the results of the competitive benchmarking, and on a more frequent basis departmental managers discuss quality problems with staff. For example, one afternoon may be set aside for the benchmark meetings followed by a 'walkabout' when the manager observes directly the activities actually taking place and compares them mentally with the competitors' operations.

The process has fifteen stages and these are all focused on trying to *measure* comparisons of competitiveness:

PLAN   Select department(s) or process group(s) for benchmarking.
         Identify best competitor, perhaps using customer feedback or industry observers.
         Identify benchmarks.
         Bring together the appropriate team to be involved.
         Decide information and data collection methodology (do not forget desk research!).
         Prepare for any visits and interact with target organizations.
         Use data collection methodology.

ANALYSE   Compare the organization and its 'competitors', using the benchmark data.
          Catalogue the information and create a 'competency centre'.
          Understand the 'enabling processes' as well as the performance measures.

DEVELOP   Set new performance level objectives/standards.
          Develop action plans to achieve goals and integrate into the organization.

IMPROVE   Implement specific actions and integrate them into the business processes.

REVIEW   Monitor the results and improvements.
          Review the benchmarks and the ongoing relationship with the target organization.

Benchmarking is very important in the administration areas, since it continuously measures services and practices against the equivalent operation in the toughest direct competitors or organizations renowned as leaders in the areas, even if they are in the same organization. An example of quantitative benchmarks in absenteeism is given in Table 7.2.

Table 7.2 *Quantitative benchmarking in absenteeism*

Organisation's absence level (%)	Productivity opportunity
Under 3	This level matches an aggressive benchmark that has been achieved in 'excellent' organizations.
3–4	This level may be viewed within the organisation as a good performance – representing a moderate productivity opportunity improvement.
5–8	This level is tolerated by many organisations but represents a major improvement opportunity.
9–10	This level indicates that a serious absenteeism problem exists.
Over 10	This level of absenteeism is extremely high and requires immediate senior management attention.

Technologies and conditions vary between different industries and markets, but the basic concepts of measurement and benchmarking are of general validity. The objective should be to produce products and services that conform to the requirements of the customer in a never-ending improvement environment. The way to accomplish this is to use the continuous improvement cycle in all the operating departments – nobody should be exempt. Measurement and benchmarking are not separate sciences or unique theories of quality management, but rather strategic approaches to getting the best out of people, processes, products, plant and programmes.

Costs of quality

Manufacturing a quality product, providing a quality service, or doing a quality job – one with a high degree of customer satisfaction – is not enough. The cost of achieving these goals must be carefully managed, so that the long-term effect on the business or organization is a desirable one. These costs are a true measure of the quality effort. A competitive product or service based on a balance between quality and cost factors is the principal goal of responsible management and may be aided by a competent analysis of the costs of quality (COQ).

The analysis of quality-related costs is a significant management tool that provides:

● A method of assessing the effectiveness of the management of quality.
● A means of determining problem areas, opportunities, savings, and action priorities.

The costs of quality are no different from any other costs. Like the costs of maintenance, design, sales, production/operations, and other activities, they can be budgeted, measured and analysed.

Having specified the quality of design, the operating units have the task of matching it. The necessary activities will incur costs that may be separated into prevention costs, appraisal costs and failure costs, the so-called P-A-F model first presented by Feigenbaum. Failure costs can be further split into those resulting from internal and external failure.

Prevention costs

These are associated with the design, implementation and maintenance of the total quality management system. Prevention costs are planned and are incurred before actual operation. Prevention includes:

Product or service requirements

The determination of requirements and the setting of corresponding specifications (which also takes account of process capability) for incoming materials, processes, intermediates, finished products and services.

Quality planning

The creation of quality, reliability, and operational, production, supervision, process control, inspection and other special plans, e.g. pre-production trials, required to achieve the quality objective.

Quality assurance

The creation and maintenance of the quality system.

Inspection equipment

The design, development and/or purchase of equipment for use in inspection work.

Training
The development, preparation and maintenance of training programmes for operators, supervisors, staff and managers, both to achieve and maintain capability.

Miscellaneous
Clerical, travel, supply, shipping, communications and other general office management activities associated with quality.

Resources devoted to prevention give rise to the '*costs of doing it right the first time*'.

Appraisal costs

These costs are associated with the supplier's and customer's evaluation of purchased materials, processes, intermediates, products and services to assure conformance with the specified requirements. Appraisal includes:

Verification
Checking of incoming material, process set-up, first-offs, running processes, intermediates and final products, including produce or service performance appraisal against agreed specifications.

Quality audits
To check that the quality system is functioning satisfactorily.

Inspection equipment
The calibration and maintenance of equipment used in all inspection activities.

Vendor rating
The assessment and approval of all suppliers, of both products and services.

Appraisal activities result in the '*costs of checking it is right*'.

Internal failure costs

These costs occur when the results of work fail to reach designed quality standards and are detected before transfer to the customer takes place. Internal failure includes the following:

Waste
The activities associated with doing unnecessary work or holding stocks as the result of errors, poor organization or poor communications, the wrong materials, etc.

Scrap
Defective product, material or stationery that cannot be repaired, used or sold.

Rework or rectification
The correction of defective material or errors to meet the requirements.

Re-inspection
The re-examination of products or work that have been rectified.

Downgrading
A product that is usable but does not meet specifications may be downgraded and sold as 'second quality' at a low price.

Failure analysis
The activity required to establish the causes of internal product or service failure.

External failure costs

These costs occur when products or services fail to reach design quality standards but are not detected until after transfer to the consumer. External failure includes:

Repair and servicing
Either of returned products or those in the field.

Warranty claims
Failed products that are replaced or services re-performed under some form of guarantee.

Complaints
All work and costs associated with handling and servicing of customers' complaints.

Returns
The handling and investigation of rejected or recalled products or materials, including transport costs.

Liability
The result of product or service liability litigation and other claims, which may include a change of contract.

Loss of goodwill
The impact on reputation and image, which impinges directly on future prospects for sales.

External and internal failure produce the '*costs of getting it wrong*'.

Order re-entry, unnecessary travel and telephone calls, conflict, are just a few examples of the wastage or failure costs often excluded. Every organization should be aware of the costs of getting it wrong, and management needs to obtain some idea how much failure is costing each year.

Clearly, this classification of cost elements may be used to interrogate any internal transformation process. Using the internal customer requirements concept as the standard for failure, these cost assessments can be made wherever information, data, materials, service or artefacts are transferred from one person or one department to another. It is the 'internal' costs of lack of quality that lead to the claim that approximately one-third of *all* our efforts are wasted.

The relationship between the quality-related costs of prevention, appraisal and failure and increasing quality awareness and improvement in the organization is shown in Figure 7.1. Where the quality awareness is low the total quality-related costs are high, the failure costs predominating. As awareness of the cost to the organization of failure gets off the ground, through initial investment in training, an increase in appraisal costs usually results. As the increased appraisal leads to investigations and further awareness, further investment in prevention is made to improve design features, processes and systems. As the preventive action takes effect, the failure *and* appraisal costs fall and the total costs reduce.

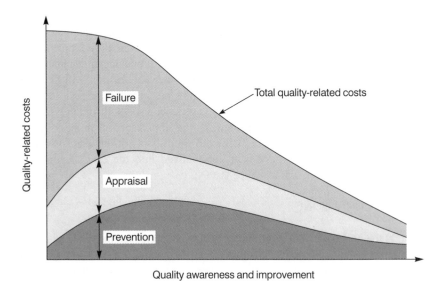

Figure 7.1 *Increasing quality awareness and improvement activities. (Source: British Standard BS 6143: 1991)*

The first presentations of the P-A-F model suggested that there may be an optimum operating level at which the combined costs are at the minimum. The author, however, has not yet found one organization in which the total costs have risen following investment in prevention.

The process model for quality costing

The P-A-F model for quality costing has a number of drawbacks. In TQM, prevention of problems, defects, errors, waste, etc., is one of the prime functions, but it can be argued that everything a well-managed organization does is directed at preventing quality problems. This makes separation of *prevention costs* very difficult. There are clearly a range of prevention activities in any manufacturing or service organization that are integral to ensuring quality but may never be included in the schedule of quality-related costs.

It may be impossible and unnecessary to categorize costs into the three categories of P-A-F. For example, a design review may be considered a prevention cost, an appraisal cost, or even a failure cost, depending on how and where it is used in the process. Another criticism of the P-A-F model is that it focuses attention on cost reduction and plays down, or in some cases even ignores, the positive contribution made to price and sales volume by improved quality.

The most serious criticism of the original P-A-F model presented by Feigenbaum and used in, for example, British Standard 6143: 1981 – 'Guide to the determination and use of quality-related costs', is that it implies an acceptable 'optimum' quality level above which there is a trade-off between investment in prevention and failure costs. Clearly, this is not in tune with the never-ending improvement philosophy of TQM. The key focus of TQM is on process improvement, and a cost categorization scheme that does not consider process costs, such as the P-A-F model, has limitations.

In a total quality-related costs system that focuses on processes rather than products or services, the operating costs of generating customer satisfaction will be of prime importance. The so-called 'process cost model', now described in the revised BS 6143: 1991 - 'Guide to economics of quality', Part 1, sets out a method for applying quality costing to any process or service. It recognizes the importance of process ownership and measurement, and uses process modelling to simplify classification. The categories of the cost of quality (COQ) have been rationalized into the cost of conformance (COC) and the cost of non-conformance (CONC):

$$COQ = COC + CONC$$

The COC is the process cost of providing products or services to the required standards, by a given specified process in the most effective manner, i.e. the cost of the ideal process where every activity is carried out according to the requirements first time, every time. The CONC is the failure cost associated with the process not being operated to the requirements, or the cost due to variability in the process. Part 2 of BS 6143: 1991 still deals with the P-A-F model, but without the 'optimum'/minimum cost theory (see Figure 7.1).

Process cost models can be used for any process within an organization and developed for the process by flowcharting. This will identify the key process steps and the parameters that are monitored in the process. The process cost elements should then be identified and recorded under the categories of product/service (outputs), and people, systems, plant or equipment, materials, environment, information (inputs). The COC and CONC for each stage of the process will comprise a list of all the parameters monitored.

Steps in process cost modelling

Process cost modelling is a methodology that lends itself to stepwise analysis, and the following are the key stages in building the model:

1 Choose a key process to be analysed, identify and name it, e.g. Retrieval of Medical Records (Acute Admissions).
2 Define the process and its boundaries.

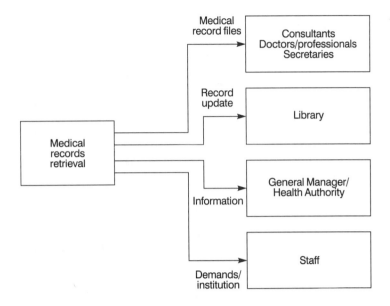

Figure 7.2 *Building the model: identify outputs and customers*

3 Construct the process diagram:
   a) Identify the outputs and customers (for example see Figure 7.2).
   b) Identify the inputs and suppliers (for example see Figure 7.3).
   c) Identify the controls and resources (for example see Figure 7.4).
4 Flowchart the process and identify the process owners (for example see Figure 7.5). Note, the process owners will form the improvement team.

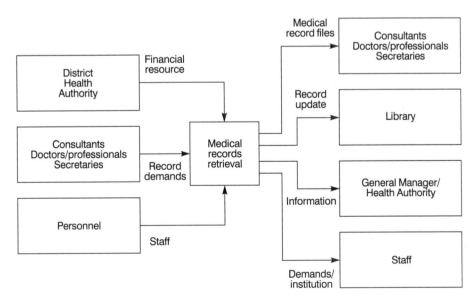

Figure 7.3 *Building the model: identify inputs and suppliers*

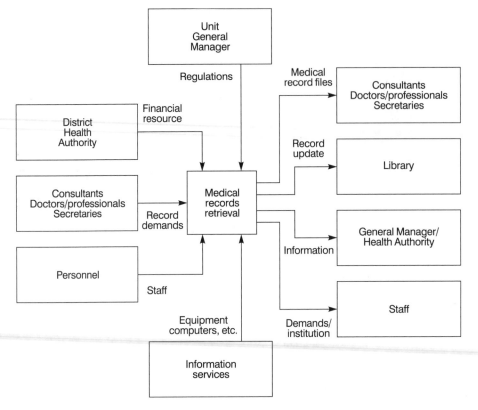

Figure 7.4 *Building the model: identify controls and resources*

5 Allocate the activities as COC or CONC (see Table 7.3).
6 Calculate or estimate the quality costs (COQ) at each stage (COC + CONC). Estimates may be required where the accounting system is unable to generate the necessary information.
7 Construct a process cost report (see Table 7.4). The report summary and results are given in Table 7.5.

There are three further steps carried out by the process owners – the improvement team – which take the process forward into the improvement stage:

8 Prioritize the failure costs and select the process stages for improvement through reduction in CONC. This should indicate any requirements for investment in prevention activities. An excessive COC may suggest the need for process redesign.
9 Review the flowchart to identify the scope for reductions in the COC. Attempts to reduce COC require a thorough process understanding, and a second flowchart of what the new process should be may help (see Chapter 4).
10 Monitor conformance and non-conformance costs on a regular basis, using the model and review for further improvements.

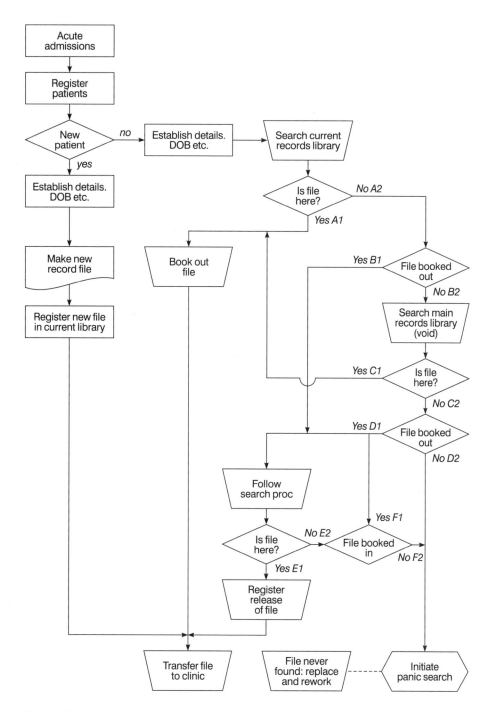

Figure 7.5 *Present practice flowchart for acute admissions, medical records retrieval*

Table 7.3 *Building the model: allocate activities as COC or CONC*

Key activities	COC	CONC
Search for files	Labour cost incurred finding a record while adhering to standard procedure	Labour cost incurred finding a record while unable to adhere to standard procedure
Make up new files	New patient files	Patients whose original files cannot be located
Rework		Cost of labour and materials for all rework files/records never found as a direct consequence of . . .
Duplication		Cost incurred in duplicating existing files

Table 7.4 *Building the model: process cost report*

Process cost report
Process: medical records retrieval (acute admissions)
Process owner: various
Time allocation: 4 days (96 hrs)

Process COC	Process CONC	Cost details		Definition	Source	
		Act	Synth			
	Labour cost incurred finding records	# ref. Sample		Cost of time required to find missing records	Medical records	£98
	Cost incurred making up replacement files		#	Labour and material costs multiplied by number of files replaced	Medical records	£40
	Rework		#	Labour and material cost of all rework	Medical records	£50
	Duplication		#		Medical records	£9

Table 7.5 *Process cost model: report summary*

Labour cost
    13.75 hrs × £5.80/hr = £80
    £80 × overhead and contribution factor 22%
    = £98

Replacement costs
    No. of files unfound 9
    Cost to replace each file £4.50
    Overall cost £40

Rework costs
    2 × Pathology reports to be retyped £50

Duplication costs
    No. of files duplicated 2
    Cost per file £4.50
    Overall cost £9

TOTAL COST £197

RESULTS
Acute admissions operated 24 hrs/day 365 days/year
This project established a cost of non-conformance of approx. £197
This equates to £197 × 365/4 = £17,976
or two personnel fully employed for 12 months

The process cost model approach must be seen as more than a simple tool to measure the financial implications of the gap between the actual and potential performance of a process. The emphasis given to the process, improving the understanding, and seeing in detail where the costs occur, should be an integral part of quality improvement.

Chapter highlights

Performance measurement and the improvement cycle

- Traditional performance measures based on cost-accounting information provide little to support TQM, because they do not map process performance and improvements seen by the customer.
- Measurement is important in identifying opportunities, and comparing performance internally and externally. Measures, typically non-financial, are used in process control and performance improvement.
- Some financial indicators, such as ROI, are often inaccurate, irrelevant and too late to be used as measures for performance improvement.
- The Deming cycle of *PLAN DO CHECK ACT* is a useful design aid for measurement systems, but firstly four basic questions about measurement should be asked: why, what, where, and how.

- In answering the question 'how to measure?', progress is important in five main areas: effectiveness, efficiency, productivity, quality and impact.
- Activity-based costing (ABC) is based on the activities performed being identified and costs traced to them. ABC uses cost drivers, which reflect the demands placed on activities.

The implementation of performance measurement systems

- The value of any measure must be compared with the cost of producing it. All critical parts of the process must be measured, but it is often better to start with the simple measures and improve them.
- Process owners should take part in defining the performance measures, which must reflect customer requirements.
- Prior to introducing TQM measurement, an audit of existing systems should be carried out to establish their effectiveness, compatibility, relationship and closeness to the customer.
- Following the audit, there are twelve basic steps for implementation, six of which are planning steps.

Benchmarking

- Benchmarking measures an organization's operations, product and services against those of its competitors. It will establish targets, priorities and operations leading to competitive advantage.
- There are four basic types of benchmarking: internal, competitive, functional and generic. The evolution of benchmarking in an organization is likely to progress through four focuses towards continuous improvement.
- The implementation of benchmarking has fifteen stages, which are categorized into plan, analyse, develop, improve and review.

Costs of quality

- A competitive product or service based on a balance between quality and cost factors is the principal goal of responsible management.
- The analysis of quality-related costs may provide a method of assessing the effectiveness of the management of quality and of determining problem areas, opportunities, savings and action priorities.
- Total quality costs may be categorized into prevention, appraisal, internal failure and external failure costs, the P-A-F model.
- Prevention costs are associated with doing it right the first time, appraisal costs with checking it is right, and failure costs with getting it wrong.
- When quality awareness in an organization is low, the total quality-related costs are high, the failure costs predominating. After an initial rise in costs, mainly through the investment in training and appraisal, increasing investment in prevention causes failure, appraisal and total costs to fall.

The process model for quality costing

- The P-A-F model or quality costing has a number of drawbacks, mainly due to estimating the prevention costs, and its association with an 'optimized' or minimum total cost.
- An alternative – the process cost model – rationalizes cost of quality (COQ) into the cost of conformance (COC) and the cost of non-conformance (CONC). COQ = COC + CONC at each process stage.
- Process cost modelling calls for choice of a process and its definition; construction of a process diagram; identification of outputs and customers, inputs and suppliers, controls and resources; flowcharting the process and identifying owners; allocating activities as COC or CONC; and calculating the costs. A process cost report with summaries and results is produced.
- The failure costs of CONC should be prioritized for improvements.

Chapter 8

Tools and techniques for quality improvement

A systematic approach

In the never-ending quest for improvement in the ways processes are operated, numbers and information will form the basis for understanding, decisions and actions; and a thorough data gathering, recording and presentation system is essential.

In addition to the basic elements of a quality system that provide a framework for recording, there exists a set of methods the Japanese quality guru Ishikawa has called the seven basic tools. These should be used to interpret and derive the maximum use from data. The simple methods listed below, of which there are clearly more than seven, will offer any organization means of collecting, presenting and analysing most of its data:

- Process flowcharting – what is done?
- Check sheets/tally charts – how often is it done?
- Histograms – what do overall variations look like?
- Scatter diagrams – what are the relationships between factors?
- Stratification – how is the data made up?
- Pareto analysis – which are the big problems?
- Cause and effect analysis and brainstorming (including CEDAC, NGT, and the five whys) – what causes the problems?
- Force-field analysis – what will obstruct or help the change or solution?
- Emphasis curve – which are the most important factors?
- Control charts – which variations to control and how?

Sometimes more sophisticated techniques, such as analysis of variance, regression analysis, and design of experiments, need to be employed.

The effective use of the tools requires their application by the people who actually work on the processes. Their commitment to this will be possible only if they are assured that management cares about improving quality. Managers must show they are serious by establishing a systematic approach and providing the training and implementation support required.

Improvements cannot be achieved without specific opportunities, commonly called problems, being identified or recognized. A focus on improvement opportunities leads to the creation of teams whose membership is determined by their work on and detailed knowledge of the process, and their ability to take improvement action. The teams must then be provided with good leadership and the right tools to tackle the job.

The systematic approach (Figure 8.1) should lead to the use of factual information, collected and presented by means of proven techniques, to open a channel of communications not available to the many organizations that do not follow this or a similar approach to problem solving and improvement. Continuous improvements in the quality of products, services and processes can often be obtained without major capital investment, if an organization marshals its resources, through an understanding and breakdown of its processes in this way.

By using reliable methods, creating a favourable environment for team-based problem solving, and continuing to improve using systematic techniques, the never-ending improvement helix (see Chapter 2) will be engaged. This approach demands the real time management of data, and actions on processes and inputs, not outputs. It will require a change in the language of many organizations from percentage defects, percentage 'prime' product, and number of errors, to *process capability*. The climate must change from the traditional approach of: 'If it meets the specification, there are no problems and no further improvements are necessary.' The driving force for this will be the need for better internal and external customer satisfaction levels, which will lead to the continuous improvement question, 'Could we do the job better?'

Some basic tools and techniques

Understanding processes so that they can be improved by means of the systematic approach requires knowledge of a simple kit of tools or techniques. What follows is a brief description of each technique, but a full description and further examples of some of them may be found in reference 1 at the end of this chapter.

Process flowcharting

The use of this technique, which is described in Chapter 4, ensures a full understanding of the inputs and flow of the process. Without that understanding, it is not possible to draw the correct flowchart of the process. In flowcharting it is important to remember that in all but the smallest tasks no single person is able to complete a chart without help from others. This makes flowcharting a powerful team-forming exercise.

Check sheets or tally charts

A check sheet is a tool for data gathering, and a logical point to start in most process control or problem-solving efforts. It is particularly useful for recording direct

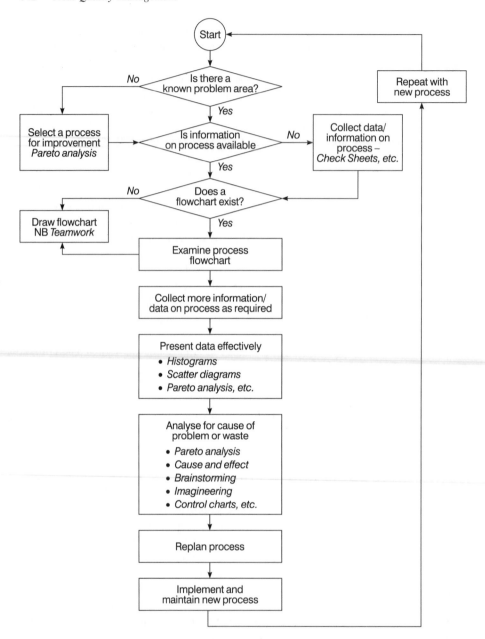

Figure 8.1 *Strategy for process improvement*

observations and helping to gather in facts rather than opinions about the process. In the recording process it is essential to understand the difference between data and numbers.

Data are pieces of information, including numerical information, that are useful in solving problems, or provide knowledge about the state of a process. Numbers alone often represent meaningless measurements or counts, which tend to confuse rather than to enlighten. Numerical data on quality will arise either from counting or measurement.

The use of simple check sheets or tally charts aids the collection of data of the right type, in the right form, at the right time. The objectives of the data collection will determine the design of the record sheet used. An example of a tally chart is shown in Figure 8.2. This gives rise to a frequency distribution.

Observer *F. Oldman*		Computer No. *148*	Date *26 June*	
Number of observations *95*			Total	Percentage
Computer in use		*HHt HHt HHt HHt HHt* *HHt HHt HHt HHt HHt* *HHt*	*55*	*57.9*
Computer idle	Repairs	*HHt*	*5*	*5.3*
	No work	*HHt HHt II*	*12*	*12.6*
	Operator absent	*HHt HHt*	*10*	*10.5*
	System failure	*HHt HHt III*	*13*	*13.7*

Figure 8.2 *Activity sampling record in an office*

Histograms

Histograms show, in a very clear pictorial way, the frequency with which a certain value or group of values occurs. They can be used to display both attribute and variable data, and are an effective means of letting the people who operate the process know the results of their efforts. Data gathered on truck turn-round times is drawn as a histogram in Figure 8.3.

Scatter diagrams

Depending on the technology, it is frequently useful to establish the association, if any, between two parameters or factors. A technique to begin such an analysis is a simple X-Y plot of the two sets of data. The resulting grouping of points on scatter diagrams (e.g. Figure 8.4) will reveal whether or not a strong or weak, positive or negative, correlation exists between the parameters. The diagrams are simple to construct and easy to interpret, and the absence of correlation can be as revealing as finding that a relationship exists.

Stratification

Stratification is simply dividing a set of data into meaningful groups. It can be used to great effect in combination with other techniques, including histograms and scatter

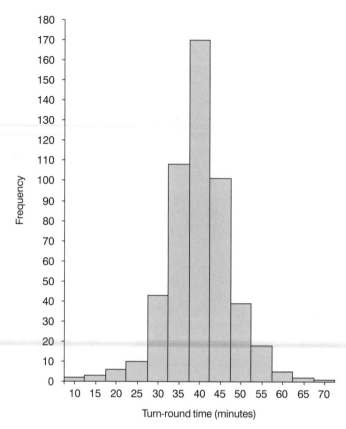

Figure 8.3 *Frequency distribution for truck turn-round times (histogram)*

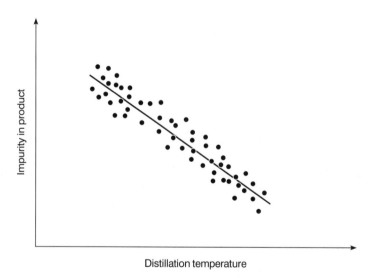

Figure 8.4 *Scatter diagram showing a negative correlation between two variables*

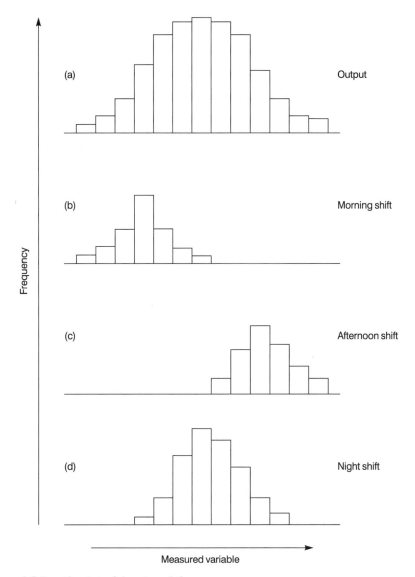

Figure 8.5 *Stratification of data into shift teams*

diagrams. If, for example, three shift teams are responsible for the output described by the histogram (a) in Figure 8.5, 'stratifying' the data into the shift groups might produce histograms (b), (c) and (d), and indicate process adjustments that were taking place at shift changeovers.

Pareto analysis

If the symptoms or causes of defective output or some other 'effect' are identified and recorded, it will be possible to determine what percentage can be attributed to any cause, and the probable results will be that the bulk (typically 80 per cent) of the errors, waste, or 'effects', derive from a few of the causes (typically 20 per cent). For example, Figure 8.6 shows a *ranked frequency distribution* of incidents in the distribution of a certain product. To improve the performance of the distribution process, therefore, the major incidents (broken bags/drums, truck scheduling, and temperature problems)

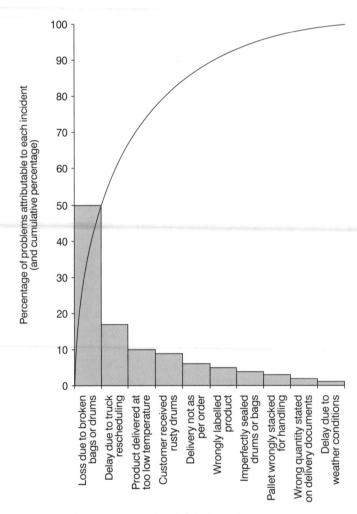

Figure 8.6 *Incidents in the distribution of a chemical product*

should be tackled first. An analysis of data to identify the major problems is known as *Pareto analysis*, after the Italian economist who realized that approximately 90 per cent of the wealth in his country was owned by approximately 10 per cent of the people. Without an analysis of this sort, it is far too easy to devote resources to addressing one symptom only because its cause seems immediately apparent.

Cause and effect analysis and brainstorming

A useful way of mapping the inputs that affect quality is the *cause and effect diagram*, also known as the Ishikawa diagram (after its originator) or the fishbone diagram (after its appearance, Figure 8.7). The effect or incident being investigated is shown at the end of a horizontal arrow. Potential causes are then shown as labelled arrows entering the main cause arrow. Each arrow may have other arrows entering it as the principal factors or causes are reduced to their subcauses and sub-subcauses by *brainstorming*.

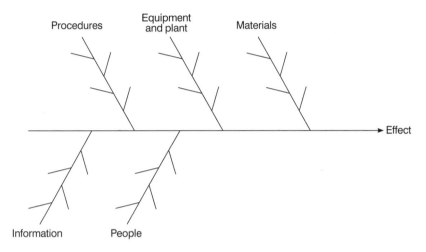

Figure 8.7 *The cause and effect, Ishikawa or fishbone diagram*

Brainstorming is a technique used to generate a large number of ideas quickly, and may be used in a variety of situations. Each members of a group, in turn, may be invited to put forward ideas concerning a problem under consideration. Wild ideas are safe to offer, as criticism or ridicule is not permitted during a brainstorming session. The people taking part do so with equal status to ensure this. The main objective is to create an atmosphere of enthusiasm and originality. All ideas offered are recorded for subsequent analysis. The process is continued until all the conceivable causes have been included. The proportion of non-conforming output attributable to each cause, for example, is then measured or estimated, and a simple Pareto analysis identifies the causes that are most worth investigating.

A useful variant on the technique is negative brainstorming and cause and effect analysis. Here the group brainstorms all the things that would need to be done to ensure a negative outcome. For example, in the implementation of TQM, it might be useful for the senior management team to brainstorm what would be needed to make sure TQM *was not* implemented. Having identified in this way the potential roadblocks, it is easier to dismantle them.

CEDAC

A variation on the cause and effect approach, which was developed at Sumitomo Electric and now is used by many major corporations across the world, is the cause and effect diagram with addition of cards (CEDAC).[1]

The effect side of a CEDAC chart is a quantified description of the problem, with an agreed and visual quantified target and continually updated results on the progress of achieving it. The cause side of the CEDAC chart uses two different coloured cards for writing facts and ideas. This ensures that the facts are collected and organized before solutions are devised. The basic diagram for CEDAC has the classic fishbone appearance.

Nominal group technique (NGT)

The nominal group technique (NGT) is a particular form of team brainstorming used to prevent domination by particular individuals. It has specific application for multi-level, multi-disciplined teams, where communication boundaries are potentially problematic.

In NGT, a carefully prepared written statement of the problem to be tackled is read out by the facilitator (F). Clarification is obtained by questions and answers and then the individual participants (P) are asked to restate the problem in their own words. The group then discusses the problem until its formulation can be satisfactorily expressed by the team (T). The method is set out in Figure 8.8. NGT results in a set of ranked ideas that are close to a team consensus view obtained without domination by one or two individuals.

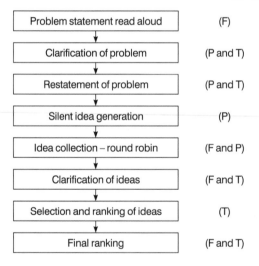

Figure 8.8 *Nominal group technique (NGT)*

Even greater discipline may be brought to brainstorming by the use of 'soft systems methodology' (SSM), developed by Peter Checkland.[2] The component stages of SSM are gaining a 'rich understanding' through 'finding out', input/output diagrams, root definition (which includes the so-called CATWOE analysis: customers, 'actors', transformations, 'world-view', owners, environment), conceptualization, comparison and recommendation.

Force field analysis

Force field analysis is a technique used to identify the forces that either obstruct or help a change that needs to be made. It is similar to negative brainstorming and cause/effect analysis and helps to plan how to overcome the barriers to change or improvement. It may also provide a measure of the difficulty in achieving the change.

The process begins with a team describing the desired change or improvement, and defining the objectives or solution. Having prepared the basic force field diagram, it identifies the favourable/positive/driving forces and the unfavourable/negative/restraining forces, by brainstorming. These forces are placed in opposition on the diagram and, if possible, rated for their potential influence on the ease of implementation. The results are evaluated. Then comes the preparation of an action plan to overcome some of the restraining forces, and increase the driving forces. Figure 8.9 shows a force field analysis produced by a senior management team considering the implementation of TQM in its organization.

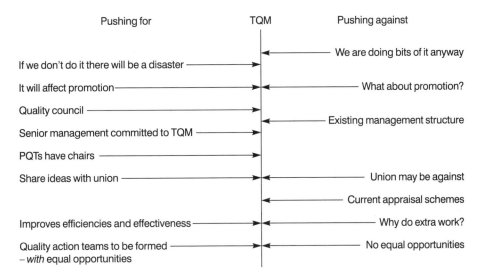

Figure 8.9 *Force field analysis*

The emphasis curve

This is a technique for ranking a number of factors, each of which cannot be readily quantified in terms of cost, frequency of occurrence, etc., in priority order. It is almost impossible for the human brain to make a judgement of the relative importance of more than three or four non-quantifiable factors. It is, however, relatively easy to judge which is the most important of two factors, using some predetermined criteria. The emphasis curve technique uses this fact by comparing only two factors at any one time.

The procedural steps for using the emphasis curve chart (Table 8.1) are as follows:

1 List the factors for ranking under 'Scope'. The number may be extended to more than ten by extending the matrix.

Table 8.1 *The emphasis technique pro forma*

Emphasis Curve to Assess ....

Assessment by .... Date ....

									No.	No. of rings
1/2	1/3	1/4	1/5	1/6	1/7	1/8	1/9	1/10	1	
	2/3	2/4	2/5	2/6	2/7	2/8	2/9	2/10	2	
		3/4	3/5	3/6	3/7	3/8	3/9	3/10	3	
			4/5	4/6	4/7	4/8	4/9	4/10	4	
				5/6	5/7	5/8	5/9	5/10	5	
					6/7	6/8	6/9	6/10	6	
						7/8	7/9	7/10	7	
							8/9	8/10	8	
								9/10	9	
									10	

Scope

....
....
....
....
....
....
....
....

Check total $= \dfrac{n(n-1)}{2}$

RANKING – Highest to lowest

10	9	8	7	6	5	4	3	2	1

2 Compare factor 1 with factor 2 and rank the most important. To assist in judging the relative importance of two factors, it may help to use weightings, e.g. degree of seriousness, capital investment, speed of completion etc., on a scale of 1 to 10.

3 Compare factor 1 with 3, 1 with 4, 1 with 5 and so on – ringing the most important number in the matrix.

4 Having compared factor 1 against the total scope, proceed to compare factor 2 with 3, 2 with 4 and so on.

5 Count the number of 'ringed' number 1s in the matrix and put the total in the right-hand (RH) column against Number 1. Next count the total number of 2s in the matrix and put the total in the RH column against Number 2 and so on.

6 Add up the numbers in the RH column and check the total, using the formula $n(n-1)/2$, where n is the number of entries in the RH column. This check ensures that all numbers have been 'ringed' in the matrix.

7 Proceed to rank by putting number 1 in the box number along the bottom of the form, which equates to the number in the RH column entered against Number 1 and so on.

8 When two or more numbers appear in one box, check the matrix to see which factor is judged to be the most important and use the original decision to give absolute ranking.

9 Generally the length of time to make a judgement between two factors does not significantly affect the outcome; therefore the rule is 'accept the first decision, record it and move quickly onto the next pair'.

An interesting exercise is to tackle the type of question often used for competitions in the national press, such as 'Rank in order of importance the following features you consider when making a decision on which motor car to buy':

 1 Style
 2 Colour
 3 Central locking
 4 Anti-lock braking
 5 Power steering
 6 Heated seats
 7 Electric sun roof
 8 Four-wheel drive
 9 Heated windscreen
10 Fuel injection
11 Five-speed manual transmission
12 Lead-free fuel
13 Four-speed automatic transmission
14 Collapsible steering wheel
15 Six-speaker radio-cassette.

Attempt to rank the features initially without the use of the emphasis curve, then use the technique and compare your results.

Control charts

A control chart is a form of traffic signal whose operation is based on evidence from the small samples taken at random during a process. A green light is given when the process should be allowed to run. All too often processes are 'adjusted' on the basis of a single measurement, check or inspection, a practice that can make a process much more variable than it is already. The equivalent of an amber light appears when trouble is possibly imminent. The red light shows that there is practically no doubt that the process has changed in some way and that it must be investigated and corrected to prevent production of defective material or information. Clearly, such a scheme can be introduced only when the process is 'in control'. Since samples taken are usually small, there are risks of errors, but these are small, calculated risks and not blind ones. The risk calculations are based on various frequency distributions.

These charts should be made easy to understand and interpret and they can become, with experience, sensitive diagnostic tools to be used by operating staff and first-line supervision to prevent errors or defective output being produced. Time and effort spent to explain the working of the charts to all concerned is never wasted.

The most frequently used control charts are simple run charts, where the data is plotted on a graph against time or sample number. There are different types of control charts for variables and attribute data: for variables mean ($\overline{X}$) and range (R) charts are used together; number defective or **np** charts and proportion defective or **p** charts are the most common ones for attributes. Other charts found in use are moving average and range charts, numbers of defects (**c** and **u**) charts, and cumulative sum (**cusum**) charts. The latter offer very powerful management tools for the detection of trends or changes in attributes and variable data.

The cusum chart is a graph that takes a little longer to draw than the conventional control chart, but gives a lot more information. It is particularly useful for plotting the evolution of processes, because it presents data in a way that enables the eye to separate true changes from a background of random variation. Cusum charts can detect small changes in data very quickly, and may be used for the control of variables and attributes. In essence, a reference or 'target value' is subtracted from each successive sample observation, and the result accumulated. Values of this cumulative sum are plotted, and 'trend lines' may be drawn on the resulting graphs. If they are approximately horizontal, the value of the variable is about the same as the target value. A downward slope shows a value less than the target and an upward slope a value greater. The technique is very useful, for example, in comparing sales forecasts with actual sales figures.

Figure 8.10 shows a comparison of an ordinary run chart and a cusum chart that have been plotted from the same data – errors in samples of 100 invoices. The change, which is immediately obvious on the cusum chart, is difficult to detect on the conventional control chart.

The range of type and use of control charts is now very wide, and within the present text it is not possible to indicate more than the basic principles underlying such charts.[1]

Failure mode, effect and criticality analysis (FMECA)

It is possible to analyse products, services and processes to determine possible modes of failure and their effects on the performance of the product or operation of the process

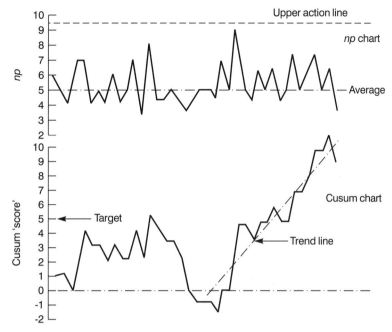

Figure 8.10 *Comparison of cusum and np charts for the same data*

or service system. Failure mode and effect analysis (FMEA) is the study of potential failures to determine their effects. If the results of an FMEA are ranked in order of seriousness, then the word CRITICALITY is added to give FMECA. The primary objective of a FMECA is to determine the features of product design, production or operation and distribution that are critical to the various modes of failure, in order to reduce failure. It uses all the available experience and expertise, from marketing, design, technology, purchasing, production/operation, distribution, service, etc., to identify the importance levels or criticality of potential problems and stimulate action to reduce these levels. FMECA should be a major consideration at the design stage of a product or service (see Chapter 3).

The elements of a complete FMECA are:

- *Failure mode* – the anticipated conditions of operation are used as the background to study the most probable failure mode, location and mechanism of the product or system and its components.
- *Failure effect* – the potential failures are studied to determine their probable effects on the performance of the whole product, process or service, and the effects of the various components on each other.
- *Failure criticality* – the potential failures on the various parts of the product or service system are examined to determine the severity of each failure effect in terms of lowering of performance, safety hazard, total loss of function, etc.

FMECA may be applied to any stage of design, development, production/operation or use, but since its main aim is to prevent failure, it is most suitably applied at the design stage to identify and eliminate causes. With more complex product or service systems, it may be appropriate to consider these as smaller units or subsystems, each one being the subject of a separate FMECA.

Special FMECA pro formas are available and they set out the steps of the analysis as follows:

1 Identify the product or system components, or process function.
2 List all possible failure modes of each component.
3 Set down the effects that each mode of failure would have on the function of the product or system.
4 List all the possible causes of each failure mode.
5 Assess numerically the failure modes on a scale from 1 to 10. Experience and reliability data should be used, together with judgement, to determine the values, on a scale 1–10, for:
   P   the probability of each failure mode occurring (1 = low, 10 = high).
   S   the seriousness or criticality of the failure (1 = low, 10 = high).
   D   the difficulty of detecting the failure before the product or service is used by the consumer (1 = easy, 10 = very difficult). See Table 8.2.
6 Calculate the product of the ratings, $C = P \times S \times D$, known as the criticality index or risk priority number (RPN) for each failure mode. This indicates the relative priority of each mode in the failure prevention activities.
7 Indicate briefly the corrective action required and, if possible, which department or person is responsible and the expected completion date.

Table 8.2 *Probability and seriousness of failure and difficulty of detection*

Value	1	2	3	4	5	6	7	8	9	10
P	low chance of occurrence _____ almost certain to occur									
S	not serious, minor nuisance _____ total failure, safety hazard									
D	easily detected _____ unlikely to be detected									

When the criticality index has been calculated, the failures may be ranked accordingly. It is usually advisable, therefore, to determine the value of *C* for each failure mode before completing the last columns. In this way the action required against each item can be judged in the light of the ranked severity and the resources available.

Moments of truth

MoT is a concept that has much in common with FMEA. The idea was created by Jan Carlzon,[3] CEO of Scandinavian Airlines (SAS) and was made popular by Albrecht and Zemke.[4] An MoT is the moment in time when a customer first comes into contact with the people, systems, procedures or products of an organization, which leads to the customer making a judgement about the quality of the organization's services or products.

In MoT analysis the points of potential dissatisfaction are identified proactively, beginning with the assembly of process flowchart-type diagrams. Every small step taken by a customer in his/her dealings with the organization's people, products or services is recorded. It may be difficult or impossible to identify all the MoTs, but the systematic approach should lead to a minimization of the number and severity of unexpected failures, and this provides the link with FMEA.

Statistical process control (SPC)

The responsibility for quality in any transformation process must lie with the operators of that process. To fulfil this responsibility, however, people must be provided with the tools necessary to:

- Know whether the process is capable of meeting the requirements.
- Know whether the process is meeting the requirements at any point in time.
- Make correct adjustment to the process or its inputs when it is not meeting the requirements.

The techniques of statistical process control (SPC) will greatly assist in these stages. To begin to monitor and analyse any process, it is necessary first of all to identify what the process is, and what the inputs and outputs are. Many processes are easily understood and relate to known procedures, e.g. drilling a hole, compressing tablets, filling cans with paint, polymerizing a chemical using catalysts. Others are less easily identifiable, e.g. servicing a customer, delivering a lecture, storing a product in a warehouse, inputting to a computer. In many situations it can be extremely difficult to define the process. For example, if the process is inputting data into a computer terminal, it is vital to know if the scope of the process includes obtaining and refining the data, as well as inputting. Process definition is so important because the inputs and outputs change with the scope of the process.

Once the process is specified, the inputs and suppliers, outputs and customers can also be defined, together with the requirements at each of the interfaces. The most difficult areas in which to do this are in non-manufacturing organizations or parts of organizations, but careful use of the questioning method, introduced in Chapter 1, should release the necessary information. Examples of outputs in non-manufacturing include training courses or programmes, typed letters, statements of intent (following a decision process), invoices, share certificates, deliveries of consignments, reports, serviced motor cars, purchase orders, wage slips, forecasts, material requirements plans, legal contracts, design change documents, clean offices, recruited trainees and advertisements. The list is endless. Some processes may produce primary and secondary outputs, such as a telephone call answered *and* a message delivered.

If the requirements are not clarified or quantified, they are often assumed or estimated. Even if this does not lead to direct complaints, it will lead to waste – lost time, confusion – and perhaps lost customers. It is salutary for some suppliers of internal customers to realize that the latter can sometimes find new suppliers, etc., if their true requirements are not properly identified and/or repeatedly not met.

Inputs to processes include: equipment, tools or plant required; materials – including paper; information – including the specification for the outputs; methods or procedures – including instructions; people (and the inputs they provide, such as skills, training, knowledge); and records. Again this is not an exhaustive list.

Prevention of failure in any transformation is possible only if the process definition, flow, inputs and outputs are properly documented and agreed. The documentation of procedures will allow reliable data about the process itself to be collected, analysis to be performed, and action to be taken to improve the process and prevent failure or non-conformance with the requirements. The target in the operation of any process is the total avoidance of failure. If the idea of no failures or error-free work is not adopted, at least as a target, then it certainly will never be achieved.

All processes can be monitored and brought 'under control' by gathering and using data – to measure the performance of the process and provide the feedback required for corrective action, where necessary. Statistical process control (SPC) methods, backed by management commitment and good organization, provide objective means of *controlling* quality in any transformation process, whether used in the manufacture of artefacts, the provision of services, or the transfer of information.

SPC is not only a tool kit, it is a strategy for reducing variability, the cause of most quality problems: variation in products, in times of deliveries, in ways of doing things, in materials, in people's attitudes, in equipment and its use, in maintenance practices, in everything. Control by itself is not sufficient. Total quality management requires that the processes should be improved continually by reducing variability. This is brought about by studying all aspects of the process, using the basic question: 'Could we do this job more consistently and on target?' The answer drives the search for improvements. This significant feature of SPC means that it is not constrained to measuring conformance, and that it is intended to lead to action on processes that are operating within the 'specification' to minimize variability.

Process control is essential, and SPC forms a vital part of the TQM strategy. Incapable and inconsistent processes render the best design impotent and make supplier quality assurance irrelevant. Whatever process is being operated, it must be reliable and consistent. SPC can be used to achieve this objective.

In the application of SPC there is often an emphasis on techniques rather than on the implied wider managerial strategies. It is worth repeating that SPC is not only about plotting charts on the walls of a plant or office, it must become part of the company-wide adoption of TQM and act as the focal point of never-ending improvement. Changing an organization's environment into one in which SPC can operate properly may take several years rather than months. For many companies SPC will bring a new approach, a new 'philosophy', but the importance of the statistical techniques should not be disguised. Simple presentation of data using diagrams, graphs and charts should become the means of communication concerning the state of control of processes. It is on this understanding that improvements will be based.

The SPC system

A systematic study of any process through answering the questions:

- Are we capable of doing the job correctly?
- Do we continue to do the job correctly?
- Have we done the job correctly?
- Could we do the job more consistently and on target?[5]

provides knowledge of the *process capability* and the sources of non-conforming outputs. This information can then be fed back quickly to marketing, design, and the 'technology' functions. Knowledge of the current state of a process also enables a more balanced judgement of equipment, both with regard to the tasks within its capability and its rational utilization.

Statistical process control procedures exist because there is variation in the characteristics of all material, articles, services and people. The inherent variability in each transformation process causes the output from it to vary over a period of time. If this variability is considerable, it is impossible to predict the value of a characteristic of any single item or at any point in time. Using statistical methods, however, it is possible to take meagre knowledge of the output and turn it into meaningful statements that may then be used to describe the process itself. Hence, statistically-based process control procedures are designed to divert attention from individual pieces of data and focus it on the process as a whole. SPC techniques may be used to measure and control the degree of variation of any purchased materials, services, processes and products, and to compare this, if required, to previously agreed specifications. In essence, SPC techniques select a representative, simple, random sample from the 'population', which can be an input to or an output from a process. From an analysis of the sample it is possible to make decisions regarding the current performance of the process.

Quality improvement techniques in non-manufacturing

Organizations that embrace the TQM concepts should recognize the value of SPC techniques in areas such as sales, purchasing, invoicing, finance, distribution, training, and in the service sector generally. These are outside the traditional areas for SPC use, but SPC needs to be seen as an organization-wide approach to reducing variation with the specific techniques integrated into a programme of change throughout. A Pareto analysis, a histogram, a flowchart or a control chart is a vehicle for communication. Data are data and, whether the numbers represent defects or invoice errors, weights or delivery times, or the information relates to machine settings, process variables, prices, quantities, discounts, sales or supply points, is irrelevant – the techniques can always be used.

In the author's experience, some of the most exciting applications of SPC have emerged from organizations and departments which, when first introduced to the methods, could see little relevance in them to their own activities. Following appropriate training, however, they have learned how to, for example:

- Using *Pareto analysis*, analyse errors on invoices to customers and industry injury data.
- Using *brainstorming and cause and effect analysis*, analyse reasons for late payment and poor purchase invoice matching.
- Using *histograms*, show defects in invoice matching and arrival of trucks at certain times during the day.
- Using *control charts*, chart the weekly demand of a product.

Distribution staff have used control charts to monitor the proportion of late deliveries, and Pareto analysis and force field analysis to look at complaints about the distribution system. Bank operators have been seen using cause and effect analysis, NGT and histograms to represent errors in the output from their services. Moving average and cusum charts have immense potential for improving processes in the marketing area.

Those organizations that have made most progress in implementing continuous improvement have recognized at an early stage that SPC is for the whole organization. Restricting it to traditional manufacturing or operational activities means that a window of opportunity for improvement has been closed. Applying the methods and techniques outside manufacturing will make it easier, not harder, to gain maximum benefit from an SPC programme.

Sales, marketing and *customer service* are areas often resistant to SPC training on the basis that it is difficult to apply. Personnel in these vital functions need to be educated in SPC methods for two reasons:

1 They need to understand the way the manufacturing or service-producing processes in their organizations work. This will enable them to have more meaningful dialogues with customers about the whole product/service/delivery system capability and control. It will also enable them to influence customers' thinking about specifications and create a competitive advantage from improving process capabilities.
2 They will be able to improve the marketing processes and activities. A significant part of the sales and marketing effort is clearly associated with building relationships, which are best built on facts (data) and not opinions. There are also opportunities to use SPC techniques directly in such areas as forecasting demand levels and market requirements, monitoring market penetration, marketing control, and product development, all of which must be viewed as processes.

SPC has considerable applications for non-manufacturing organizations, including universities! Data and information on patients in hospitals, students in universities, polytechnics, colleges and schools, people who pay (and do not pay) tax, draw social security benefit, shop at Sainsbury's or Macy's, are available in abundance. If the information were to be used in a systematic way, and all operations treated as processes, far better decisions could be made concerning past, present and future performances of some service sectors.

Chapter highlights

A systematic approach

- Numbers and information will form the basis for understanding, decisions and actions in never-ending improvement.
- A set of simple tools is needed to interpret fully and derive maximum use from data. More sophisticated techniques may need to be employed occasionally.
- The effective use of the tools requires the commitment of the people who work on the processes. This in turn needs management support and the provision of training.

Some basic tools and techniques

- The basic tools and the questions answered are:

Process flowcharting	– what is done?
Check/tally charts	– how often is it done?
Histograms	– what do variations look like?
Scatter diagrams	– what are the relationships between factors?
Stratification	– how is the data made up?
Pareto analysis	– which are the big problems?
Cause and effect analysis and brainstorming (also CEDAC and NGT)	– what causes the problem?
Force field analysis	– what will obstruct or help the change or solution?
Emphasis curve	– which are the most important factors?
Control charts (including cusum)	– which variations to control and how?

Failure mode, effect and criticality analysis (FMECA)

- FMEA is the study of potential product, service or process failures and their effects. When the results are ranked in order of criticality, the technique is called FMECA. Its aim is to reduce the probability of failure.
- The elements of a complete FMECA are to study failure mode, effect and criticality. It may be applied at any stage of design, development, production/operation or use.
- Moments of truth (MoT) is a similar concept to FMEA. It is the moment in time when a customer first comes into contact with an organization, leading to a judgement about quality.

Statistical process control (SPC)

- People operating a process must know whether it is capable of meeting the requirements, know whether it is actually doing so at any time, and make correct adjustments when it is not. SPC techniques will help here.

- Before using SPC, it is necessary to identify what the process is, what the inputs/outputs are, and how the suppliers and customers and their requirements are defined. The most difficult areas for this can be in non-manufacturing.
- All processes can be monitored and brought 'under control' by gathering and using data. SPC methods, with management commitment, provide objective means of controlling quality in any transformation process.
- SPC is not only a tool kit, it is a strategy for reducing variability, part of never-ending improvement. This is achieved by answering the following questions:

     Are we capable of doing the job correctly?
     Do we continue to do the job correctly?
     Have we done the job correctly?
     Could we do the job more consistently and on target?

  This provides knowledge of process capability.

Quality improvement techniques in non-manufacturing

- SPC techniques have value in the service sector and in the non-manufacturing areas, such as marketing and sales, purchasing, invoicing, finance, distribution, training and personnel.

References

1. Oakland, J.S., *Statistical Process Control* (4th edition), Butterworth-Heinemann, 1999.
2. Checkland, P., *Soft Systems Methodology in Action*, Wiley, 1990.
3. Carlzon, J., *Moments of Truth*, Harper & Row, 1987.
4. Albrecht, K. and Zemke, R., *Service America! – Doing Business in the New Economy*, Dow Jones-Irwin, Homewood, Ill. (USA), 1985.
5. This system for process capability and control is based on Frank Price's very practical framework for thinking about quality in manufacturing:

     Can we make it OK?
     Are we making it OK?
     Have we made it OK?
     Could we make it better?

   which he presented in this excellent book *Right First Time*, Gower, 1985.

Chapter 9

Some additional techniques for process design and improvement

Seven new tools for quality design

Seven new tools may be used as part of quality function deployment (see Chapter 3) to improve the innovation processes. These do not replace the basic systematic tools described in Chapter 8, neither are they extensions of these. The new tools are systems and documentation methods used to achieve success in design by identifying objectives and intermediate steps in the finest detail. The seven new tools are:

1 Affinity diagram
2 Interrelationship diagraph
3 Tree diagram
4 Matrix diagram or quality table
5 Matrix data analysis
6 Process decision programme chart (PDPC)
7 Arrow diagram.

The tools are interrelated, as shown in Figure 9.1. The promotion and use of the tools by the QFD team should obtain better designs in less time. They are summarized below.

I Affinity diagram

This is used to gather large amounts of language data (ideas, issues, opinions) and organizes them into groupings based on the natural relationship between the items. In other words, it is a form of brainstorming. One of the obstacles often encountered in

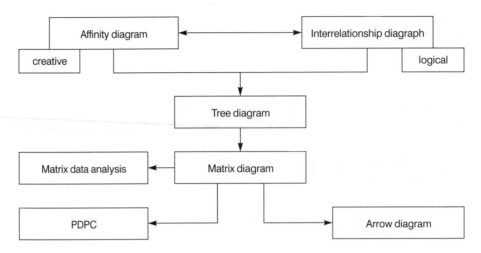

Figure 9.1 *The seven new tools of quality design*

the quest for improvement is past success or failure. It is assumed that what worked or failed in the past will continue to do so in the future. Although the lessons of the past should not be ignored, unvarying patterns of thought, which can limit progress, should not be enforced. This is especially true in QFD, where *new* logical patterns should always be explored.

The affinity diagram, like other brainstorming methods, is part of the creative process. It can be used to generate ideas and categories that can be used later with more strict, logic-based tools. This tool should be used to 'map the geography' of an issue when:

● Facts or thoughts are in chaos and the issues are too large or complex to define easily.
● Breakthroughs in traditional concepts are needed to replace old solutions and to expand a team's thinking.
● Support for a solution is essential for successful implementation.

The affinity diagram is not recommended when a problem is simple or requires a very quick solution.

The steps for generating an affinity diagram are as follows:

1 Assemble a group of people familiar with the problem of interest. Six to eight members in the group works best.
2 Phrase the issue to be considered. It should be vaguely stated so as not to prejudice the responses in a predetermined direction. For example, if you are brainstorming on why issues are not followed up in an organization, it would be best to state the question as, 'Why do issues remain unresolved?' rather than, 'Why don't people take the responsibility to complete their assignments?'
3 Give each member of the group a stack of cards and allow 5–10 minutes for everyone in the group to record ideas on the cards, one per card. During this time the

objective is to write down as many ideas as possible, as concisely as possible. There should be no communication between members of the group during the 5–10 minutes.

4 At the end of the 5–10 minutes each member of the group, in turn, reads out one of his/her ideas and places it on the table for everyone to see. There should be no criticism or justification of ideas, and it is allowable to write new ideas during this time if fresh thoughts are generated.

5 When all ideas are presented, members of the group place together all cards with related ideas. This process is repeated until the ideas are in approximately ten groups.

6 Look for one card in each group that captures the meaning of that group.

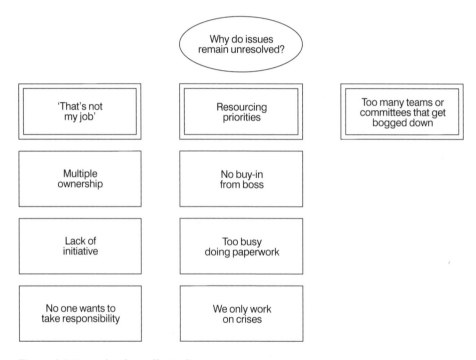

Figure 9.2 *Example of an affinity diagram*

The output of this exercise is a compilation of a maximum number of ideas under a limited number of major headings (see, for example, Figure 9.2). This data can then be used with other tools to define areas for attack. One of these tools is the interrelationship diagraph.

2 Interrelationship diagraph

This tool is designed to take a central idea, issue or problem, and map out the logical or sequential links among related factors. While this still requires a very creative process, the interrelationship diagraph begins to draw the logical connections that surface in the affinity diagram.

In designing, planning and problem solving it is obviously not enough to just create an explosion of ideas. The affinity diagram allows some organized creative patterns to emerge but the interrelationship diagraph lets *logical* patterns become apparent. The diagraph is based on a principle that the Japanese frequently apply regarding the natural emergence of ideas. This tool starts therefore from a central concept, leads to the generation of large quantities of ideas, and finally to the delineation of observed patterns. To some this may appear to be like reading tea leaves, but it works incredibly well. Like the affinity diagram, the interrelationship diagraph allows unanticipated ideas and connections to rise to the surface.

The interrelationship diagraph is adaptable to both specific operational issues and general organizational questions. For example, a classic use of this tool at Toyota focused on all the factors behind the establishment of a 'billboard system' as part of their JIT programme. On the other hand, it has also been used to deal with issues underlying the problem of getting top management support for TQM.

In summary, the interrelationship diagraph should be used when:

a) An issue is sufficiently complex that the interrelationship between ideas is difficult to determine.
b) The correct sequencing of management actions is critical.
c) There is a feeling or suspicion that the problem under discussion is only a symptom.
d) There is ample time to complete the required reiterative process and define cause and effect.

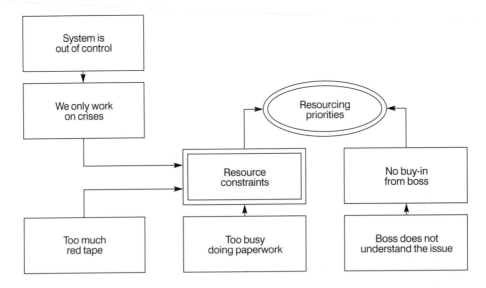

Figure 9.3 *Example of the interrelationship diagraph*

The interrelationship diagraph can be used by itself, or it can be used after the affinity diagram, using data from the previous effort as input. The steps for using this tool are:

1 Clearly define one statement that describes the key issue to be discussed. Record this statement on a card and place it on the wall or a table, in the centre of a large sheet of paper. Mark this card in some way so that it can be easily identified as the central idea, e.g. use a double circle around the text.
2 Generate related issues or problems. This may be done in wide-open brainstorming, or may be taken directly from an affinity diagram. Place each of the ideas on a card and place the cards around the central idea card.
3 Use arrows to indicate which items are related and what leads to what. Look for possible relationships between all items.
4 Look for patterns of arrows to determine key factors or causes. For example, if one card has seven arrows coming from it to other issues, the idea on that card is a key factor or cause. Mark these key factors in a tree diagram for further analysis.

Figure 9.3 gives an example of a simple interrelationship diagraph.

3 Systems flow/tree diagram

The systems flow/tree diagram (usually referred to as a tree diagram) is used to systematically map out the full range of activities that must be accomplished in order to reach a desired goal. It may also be used to identify all the factors contributing to a problem under consideration. As mentioned above, major factors identified by an interrelationship diagraph can be used as inputs for a tree diagram. One of the strengths of this method is that it forces the user to examine the logical and chronological link between tasks. This assists in preventing a natural tendency to jump directly from goal or problem statement to solution (Ready ... Fire ... Aim!).

The tree diagram is indispensable when a thorough understanding of what needs to be accomplished is required, together with how it is to be achieved, and the relationships between these goals and methodologies. It has been found to be most helpful in situations when:

a) Very ill-defined needs must be translated into operational characteristics, and used to identify which characteristics can presently be controlled.
b) All the possible causes of a problem need to be explored. This use is closest to the cause and effect diagram or fishbone chart.
c) Identifying the first task that must be accomplished when aiming for a broad organizational goal.
d) The issue under question has sufficient complexity and time available for solution.

Depending on the type of issue being addressed, the tree diagram will be similar to either a cause and effect diagram (Chapter 8) or a flowchart (Chapter 4), although it may be easier to interpret because of its clear linear layout. If a problem is being considered, each branch of the tree diagram will be similar to a cause and effect diagram. If a general objective is being considered, each branch may represent chronological activities, in which case the diagram will be similar to a flowchart. Although this tool is similar to other tools, suggestions on the stepwise procedure are included below. The procedure is based on trying to accomplish a goal, but it can be easily modified for use in problem solving:

1 Start with one statement that clearly and simply states the issue or goal. Write the idea on a card and place it on the left side of a flip chart or table.
2 Ask: 'What method or task is needed to accomplish this goal or purpose?' Use the interrelationship diagraph to find ideas that are most closely related to that statement, and place them directly to the right of the statement card.
3 Look at each of these 'second tier' ideas and ask the same question. Place these ideas to the right of the ones that they relate to. Continue this process until all the ideas are gone. *Note*: If none of the existing ideas on the interrelationship diagraph can adequately answer the question, new ideas may be developed so as not to leave holes in the tree diagram.
4 Review the entire tree diagram by starting on the right and asking: 'If this is done, will it lead to the accomplishment of the next idea or task?' The diagram produced will be similar to an organization chart.

An example is shown in Figure 9.4.

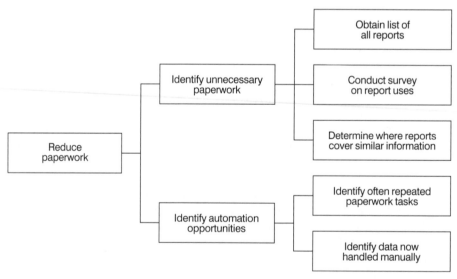

Figure 9.4 *An example of the tree diagram*

4 Matrix diagrams

The matrix diagram is the heart of the seven new tools and the house of quality described in Chapter 3. The purpose of the matrix diagram is to outline the interrelationships and correlations between tasks, functions or characteristics, and to

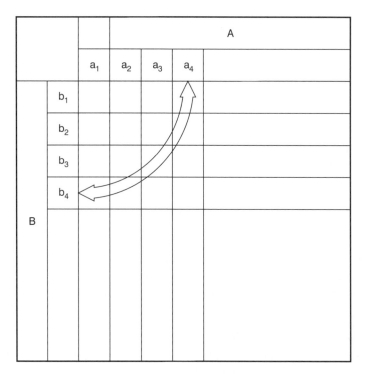

Figure 9.5 *L-shaped matrix*

show their relative importance. There are many versions of the matrix diagram, but the most widely used is a simple L-shaped matrix known as the *quality table*.

L-shaped matrix diagram

This is the most basic form of matrix diagram. In the L-shape, two interrelated groups of items are presented in line and row format. It is a simple two-dimensional representation that shows the intersection of related pairs of items as shown in Figure 9.5. It can be used to display relationships between items in *all* operational areas, including administration, manufacturing, personnel, R&D, etc., to identify all the organizational tasks that need to be accomplished and how they should be allocated to individuals. In a QFD it is even more interesting if each person completes the matrix individually and then compares the coding with everyone in the work group.

Quality table

In a *quality table*, customer demands (the whats) are analysed with respect to substitute quality characteristics (the hows) – see Figure 9.6. Correlations between the two are categorized as strong, moderate and possible. The customer demands shown on the left of the matrix are determined in co-operation with the customer. This effort requires a kind of a verbal 'ping-pong' with the customer to be truly effective: ask the customer what he wants, write it down, show it to him and ask

Substitute quality characteristics

	MFR	Ash	Importance	Current	Best competitor	Plan	IR	SP	RQW
No film breaks	◎ 17	▲ 6	4	4	4	4	1	○	5.6
High rates	◉ 23		3	3	4	4	1.3		4.6
Low gauge variability	◉ 37	▲ 7	4	3	4	4	1.3	○	7.3

Customer demands (row label, left side)

◉   Strong correlation
○   Some correlation
▲   Possible correlation
IR   Improvement ratio
SP   Sales point
RQW Relative quality weight

Figure 9.6 *An example of the matrix diagram (quality table)*

him if that is what he meant, then revise and repeat the process as necessary. This should be done in a joint meeting with the customer, if at all possible. It is often of value to use a tree diagram to give structure to this effort.

The right side of the chart is often used to compare current performance to competitors' performance, company plan, and potential sales points with reference to the customer demands. Weights are given to these items to obtain a 'relative quality weight', which can be used to identify the key customer demands. The relative quality weight is then used with the correlations identified on the matrix to determine the key quality characteristics.

A modification that is added to create the house of quality table is a second matrix that explores the correlations between the quality characteristics. This is done so that errors caused by the manipulation of variables in a one-at-a-time fashion can be avoided. This also gives indications of where designed experiments would be of use in the design process. In the training required for use of this technique, several hours should be dedicated to a detailed explanation of the steps in the construction of a quality table, and the system to be used to compare numerically the various items.

T-shaped matrix diagram

The T-shaped matrix is nothing more than the combination of two L-shaped matrix diagrams. As can be seen in Figure 9.7, it is based on the premise that two separate sets of items are related to a third set. Therefore A items are somehow related to both B and C items.

Figure 9.8 shows one application. In this case it shows the relationship between a set of courses in a curriculum and two important sets of considerations: who should do the training for each course and which would be the most appropriate functions to attend each of the courses. It has also been widely used to develop new materials by simultaneously relating different alternative materials to two sets of desirable properties.

There are other matrices that deal with ideas such as product or service function, cost, failure modes, capabilities, etc., and there are at least forty different types of matrix diagrams available.

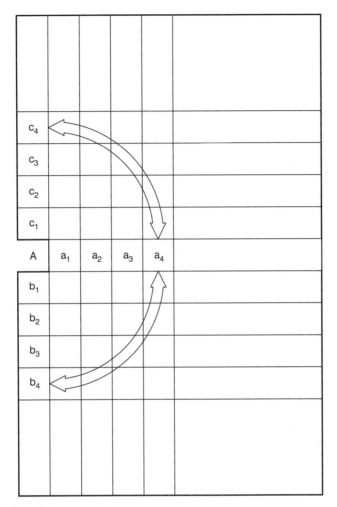

Figure 9.7 *T-shaped matrix*

5 Matrix data analysis

Matrix data analysis is used to take data displayed in a matrix diagram and arrange them so that they can be more easily viewed and show the strength of the relationship between variables. It is used most often in marketing and product research. The concept behind matrix data analysis is fairly simple, but its execution (including data gathering) is complex.

A good idea of the uses and value of the construction of a chart for matrix data analysis may be shown in a simple example in which types of pain relievers are compared based on gentleness and effectiveness (Figure 9.9). This information could be used together with some type of demographic analysis to develop a marketing plan. Based on the information, advertising and product introduction could be effectively

Who trains?

	Courses	SQC	7 Old tools	7 New tools	Reliability	Design review	QC basics	QCC facilitator	Diagnostic tools	Problem solving	Communication skills	Organize for quality	Design of experiments	Company mission	Quality planning	Just-in-time	New superv. training	Company TQM system	Group dynamics skills	SQC course/execs.
Human resources dept.																				
Managers																				
Operators*																				
Consultants																				
Production operator																				
Craft foreman																				
GLSPC co-ordinator																				
Plant SPC co-ordinator																				
University																				
Technology specialists																				
Engineers																				

* Need to tailor to groups

X = Full
O = Overview

Who attends?

	Courses	SQC	7 Old tools	7 New tools	Reliability	Design review	QC basics	QCC facilitator	Diagnostic tools	Problem solving	Communication skills	Organize for quality	Design of experiments	Company mission	Quality planning	Just-in-time	New superv. training	Company TQM system	Group dynamics skills	SQC course/execs.
Executives																				
Top management																				
Middle management																				
Production supervisors																				
Supervisor functional																				
Staff																				
Marketing																				
Sales																				
Engineers																				
Clerical																				
Production worker																				
Quality professional																				
Project team																				
Employee involvement																				
Suppliers																				
Maintenance																				

Figure 9.8 *T-matrix diagram on company-wide training*

tailored for specific areas. New product development could also be carried out to attack specific niches in markets that would be profitable.

6 Process decision programme chart

A process decision programme chart (PDPC) is used to map out each event and contingency that can occur when progressing from a problem statement to its solution. The PDPC is used to anticipate the unexpected and plan for it. It includes plans for counter-measures on deviations. The PDPC is related to a failure mode and effect analysis (see Chapter 8) and its structure is similar to that of a tree diagram. (An

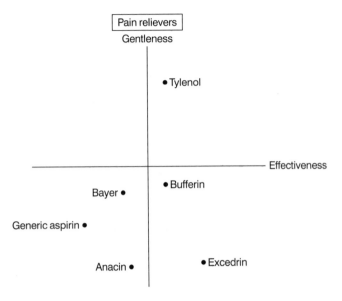

Figure 9.9 *An example of matrix data analysis*

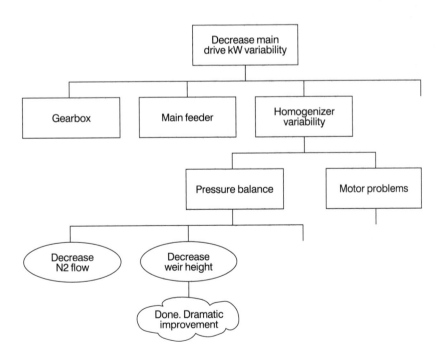

Figure 9.10 *Process decision programme chart*

example of the PDPC is shown in Figure 9.10.) Suggested steps for constructing a PDPC are as follows:

1 Construct a tree diagram as described previously.
2 Take one major branch of the tree diagram (an item just to the right of the main goal or purpose). Ask 'What could go wrong at this step?' or 'What other path could this step take?'
3 Answer the questions by branching off the original path in 'organization chart' manner.
4 Off to the side of each step, list actions or counter-measures that could be taken.
5 Continue the process until the branch is exhausted.
6 Repeat with other main branches.

The PDPC is very simply an attempt to be proactive in the analysis of failure and to construct, on paper, a 'dry run' of the process so that the 'check' part of the improvement cycle can be defined in advance. PDPC is likely to enjoy widespread use because of increasing attention to product liability.

7 Arrow diagram

The arrow diagram is used to plan or schedule a task. To use it, one must know the subtask sequence and duration. This tool is essentially the same as the standard Gantt chart shown in Figure 9.11. Figure 9.12 is the same sequence shown as an arrow diagram. Although it is a simple and well-known tool for planning work, it is surprising how often it is ignored. The arrow diagram is useful in analysing a repetitive job in order to make it more efficient. Some suggestions on constructing arrow diagrams are:

1 Use a team of people working on a job or project, e.g. a QFD team, to list all the tasks necessary to complete the job, and write them on individual cards. On the bottom half of the card, write the time required to complete the task.
2 Place related tasks together. Place them in chronological order.
3 Summarize the cards on a chart similar to Figure 9.12.

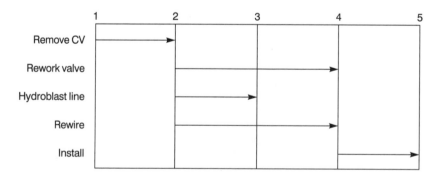

Figure 9.11 *Gantt chart*

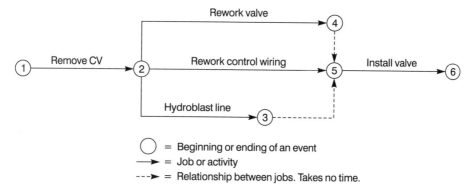

Figure 9.12 *The arrow diagram*

Summary

What has been described in this section is a system for improving the design of products, processes and services by means of seven new tools, sometimes called the quality function deployment tools. For the most part the seven tools are neither new nor revolutionary, but rather a compilation and modification of some tools that have been around for a long time. The tools do not replace statistical methods or other tools, but they are meant to be used together as part of the design process.

The tools work best when representatives from all parts of an organization take part in their use and execution of the results. Besides the structure that the tools provide, the co-operation between functions or departments that is required will help break down barriers within the organizations.

While designers and marketing personnel will see the most direct applications for these tools, proper use of the 'philosophy' behind them requires participation from all parts of an organization. In addition, some of the seven new tools can be used in problem-solving activities not directly related to design.

Taguchi methods for process improvement

Genichi Taguchi was a noted Japanese engineering specialist who advanced 'quality engineering' as a technology to reduce costs and improve quality simultaneously. The popularity of Taguchi methods today testifies to the merit of his philosophies on quality. The basic elements of Taguchi's ideas, which have been extended here to all aspects of product, service and process quality, may be considered under four main headings.

I Total loss function

An important aspect of the quality of a product or service is the total 'loss' to society that it generates. Taguchi's definition of product quality as 'the loss imparted to society from the time a product is shipped' is rather strange, since the word 'loss' denotes the very opposite of what is normally conveyed by using the word quality. The essence of his definition is that the smaller the loss generated by a product or service from the time it is transferred to the customer, the more desirable it is.

The main advantage of this idea is that it encourages a new way of thinking about investment in quality improvement projects, which become attractive when the resulting savings to customers are greater than the cost of improvements.

Taguchi claims with some justification that any variation about a target value for a product or process parameter causes loss to the customer. The loss may be some simple inconvenience, but it can represent actual cash losses, owing to rework or badly fitting parts, and it may well appear as loss of customer goodwill and eventually market share. The loss (or cost) increases exponentially as the parameter value moves away from the target, and is at a minimum when the product or service is at the target value.

2 Design of products, services and processes

In any product or service development three stages may be identified: product or service design, process design, and production or operations. Each of these overlapping stages has many steps, the output of one often being the input to others. The output/input transfer points between steps clearly affect the quality and cost of the final product or service. The complexity of many modern products and services demands that the crucial role of design be recognized. Indeed the performance of the quality products from the Japanese automotive, banking, camera and machine tool industries can be traced to the robustness of their product and process designs.

The prevention of problems in using products or services under varying operations and environmental conditions must be built in at the design stage. Equally, the costs during production or operation are determined very much by the actual manufacturing or operating process. Controls, including SPC methods, added to processes to reduce imperfections at the operational stage are expensive, and the need for controls *and* the production of non-conformance can be reduced by correct initial designs of the process itself.

Taguchi distinguishes between *off-line* and *on-line* quality control methods, 'quality control' being used here in the very broad sense to include quality planning, analysis and improvement. Off-line QC uses technical aids in the *design* of products and processes, whereas on-line methods are technical aids for controlling quality and costs in the *production* of products or services. Too often the off-line QC methods focus on evaluation rather than improvement. The belief by some people (often based on experience!) that it is unwise to buy a new model of a motor car 'until the problems have been sorted out' testifies to the fact that insufficient attention is given to improvement at the product and process design stages. In other words, the bugs should be removed *before* not after product launch. This may be achieved in some organizations by replacing detailed quality and reliability evaluation methods with approximate estimates, and using the liberated resources to make improvements.

3 Reduction of variation

The objective of a continuous quality improvement programme is to reduce the variation of key products' performance characteristics about their target values. The widespread practice of setting specifications in terms of simple upper and lower limits conveys the wrong idea that the customer is satisfied with all values inside the specification band, but is suddenly not satisfied when a value slips outside one of the limits. The practice of stating specifications as tolerance intervals only can lead manufacturers to produce and despatch goods whose parameters are just inside the specification band. Owing to the interdependence of many parameters of component parts and assemblies, this is likely to lead to quality problems.

The target value should be stated and specified as the ideal, with known variability about the mean. For those performance characteristics that cannot be measured on the continuous scale, the next best thing is an ordered categorical scale such as excellent, very good, good, fair, unsatisfactory, very poor, rather than the binary classification of 'good' or 'bad' that provides meagre information with which the variation reduction process can operate.

Taguchi has introduced a three-step approach to assigning nominal values and tolerances for product and process parameters:

a) *System design* – the application of scientific engineering and technical knowledge to produce a basic functional prototype design. This requires a fundamental understanding of the needs of the customer *and* the production environment.

b) *Parameter design* – the identification of the settings of product or process parameters that reduce the sensitivity of the designs to sources of variation. This requires a study of the whole process system design to achieve the most robust operational settings, in terms of tolerance to ranges of the input variables. This is similar to the experiments needed to identify the plant varieties that can tolerate variations in weather conditions, soil and handling. Manual processes that can tolerate the ranges of dimensions of the human body provide another example.

c) *Tolerance design* – the determination of tolerances around the nominal settings identified by parameter design. This requires a trade-off between the customer's loss due to performance variation and the increase in production or operational costs.

4 Statistically planned experiments

Taguchi has pointed out that statistically planned experiments should be used to identify the settings of product and process parameters that will reduce variation in performance. He classifies the variables that affect the performance into two categories: design parameters and sources of 'noise'. As we have seen earlier, the nominal settings of the *design parameters* define the specification for the product or process. The *sources of noise* are all the variables that cause the performance characteristics to deviate from the target values. The *key* noise factors are those that represent the major sources of variability, and these should be identified and included in the experiments to design the parameters at which the effect of the noise factors on the performance is minimum. This is done by systematically varying the design parameter settings and comparing the effect of the noise factors for each experimental run.

Statistically planned experiments may be used to identify:

a) The design parameters that have a large influence on the product or performance characteristic.
b) The design parameters that have no influence on the performance characteristics (the tolerances of these parameters may be relaxed).
c) The settings of design parameters at which the effect of the sources of noise on the performance characteristic is minimal.
d) The settings of design parameters that will reduce cost without adversely affecting quality.[1]

Taguchi methods have stimulated a great deal of interest in the application of statistically planned experiments to product and process designs. The use of 'design of experiments' to improve industrial products and processes is not new – Tippett used these techniques in the textile industry more than 50 years ago. What Taguchi has done, however, is to acquaint us with the scope of these techniques in off-line quality control.

Taguchi's methods, like all others, should not be used in isolation, but should be an integral part of continuous improvement.

Adding the tools to the TQM model

Having looked at some of the many tools and techniques of measurement and improvement, we see that the generic term 'tools' may be added, as the second hard management necessity, to the TQM model (Figure 9.13). The systems manage the

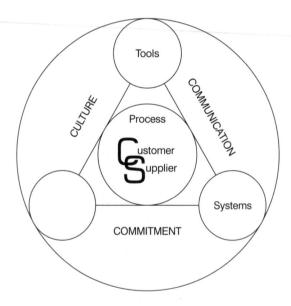

Figure 9.13 *Total quality management model – the basic tools*

processes, and the tools are used to progress further round the improvement cycle by creating better customer–supplier relationships, both externally and internally. They provide the means for analysis, correlation and prediction of what *action* to take on the systems.

Chapter highlights

Seven new tools for quality design

- Seven new tools may be used as part of quality function deployment (QFD, see Chapter 3) to improve the innovation processes. These are systems and documentation methods for identifying objectives and intermediate steps in the finest detail.
- The seven new tools are: affinity diagram, interrelationship diagraph, tree diagram, matrix diagrams or quality table, matrix data analysis, process decision programme chart (PDPC), and arrow diagram.
- The tools are interrelated and their promotion and use should lead to better designs in less time. They work best when people from all parts of an organization are using them. Some of the tools can be used in problem-solving activities not related to design.

Taguchi methods for process improvement

- Genichi Taguchi has advanced 'quality engineering' as a technology to reduce costs and make improvements.
- Taguchi's approach may be classified under four headings: total loss function; design of products, services and processes; reduction in variation; and statistically planned experiments.
- Taguchi methods, like all others, should not be used in isolation, but as an integral part of continuous improvement.

Adding the tools to the TQM model

- A second hard management necessity – the tools – may be added, with the systems, to the TQM model to progress further round the never-ending improvement cycle.

Reference

1. Caulcutt, R., *Statistics in Research and Development* (2nd edition), Chapman and Hall, London, 1991.

Part Three

Discussion questions

1 a) Using the expression: 'if you don't measure you can't improve', discuss this in the context of TQM. Why is measurement important?
   b) What is the difference between measuring for results and measuring for process improvement? Using your knowledge of process management, where do you think measurement should take place and how should it be conducted?

2 Discuss the important features of a performance measurement system based on a TQM approach. Suggest an implementation strategy for a performance measurement system in a progressive company which is applying TQM principles to its business processes.

3 It is often said that 'you can't control what you can't measure and you can't manage what you can't control'. Measurement is, therefore, considered to be at the heart of managing business processes, activities and tasks. What do you understand by improvement-based performance measurement? Why is it important? Suggest a strategy for introducing TQM-based performance measurement into an organization in the public sector.

4 Benchmarking is a development in which most progressive organizations are interested. What do you understand by benchmarking? How does benchmarking link with performance measurement? Suggest a strategy for integrating benchmarking into a TQM programme.

5 a) Some people would say that benchmarking is not different from competitor analysis and is a practice that organizations have always carried out. Do you agree with this? How would you define benchmarking and what are its key elements?
   b) Suggest a benchmarking approach for a progressive small company that has no previous knowledge or experience of doing this.

6 a) What are the major limitations of the 'Prevention-Appraisal-Failure (P-A-F)' costing model? Why would the process cost model be a better alternative?
   b) Discuss the link between benchmarking and quality costing.
   c) Suggest an implementation plan for benchmarking in a large company in the telecommunications sector which is highly committed to TQM.

7 A construction company is concerned about its record of completing projects on time. Considerable penalty costs are incurred if the company fails to meet the agreed contractual completion date. How would you investigate this problem and what methodology would you adopt?

8 English Aerospace is concerned about its poor delivery performance with the EA911. Considerable penalty costs are incurred if the company fails to meet agreed delivery dates. As the company's TQM Manager you have been asked to investigate this problem using a systematic approach. Describe the methodology you would adopt.

9 The Marketing Department of a large chemical company is reviewing its sales forecasting activities. Over the last three years the sales forecasts have been grossly inaccurate. As a result, a Quality Improvement Team has been formed to look at this problem. Give a systematic account of how the 'systematic tools' of TQM could be used in this situation.

10 It has been suggested by Deming and Ishikawa that statistical techniques can be used by staff at all levels within an organization. Explain how such techniques can help:
   a) senior managers to assess performance
   b) sales staff to demonstrate process capability to customers
   c) process teams to achieve quality improvement.

TQM – The Organizational, Communication and Teamwork Requirements

Dust as we are, the immortal spirit grows
Like harmony in music; there is a dark
Inscrutable workmanship that reconciles
Discordant elements, makes them cling together
In one society.

William Wordsworth, 1770–1850

Teams

CULTURE

COMMUNICATION

Process

Customer
Supplier

Systems

Tools

COMMITMENT

Chapter 10

Organization for quality

The quality function and the quality director or manager

In many organizations management systems are viewed in terms of the internal dynamics between marketing, design, sales, production/operations, distribution, accounting, etc. A change is required from this to a larger process-based system that encompasses and integrates the business interests of customers and suppliers. Management needs to develop an in-depth understanding of these relationships and how they may be used to cement the partnership concept. A quality function can be the organization's focal point in this respect, and should be equipped to gauge internal and external customers' expectations and degree of satisfaction. It should also identify deficiencies in all business functions, and promote improvements.

The role of the quality function is to make quality an inseparable aspect of every employee's performance and responsibility. The transition in many companies from quality departments with line functions will require careful planning, direction and monitoring. Quality professionals have developed numerous techniques and skills, focused on product or service quality. In many cases there is a need to adapt these to broader, process applications. The first objectives for many 'quality managers' will be to gradually disengage themselves from line activities, which will then need to be dispersed throughout the appropriate operating departments. This should allow quality to be understood as a 'process' at a senior level, and to be concerned with the following throughout the organization:

● Encouraging and facilitating quality improvement.
● Monitoring and evaluating the progress of quality improvement.
● Promoting the 'partnership' in quality, in relations with customers and suppliers.
● Planning, managing, auditing and reviewing quality management systems.

- Planning and providing quality training and counselling or consultancy.
- Giving advice to management on:
  - establishment of quality management and process control
  - relevant statutory/legislation requirements with respect to quality
  - quality and process improvement programmes
  - inclusion of quality elements in all job instructions and procedures.

Quality directors and managers have an initial task, however, to help those who control the means to implement this concept – the leaders of industry and commerce – to really believe that quality must become an integral part of all the organization's operations.

The author has a vision of quality as a strategic business management function that will help organizations to change their cultures. To make this vision a reality, quality professionals must expand the application of quality concepts and techniques to all business processes and functions, and develop new forms of providing assurance of quality at every supplier–customer interface. They will need to know the entire cycle of products or services, from concept to the *ultimate* end user. An example of this was observed in the case of a company manufacturing pharmaceutical seals, whose customer expressed concern about excess aluminium projecting below and round a particular type of seal. This was considered a cosmetic defect by the immediate customer, the Health Service, but a safety hazard by a blind patient – the *customer's customer*. The prevention of this 'curling' of excess metal meant changing practices at the mill that rolled the aluminium – at the *supplier's supplier*. Clearly, the quality professional dealing with this problem needed to understand the supplier's processes and the ultimate customer's needs, in order to judge whether the product was indeed capable of meeting the requirements.

The shift in 'philosophy' will require considerable staff education in many organizations. Not only must people in other functions acquire quality-related skills, but quality personnel must change old attitudes and acquire new skills – replacing the inspection, calibration, specification-writing mentality with knowledge of defect prevention, wide-ranging quality management systems design and audit. Clearly, the challenge for many quality professionals is not so much making changes in their organization, as recognizing the changes required in themselves. It is more than an overnight job to change the attitudes of an inspection police force into those of a consultative, team-oriented improvement force. This emphasis on prevention and improvement-based systems elevates the role of quality professionals from a technical one to that of general management. A narrow departmental view of quality is totally out of place in an organization aspiring to TQM, and many quality managers will need to widen their perspective and increase their knowledge to encompass all facets of the organization.

To introduce the concepts of process management required for TQM will require not only a determination to implement change but sensitivity and skills in interpersonal relations. This will depend very much of course on the climate within the organization. Those whose management is truly concerned with co-operation and concerned for the people will engage strong employee support for the quality manager or director in his or her catalytic role in the improvement process. Those with aggressive, confrontational management will create for the quality professional impossible difficulties in obtaining support from the rank and file.

TQM appointments

Many organizations have realized the importance of the contribution a senior, qualified director of quality can make to the prevention strategy. Smaller organizations may well feel that the cost of employing a full-time quality manager is not justified, other than in certain very high-risk areas. In these cases a member of the management team may be appointed to operate on a part-time basis, performing the quality management function in addition to his/her other duties. To obtain the best results from a quality director/manager, he/she should be given sufficient authority to take necessary action to secure the implementation of the organization's quality policy, and must have the personality to be able to communicate the message to all employees, including staff, management and directors. Occasionally the quality director/manager may require some guidance and help on specific technical quality matters, and one of the major attributes required is the knowledge and wherewithal to acquire the necessary information and assistance.

In large organizations, then, it may be necessary to make several specific appointments or to assign details to certain managers. The following actions may be deemed to be necessary.

Assign a quality director, manager or co-ordinator

This person will be responsible for the planning and implementation of TQM. He or she will be chosen first for process, project and people management abilities rather than detailed knowledge of quality assurance matters. Depending on the size and complexity of the organization, and its previous activities in quality management, the position may be either full- or part-time, but it must report directly to the Chief Executive.

Appoint a quality management adviser

A professional expert on quality management will be required to advise on the 'technical' aspects of planning and implementing TQM. This is a consultancy role, and may be provided from within or without the organization, full- or part-time. This person needs to be a persuader, philosopher, teacher, adviser, facilitator, reporter and motivator. He or she must clearly understand the organization, its processes and interfaces, be conversant with the key functional languages used in the business, and be comfortable operating at many organizational levels. On a more general level this person must fully understand and be an effective advocate and teacher of TQM, be flexible and become an efficient agent of change.

Steering committees and teams

Devising and implementing total quality management for an organization takes considerable time and ability. It must be given the status of a senior executive project. The creation of cost-effective quality improvement is difficult, because of the need for full integration with the organization's strategy, operating philosophy and management systems. It may require an extensive review and substantial revision of existing systems of management and ways of operating. Fundamental questions may have to be asked, such as 'Do the managers have the necessary authority, capability and time to carry this through?'

Any review of existing management and operating systems will inevitably 'open many cans of worms' and uncover problems that have been successfully buried and smoothed over – perhaps for years. Authority must be given to those charged with following TQM through with actions that they consider necessary to achieve the goals. The commitment will be continually questioned and will be weakened, perhaps destroyed, by failure to delegate authoritatively.

The following steps are suggested in general terms. Clearly, different types of organization will have need to make adjustments to the detail, but the component parts are the basic requirements.

Figure 10.1 *Employee participation through the TQM structure*

A disciplined and systematic approach to continuous improvement may be established in a TQM or Business Excellence 'Steering Committee' or 'Council' (Figure 10.1). The Committee/Council should meet at least monthly to review strategy, implementation progress, and improvement. It should be chaired by the Chief Executive, who must attend every meeting – only death or serious illness should prevent him/her being there. Clearly, postponement may be necessary occasionally, but the council should not carry on meeting without the Chief Executive present. The council members should include the top management team and the chairmen of any 'site' TQM steering committees or process quality teams, depending on the size of the organization. The objectives of the council are to:

● Provide strategic direction on TQM for the organization.
● Establish plans for TQM on each 'site'.
● Set up and review the process quality teams that will own the key or critical business processes.
● Review and revise quality plans for implementation.

The process quality teams (PQTs) and any site TQM steering committees should also meet monthly, shortly before the senior steering committee/council meetings. Every senior manager should be a member of at least one PQT. This system provides the 'top-down' support for employee participation in process management and development, through either a quality improvement team or a quality circle programme. It also ensures that the commitment to TQM at the top is communicated effectively through the organization.

The three-tier approach of steering committee, process quality teams (PQTs) and quality improvement teams (QITs) allows the first to concentrate on quality strategy, rather than become a senior problem-solving group. Progress is assured if the PQT chairmen are required to present a status report at each meeting.

The process quality teams or steering committees control all the QITs and have responsibility for:

- The selection of projects for the QITs.
- Providing an outline and scope for each project to give to the QITs.
- The appointment of team members and leaders.
- Monitoring and reviewing the progress and results from each QIT project.

As the focus of this work will be the selection of projects, some attention will need to be given to the sources of nominations. Projects may be suggested by:

a) Steering Committee/Council members representing their own departments, process quality teams, their suppliers or their customers, internal and external.
b) Quality improvement teams.
c) Quality circles (if in existence).
d) Suppliers.
e) Customers.

The PQT members must be given the responsibility and authority to represent their part of the organization in the process. The members must also feel that they represent the team to the rest of the organization. In this way the PQT will gain knowledge and respect and be seen to have the authority to act in the best interests of the organization, with respect to their process.

Process and quality improvement teams

Process and quality improvement teams (PQTs and QITs) are groups of people with the appropriate knowledge, skills and experience who are brought together specifically by management to improve processes and/or tackle and solve a particular problem, usually on a project basis. They are cross-functional and often multi-disciplinary.

The 'task force' has long been a part of the culture of many organizations at the 'technology' and management levels. But process/quality improvement teams go a step further; they expand the traditional definition of 'process' to cover the entire production or operating system. This includes technology, paperwork, communication and other units, operating procedures, and the process equipment itself. By taking this broader view, the teams can address new problems. The actual running of process/ quality improvement teams calls several factors into play:

- Team selection and leadership
- Team objectives
- Team meetings
- Team assignments
- Team dynamics
- Team results and reviews.

Team selection and leadership

The most important element of a PQT or QIT is its members. People with knowledge and experience relevant to the process or solving the problem are clearly required. However, there should be a limit of five to ten members to keep the team small enough to be manageable but allow a good exchange of ideas. Membership should include appropriate people from groups outside the operational and technical areas directly 'responsible' for the process or problem, if their presence is relevant or essential. In the selection of team members it is often useful to start with just one or two people concerned directly with the problem. If they try to draw maps or flowcharts (see Chapter 4) of the relevant processes, the requirement to include other people, in order to understand the process and complete the charts, will aid the team selection. This method will also ensure that all those who can make a significant contribution to the process improvement are represented.

The team leader has a primary responsibility for team management and maintenance, and his/her selection and training is crucial to success. The leader need not be the highest ranking person in the team, but must be concerned about accomplishing the team objectives (this is sometimes described as 'task concern') and the needs of the members (often termed 'people concern'). Weakness in either of these areas will lessen the effectiveness of the team in solving problems. Team leadership training should be directed at correcting deficiencies in these crucial aspects.

Team objectives

At the beginning of any PQT or QIT project, and at the start of every meeting, the objectives should be stated as clearly as possible by the leader. This can take a simple form: 'This meeting is to continue the discussion from last Tuesday on the provision of current price data from salesmen to invoice preparation, and to generate suggestions for improvement in its quality.' Project and/or meeting objectives enable the team members to focus thoughts and efforts on the aims, which may need to be restated if the team becomes distracted by other issues.

Team meetings

An agenda should be prepared by the leader and distributed to each team member before every meeting. It should include the following information:

- Meeting place, time and how long it will be.
- A list of members (and co-opted members) expected to attend.
- Any preparatory assignments for individual members or groups.
- Any supporting material to be discussed at the meeting.

Early in a project the leader should orient the team members in terms of the approach, methods and techniques they will use to solve the problem. This may require a review of the:

1 Systematic approach (Chapter 8).
2 Procedures and rules for using some of the basic tools, e.g. brainstorming – no judgement of initial ideas.
3 Role of the team in the continuous improvement process.
4 Authority of the team.

A team secretary should be appointed to take the minutes of meetings and distribute them to members as soon as possible after each meeting. The minutes should not be formal, but reflect decisions and carry a clear statement of the action plans, together with assignments of tasks. They may be handwritten initially, copied and given to team members at the end of the meeting, to be followed later by a more formal document that will be seen by any member of staff interested in knowing the outcome of the meeting. In this way the minutes form an important part of the communication system, supplying information to other teams or people needing to know what is going on.

Team assignments

It is never possible to solve problems by meetings alone. What must come out of those meetings is a series of action plans that assign specific tasks to team members. This is the responsibility of the team leader. Agreement must be reached regarding the responsibilities for individual assignments, together with the time scale, and this must be made clear in the minutes. Task assignments must be decided while the team is together and not by separate individuals in after-meeting discussions.

Team dynamics

In any team activity the interactions between the members are vital to success. If solutions to problems are to be found, the meetings and ensuring assignments should assist and harness the creative thinking process. This is easier said than done, because many people have either not learned or been encouraged to be innovative. The team leader clearly has a role here to:

- Create a 'climate' for creativity.
- Encourage all team members to speak out and contribute their own ideas or build on others.
- Allow differing points of view and ideas to emerge.
- Remove barriers to idea generation, e.g. incorrect preconceptions, which are usually destroyed by asking 'Why?'
- Support all team members in their attempts to become creative.

In addition to the team leader's responsibilities, the members should:

a) Prepare themselves well for meetings, by collecting appropriate data or information (*facts*) pertaining to a particular problem.
b) Share ideas and opinions.
c) Encourage other points of view.
d) Listen 'openly' for alternative approaches to a problem or issue.
e) Help the team determine the best solutions.
f) Reserve judgement until all the arguments have been heard *and* fully understood.
g) Accept individual responsibility for assignments and group responsibility for the efforts of the team.

Further details of teamworking are given in Chapter 11.

Team results and reviews

A PQT/QIT approach to process improvement and problem-solving functions is most effective when the results of the work are communicated and acted upon. Regular feedback to the teams, via their leaders, will assist them to focus on objectives and review progress.

Reviews also help to deal with certain problems that may arise in teamwork. For example, certain members may be concerned more with their own personal objectives than those of the team. This may result in some manipulation of the problem-solving process to achieve different goals, resulting in the team splitting apart through self-interest. If recognized, the review can correct this effect and demand greater openness and honesty.

A different type of problem is the failure of certain members to contribute and take their share of individual and group responsibility. Allowing other people to do their work results in an uneven distribution of effort, and leads to bitterness. The review should make sure that all members have assigned and specific tasks, and perhaps lead to the documentation of duties in the minutes. A team roster may even help.

A third area of difficulty, which may be improved by reviewing progress, is the ready-fire-aim syndrome of action before analysis. This often results from team leaders being too anxious to deal with a problem. A review should allow the problem to be redefined adequately and expose the real cause(s). This will release the trap the team may be in of doing something before they really know what should be done. The review will provide the opportunity to rehearse the steps in the systematic approach:

Record data	– all processes can and should be measured
	– all measurements should be recorded
Use data	– if data are recorded and not used they will be abused.
Analyse data systematically	– data analysis should be carried out by means of the basic tools (Chapter 8)
Act on the results	– recording and analysis of data without action leads to frustration.

Quality circles or Kaizen teams

Kaizen is a philosophy of continuous improvement of all the employees in an organization so that they perform their tasks a little better each day. It is a never-ending journey centred on the concept of starting anew each day with the principle that methods can always be improved.

Kaizen Teian is a Japanese system for generating and implementing employee ideas. Japanese suggestion schemes have helped companies to improve quality and productivity, and reduced prices to increase market share. They concentrate on participation and the rates of implementation, rather than on the 'quality' or value of the suggestion. The emphasis is on encouraging everyone to make improvements.

Kaizen Teian suggestions are usually small-scale ones, in the worker's own area, and are easy and cheap to implement. Key points are that the rewards given are small, and implementation is rapid, which results in many small improvements that accumulate to massive total savings and improvements.

One of the most publicized aspects of the Japanese approach to quality has been these quality circles or Kaizen teams. The quality circle may be defined then as a group of workers doing similar work who meet:

● Voluntarily
● Regularly
● In normal working time
● Under the leadership of their 'supervisor'
● To identify, analyse and solve work-related problems
● To recommend solutions to management.

Where possible, quality circle members should implement the solutions themselves.

The quality circle concept first originated in Japan in the early 1960s, following a postwar reconstruction period during which the Japanese placed a great deal of emphasis on improving and perfecting their quality control techniques. As a direct result of work carried out to train foremen during that period, the first quality circles were conceived, and the first three circles registered with the Japanese Union of Scientists and Engineers (JUSE) in 1962. Since that time the growth rate has been phenomenal. The concept has spread to Taiwan, the USA and Europe, and circles in many countries have been successful. Many others have failed.

It is very easy to regard quality circles as the magic ointment to be rubbed on the affected spot, and unfortunately many managers in the West first saw them as a panacea for all ills. There are no panaceas, and to place this concept into perspective, Juran, who has been an important influence in Japan's improvement in quality, has stated that quality circles represent only 5–10 per cent of the canvas of the Japanese success. The rest is concerned with understanding quality, its related costs and the organization, systems and techniques necessary for achieving customer satisfaction.

Given the right sort of commitment by top management, introduction, and environment in which to operate, quality circles can produce the 'shop floor' motivation to achieve quality performance at that level. Circles should develop out of an understanding and knowledge of quality on the part of senior management. They must not be introduced as a desperate attempt to do something about poor quality. The term 'quality circle' may be replaced with a number of acronyms but the basic concepts and operational aspects may be found in many organizations.

The structure of a quality circle organization

The unique feature about quality circles or Kaizen teams is that people are asked to join and not told to do so. Consequently, it is difficult to be specific about the structure of such a concept. It is, however, possible to identify four elements in a circle organization:

- Members
- Leaders
- Facilitators or co-ordinators
- Management.

Members form the prime element of the concept. They will have been taught the basic problem-solving and process control techniques and, hence, possess the ability to identify and solve work-related problems.

Leaders are usually the immediate supervisors or foremen of the members. They will have been trained to lead a circle and bear the responsibility of its success. A good leader, one who develops the abilities of the circle members, will benefit directly by receiving valuable assistance in tackling nagging problems.

Facilitators are the managers of the quality circle programmes. They, more than anyone else, will be responsible for the success of the concept, particularly within an organization. The facilitators must co-ordinate the meetings, the training and energies of the leaders and members, and form the link between the circles and the rest of the organization. Ideally the facilitator will be an innovative industrial teacher, capable of communicating with all levels and with all departments within the organization.

Management support and commitment are necessary to quality circles or, like any other concept, they will not succeed. Management must retain its prerogatives, particularly regarding acceptance or non-acceptance of recommendations from circles, but the quickest way to kill a programme is to ignore a proposal arising from it. One of the most difficult facts for management to accept, and yet one forming the cornerstone of the quality circle philosophy, is that the real 'experts' on performing a task are those who do it day after day.

Training quality circles

The training of circle/Kaizen leaders and members is the foundation of all successful programmes. The whole basis of the training operation is that the ideas must be easy to take in and be put across in a way that facilitates understanding. Simplicity must be the key word, with emphasis being given to the basic techniques. Essentially there are eight segments of training:

1 Introduction to quality circles.
2 Brainstorming.

3 Data gathering and histograms.
4 Cause and effect analysis.
5 Pareto analysis.
6 Sampling and stratification.
7 Control charts.
8 Presentation techniques.

Managers should also be exposed to some training in the part they are required to play in the quality circle philosophy. A quality circle programme can only be effective if management believes in it and is supportive and, since changes in management style may be necessary, managers' training is essential.

Operation of quality circles/Kaizen teams

There are no formal rules governing the size of a quality circle/Kaizen team. Membership usually varies from three to fifteen people, with an average of seven to eight. It is worth remembering that, as the circle becomes larger than this, it becomes increasingly difficult for all members of the circle to participate.

Meetings should be held away from the work area, so that members are free from interruptions, and are mentally and physically at ease. The room should be arranged in a manner conducive to open discussion, and any situation that physically emphasizes the leader's position should be avoided.

Meeting length and frequency are variable, but new circles meet for approximately one hour once per week. Thereafter, when training is complete, many circles continue to meet weekly; others extend the interval to 2 or 3 weeks. To a large extent the nature of the problems selected will determine the interval between meetings, but this should never extend to more than 1 month, otherwise members will lose interest and the circle will cease to function.

Great care is needed to ensure that every meeting is productive, no matter how long it lasts or how frequently is it held. Any of the following activities may take place during a circle meeting:

● Training – initial or refresher
● Problem identification
● Problem analysis
● Preparation and recommendation for problem solution
● Management presentations
● Quality circle administration.

A quality circle usually selects a project to work on through discussion within the circle. The leader then advises management of this choice and, assuming that no objections are raised, the circle proceeds with the work. Other suggestions for projects come from management, quality assurance staff, the maintenance department, various staff personnel, and other circles.

It is sometimes necessary for quality circles to contact experts in a particular field, e.g. engineers, quality experts, safety officers, maintenance personnel. This communication should be strongly encouraged, and the normal company channels should be used to invite specialists to attend meetings and offer advice. The experts may be considered to be 'consultants', the quality circle retaining responsibility for improving a process or solving the particular problem. The overriding purpose of quality circles or Kaizen teams is to provide the powerful motivation of allowing people to take some part in deciding their own actions and futures.

Departmental purpose analysis

'Quality is everyone's business' is an often quoted cliché, but 'Everything is everyone's business', and so quality often becomes nobody's business. The responsibility for quality begins with the determination of the customer's quality requirements and continues until the service or product is accepted by a satisfied customer. The department purpose analysis (DPA) technique, developed by IBM, helps to define the real purpose of each department, with the objective of improving performance and breaking down departmental barriers. It leads to an understanding and agreement on the key processes of each group. The department can then liaise with its immediate 'suppliers' and 'customers', often internally, to identify potential or actual problem areas and simultaneously carry out an analysis of what proportion of time is spent on the key activities. This begins the change from departmental to process management thinking.

Group discussions during the DPA process usually yield many good ideas for improvement, either eliminating wasteful activity or improving the quality of output from the department. Everyone becomes and should then remain aware of the prime purpose of the department, and the focus on efficiency and reducing waste usually carries through to all work activities. The manager of the department, who should run the exercise, must understand the DPA process and why it is necessary and important. He/she needs to be open-minded towards change, and to encourage departmental staff to question whether all their activities add value to the product, service or business. One of the greatest barriers to improvements through DPA is the 'but we've always done it that way' response.

The basic steps of DPA are:

1 Form the DPA group.
2 Brainstorm to list all the departmental tasks (see Chapter 8).
3 Agree which are the five main tasks.
4 Define the position and role of the departmental manager.
5 Review the main activities, and for each one identify the 'customer(s)' and 'supplier(s)'.
6 Consult the customer(s) and supplier(s) by means of a suitable questionnaire. This should be very similar to the list of questions suggested in Chapter 1 for interrogating any customer–supplier interface.
7 Review the customer–supplier survey results and brainstorm how improvements can be made.
8 Prioritize improvements to list those to be tackled first, and plan how.

9 Implement the improvement action plan, maintaining encouragement and support.
10 Review the progress made and repeat the DPA.

As with any new group activity, some successes are desirable early in the programme, if the department is to build confidence in its ability to make improvements and solve problems. For this reason DPA should confine itself, initially at least, to resolving issues that are within its control. It is unlikely, for example, that a sales team will be successful in getting a product redesigned in its first improvement project. Experience at IBM shows that, as confidence builds through continued management encouragement, the DPA groups will tackle increasingly difficult business processes and problems, with an increasing return of the investment in time.

Chapter highlights

The quality function and the quality director or manager

- The quality function should be the organization's focal point of the integration of the business interests of customers and suppliers into the internal dynamics of the organization.
- Its role is to encourage and facilitate quality and process improvement; monitor and evaluate progress; promote the quality chains; plan, manage, audit and review systems; plan and provide quality training, counselling and consultancy; and give advice to management.
- In larger organizations a quality director will contribute to the prevention strategy. Smaller organizations may appoint a member of the management team to this task on a part-time basis. An external TQM adviser is usually required.

Steering committees and teams

- In devising and implementing TQM for an organization, it may be useful to ask first if the managers have the authority, capability and time to carry it through.
- A disciplined and systematic approach to continuous improvement may be established in a steering committee/council, whose members are the senior management team.
- Reporting to the steering committee are the process quality teams (PQTs) or any site steering committees, which in turn control the quality improvement teams (QITs) and quality circles.

Process and quality improvement teams

- A PQT or QIT is a group brought together by management to improve a process or tackle a particular problem on a project basis. The running of PQTs and QITs includes several team factors: selection and leadership, objectives, meetings, assignments, dynamics, results and reviews.

Quality circles or Kaizen teams

- Kaizen is a philosophy of small-step continuous improvement, by all employees. In Kaizen teams the suggestions and rewards are small but the implementation is rapid.
- A quality circle or Kaizen team is a group of people who do similar work meeting voluntarily, regularly, in normal working time, to identify, analyse and solve work-related problems, under the leadership of their supervisor. They make recommendations to management. Alternative names may be given to the teams, other than 'quality circles'.

Departmental purpose analysis

- DPA helps to define the real purpose of each department, with the objective of improving performance and breaking down barriers. It leads to an understanding and agreement on the key processes of each group.
- The departmental manager runs the exercise and must understand DPA. The basic steps are: form DPA group; list all departmental tasks; agree five main tasks; define position and role of manager; identify task customer(s) and supplier(s), and consult, review and brainstorm improvements; prioritize; implement plan; review progress and repeat DPA.

Chapter 11

Culture change through teamwork for quality

The need for teamwork

The complexity of most of the processes that are operated in industry, commerce and the services places them beyond the control of any one individual. The only really efficient way to tackle process improvement or problems is through the use of some form of teamwork. The use of the team approach to problem solving has many advantages over allowing individuals to work separately:

● A greater variety of complex problems may be tackled – those beyond the capability of any one individual or even one department – by the pooling of expertise and resources.
● Problems are exposed to a greater diversity of knowledge, skill, experience, and are solved more efficiently.
● The approach is more satisfying to team members, and boosts morale and ownership through participation in problem solving and decision making.
● Problems that cross departmental or functional boundaries can be dealt with more easily, and the potential/actual conflicts are more likely to be identified and solved.
● The recommendations are more likely to be implemented than individual suggestions, as the quality of decision making in *good teams* is high.

Most of these factors rely on the premise that people are willing to support any effort in which they have taken part or helped to develop.

When properly managed and developed, teams improve the process of problem solving, producing results quickly and economically. Teamwork throughout any

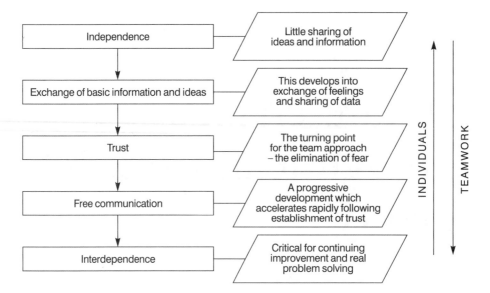

Figure 11.1 *Independence to interdependence through teamwork*

organization is an essential component of the implementation of TQM, for it builds trust, improves communications and develops interdependence. Much of what has been taught previously in management has led to a culture in the West of independence, with little sharing of ideas and information. Knowledge is very much like organic manure – if it is spread around it will fertilize and encourage growth; if it is kept closed in, it will eventually fester and rot.

Teamwork devoted to quality improvement changes the independence to inter-dependence through improved communications, trust and the free exchange of ideas, knowledge, data and information (Figure 11.1). The use of the face-to-face interaction method of communication, with a common goal, develops over time the sense of dependence on each other. This forms a key part of any quality improvement process, and provides a methodology for employee recognition and participation, through active encouragement in group activities.

Teamwork provides an environment in which people can grow and use all the resources effectively and efficiently to make continuous improvements. As individuals grow, the organization grows. It is worth pointing out, however, that employees will not be motivated towards continual improvement in the absence of:

- Commitment to quality from top management.
- The organizational quality 'climate'.
- A mechanism for enabling individual contributions to be effective.

All these are focused essentially at enabling people to feel, accept and discharge responsibility. More than one organization has made this part of their quality strategy – to 'empower people to act'. If one hears from employees comments such as, 'We know this is not the best way to do this job, but if that is the way management want us to do it, that is the way we will do it', then it is clear that the expertise existing at the point of operation has not been harnessed and the people do not feel responsible for the outcome of their actions. Responsibility and accountability foster pride, job satisfaction and better work.

Empowerment to act is very easy to express conceptually, but it requires real effort and commitment on the part of all managers and supervisors to put into practice. Recognition that only partially successful but good ideas or attempts are to be applauded and not criticized is a good way to start. Encouragement of ideas and suggestions from the workforce, particularly through their part in team or group activities, requires investment. The rewards are total commitment, both inside the organization and outside through the supplier and customer chains.

Teamwork for quality improvement has several components. It is driven by a strategy, needs a structure, and must be implemented thoughtfully and effectively. The strategy that drives the quality improvement teams at the various levels was outlined in Part 1, and will be dealt with in more detail in the final chapter of this book, but in essence it comprises:

- The mission of the organization.
- The critical success factors.
- The core process.

The structure of having the top management team in a senior steering committee or council, and the key processes being owned by process management teams, which manage projects through QITs and quality circles was detailed in Chapter 10, on the organizational requirements for quality. The remainder of this chapter will concentrate on teamwork and its implementation.

Teamwork and action-centred leadership

Over the years there has been much academic work on the psychology of teams and on the leadership of teams. Three points on which all authors are in agreement are that teams develop a personality and culture of their own, respond to leadership, and are motivated according to criteria usually applied to individuals.

Key figures in the field of human relations, like Douglas McGregor (Theories X & Y), Abraham Maslow (Hierarchy of Needs) and Fred Hertzberg (Motivators and Hygiene Factors), all changed their opinions on group dynamics over time as they came to realize that groups are not the democratic entity that everyone would like them to be, but respond to individual, strong, well-directed leadership, both from without and within the group, just like individuals.

Action-centred leadership

During the 1960s John Adair, senior lecturer in Military History and the Leadership Training Adviser at the Military Academy, Sandhurst, and later assistant director of the Industrial Society, developed what he called the action-centred leadership model, based

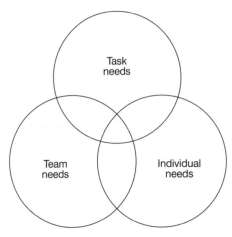

Figure 11.2 *Adair's model*

on his experiences at Sandhurst, where he had the responsibility to ensure that results in the cadet training did not fall below a certain standard. He had observed that some instructors frequently achieved well above average results, owing to their own natural ability with groups and their enthusiasm. He developed this further into a team model, which is the basis of the approach of the author and his colleagues to this subject.

In developing his model for teamwork and leadership, Adair brought out clearly that for any group or team, big or small, to respond to leadership, they need a clearly defined *task*, and the response and achievement of that task are interrelated to the needs of the *team* and the separate needs of the *individual members* of the team (Figure 11.2).

The value of the overlapping circles is that it emphasizes the unity of leadership and the interdependence and multifunctional reaction to single decisions affecting any of the three areas.

Leadership tasks

Drawing upon the discipline of social psychology, Adair developed and applied to training the functional view of leadership. The essence of this he distilled into the three interrelated but distinctive requirements of a leader. These are to define and achieve the job or task, to build up and co-ordinate a team to do this, and to develop and satisfy the individuals within the team (Figure 11.3).

1 *Task needs.* The difference between a team and a random crowd is that a team has some common purpose, goal or objective, e.g. a football team. If a work team does not achieve the required results or meaningful results, it will become frustrated. Organizations have to make a profit, to provide a service, or even to survive. So anyone who manages others has to achieve results; in production, marketing, selling or whatever. Achieving objectives is a major criterion of success.

2 *Team needs.* To achieve these objectives, the group needs to be held together. People need to be working in a co-ordinated fashion in the same direction. Teamwork will ensure that the team's contribution is greater than the sum of its parts. Conflict within

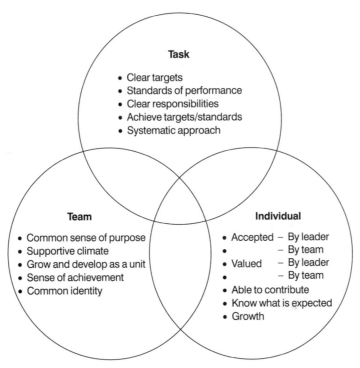

Figure 11.3 *The leadership needs*

the team must be used effectively; arguments can lead to ideas or to tension and lack of co-operation.

3 *Individual needs*. Within working groups, individuals also have their own set of needs. They need to know what their responsibilities are, how they will be needed, how well they are performing. They need an opportunity to show their potential, take on responsibility and receive recognition for good work.

The task, team and individual functions for the leader are as follows:

a) *Task functions*   Defining the task.
                      Making a plan.
                      Allocating work and resources.
                      Controlling quality and tempo of work.
                      Checking performance against the plan.
                      Adjusting the plan.
b) *Team functions*   Setting standards.
                      Maintaining discipline.
                      Building team spirit.
                      Encouraging, motivating, giving a sense of purpose.
                      Appointing subleaders.
                      Ensuring communication within the group.
                      Training the group.

c) *Individual functions*   Attending to personal problems.
Praising individuals.
Giving status.
Recognizing and using individual abilities.
Training the individual.

The team leader's or facilitator's task is to concentrate on the small central area where all three circles overlap. In a business that is introducing TQM this is the 'action to change' area, where the leaders are attempting to manage the change from *business as usual*, through total quality management, to *TQM equals business as usual*, using the cross-functional quality improvement teams at the strategic interface.

In the action area the facilitator's or leader's task is similar to the task outlined by John Adair. It is to try to satisfy all three areas of need by achieving the task, building the team, and satisfying individual needs. If a leader concentrates on the task, e.g. in going all out for production schedules, while neglecting the training, encouragement and motivation of the team and individuals, he/she may do very well in the short term. Eventually, however, the team members will give less effort than they are capable of. Similarly, a leader who concentrates only on creating team spirit, while neglecting the task and the individuals, will not receive maximum contribution from the people. They may enjoy working in the team but they will lack the real sense of achievement that comes from accomplishing a task to the utmost of the collective ability.

So the leader/facilitator must try to achieve a balance by acting in all three areas of overlapping need. It is always wise to work out a list of required functions within the context of any given situation, based on a general agreement on the essentials. Here is Adair's original Sandhurst list, on which one's own adaptation may be based:

- *Planning,* e.g. seeking all available information.
  Defining group task, purpose or goal.
  Making a workable plan (in right decision-making framework).
- *Initiating,* e.g. briefing group on the aims and the plan.
  Explaining why aim or plan is necessary.
  Allocating tasks to group members.
- *Controlling*, e.g. maintaining group standard.
  Influencing tempo.
  Ensuring all actions are taken towards objectives.
  Keeping discussions relevant.
  Prodding group to action/decision
- *Supporting,* e.g. expressing acceptance of persons and their contribution.
  Encouraging group/individuals.
  Disciplining group/individuals.
  Creating team spirit.
  Relieving tension with humour.
  Reconciling disagreements or getting others to explore them.
- *Informing,* e.g. clarifying task and plan.
  Giving new information to the group, i.e. keeping them 'in the picture'.
  Receiving information from the group.
  Summarizing suggestions and ideas coherently.

- *Evaluating,* e.g. checking feasibility of an idea.
  Testing the consequences of a proposed solution.
  Evaluating group performance.
  Helping the group to evaluate its own performance against standards.

Situational leadership

In dealing with the task, the team, and with any individual in the team, a style of leadership appropriate to the situation must be adopted. The teams and the individuals within them will, to some extent, start 'cold', but they will develop and grow in both strength and experience. The interface with the leader must also change with the change in the team, according to the Tannenbaum and Schmidt model (Figure 11.4).[1]

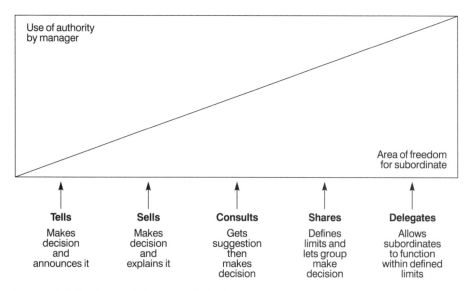

Figure 11.4 *Continuum of leadership behaviour*

Initially a very directive approach may be appropriate, giving clear instructions to meet agreed goals. Gradually, as the teams become more experienced and have some success, the facilitating team leader will move through coaching and support to less directing and eventually a less supporting and less directive approach – as the more interdependent style permeates the whole organization.

This equates to the modified Blanchard model[1] in Figure 11.5, where directive behaviour moves from high to low as people develop and are more easily empowered. When this is coupled with the appropriate level of supportive behaviour, a directing style of leadership can move through coaching and supporting to a delegating style. It must be stressed, however, that effective delegation is only possible with developed 'followers', who can be fully empowered.

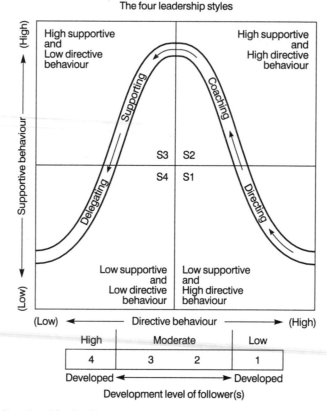

Figure 11.5 *Situational leadership – progressive empowerment through TQM*

One of the great mistakes in recent years has been the expectation by management that teams can be put together with virtually no training or development (S1 in Figure 11.5) and that they will perform as a mature team (S4). The Blanchard model emphasizes that there is no quick and easy 'tunnel' from S1 to S4. The only route is the laborious climb through S2 and S3.

Stages of team development.

Original work by Tuckman[1] suggested that when teams are put together, there are four main stages of team development, the so-called forming (awareness), storming (conflict), norming (co-operation), and performing (productivity). The characteristics of each stage and some key aspects to look out for in the early stages are given below.

Forming – awareness

Characteristics:

- Feelings, weaknesses and mistakes are covered up.
- People conform to established lines.
- Little care is shown for others' values and views.
- There is no shared understanding of what needs to be done.

Watch out for:

- Increasing bureaucracy and paperwork.
- People confining themselves to defined jobs.
- The 'boss' is ruling with a firm hand.

Storming – conflict

Characteristics:

- More risky, personal issues are opened up.
- The team becomes more inward-looking.
- There is more concern for the values, views and problems of others in the team.

Watch out for:

- The team becomes more open, but lacks the capacity to act in a unified, economic and effective way.

Norming – co-operation

Characteristics:

- Confidence and trust to look at how the team is operating.
- A more systematic and open approach, leading to a clearer and more methodical way of working.
- Greater valuing of people for their differences.
- Clarification of purpose and establishing of objectives.
- Systematic collection of information.
- Considering all options.
- Preparing detailed plans.
- Reviewing progress to make improvements.

Performing – productivity

Characteristics:

- Flexibility.
- Leadership decided by situations, not protocols.

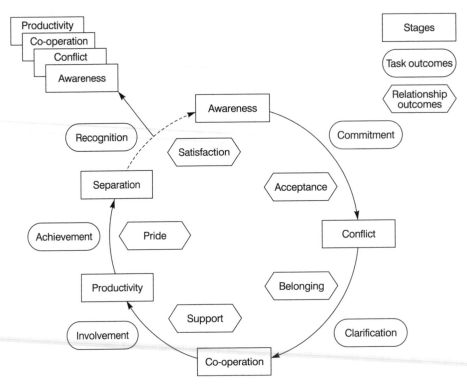

Figure 11.6 *Team stages and outcomes. (Derived from Kormanski and Mozenter, 1987[1])*

- Everyone's energies utilized.
- Basic principles and social aspects of the organization's decisions considered.

The team stages, the task outcomes and the relationship outcomes are shown together in Figure 11.6. This model, which has been modified from Kormanski, may be used as a framework for the assessment of team performance. The issues to look for are:

1 How is leadership exercised in the team?
2 How is decision making accomplished?
3 How are team resources utilized?
4 How are new members integrated into the team?

Teams which go through these stages successfully should become effective teams and display the following attributes.

Attributes of successful teams

Clear objectives and agreed goals.
No group of people can be effective unless they know what they want to achieve, but it is more than knowing what the objectives are. People are only likely to be committed

to them if they can identify with and have ownership of them – in other words, objectives and goals are agreed by team members.

Often this agreement is difficult to achieve but experience shows that it is an essential prerequisite for the effective group.

Openness and confrontation

If a team is to be effective, then the members of it need to be able to state their views, their differences of opinion, interests and problems, without fear of ridicule or retaliation. No teams work effectively if there is a cut-throat atmosphere, where members become less willing or able to express themselves openly; then much energy, effort and creativity are lost.

Support and trust

Support naturally implies trust among team members. Where individual group members do not feel they have to protect their territory or job, and feel able to talk straight to other members, about both 'nice' and 'nasty' things, then there is an opportunity for trust to be shown. Based on this trust, people can talk freely about their fears and problems and receive from others help they need to be more effective.

Co-operation and conflict

When there is an atmosphere of trust, members are more ready to participate and are committed. Information is shared rather than hidden. Individuals listen to the ideas of others and build on them. People find ways of being more helpful to each other and the group generally. Co-operation causes high morale – individuals accept each other's strengths and weaknesses and contribute from their pool of knowledge of skill. All abilities, knowledge and experience are fully utilized by the group; individuals have no inhibitions about using other people's abilities to help solve their problems, which are shared.

Allied to this, conflicts are seen as a necessary and useful part of the organizational life. The effective team works through issues of conflict and uses the results to help objectives. Conflict prevents teams from becoming complacent and lazy, and often generates new ideas.

Good decision making

As mentioned earlier, objectives need to be clearly and completely understood by all members before good decision making can begin. In making decisions effective, teams develop the ability to collect information quickly then discuss the alternatives openly. They become committed to their decisions and ensure quick action.

Appropriate leadership

Effective teams have a leader whose responsibility it is to achieve results through the efforts of a number of people. Power and authority can be applied in many ways, and team members often differ on the style of leadership they prefer. Collectively, teams may come to different views of leadership but, whatever their view, the effective team usually sorts through the alternatives in an open and honest way.

Review of the team processes

Effective teams understand not only the group's character and its role in the organization, but also how it makes decisions, deals with conflicts, etc. The team process allows the team to learn from experience and consciously to improve teamwork. There are numerous ways of looking at team processes – use of an observer, by a team member giving feedback, or by the whole group discussing members' performance.

Sound inter-group relationships

No human being or group is an island; they need the help of others. An organization will not achieve maximum benefit from a collection of quality improvement teams that are effective within themselves but fight among each other.

Individual development opportunities

Effective teams seek to pool the skills of individuals, and it necessarily follows that they pay attention to development of individual skills and try to provide opportunities for individuals to grow and learn, and of course have FUN.

Once again, these ideas are not new but are very applicable and useful in the management of teams for quality improvements, just as Newton's theories on gravity still apply!

Personality types and the MBTI

No one person has a monopoly of 'good characteristics. Attempts to list the qualities of the ideal manager, for example, demonstrate why that paragon cannot exist. This is because many of the qualities are mutually exclusive, for example:

Highly intelligent	*v*	Not *too* clever
Forceful and driving	*v*	Sensitive to people's feelings
Dynamic	*v*	Patient
Fluent communicator	*v*	Good listener
Decisive	*v*	Reflective

Although no individual can possess all these and more desirable qualities, a team often does.

A powerful aid to team development is the use of the Myers–Briggs Type Indicator (MBTI).[1] This is based on an individual's preferences on four scales for:

- Giving and receiving 'energy'
- Gathering information
- Making decisions
- Handling the outer world.

Its aim is to help individuals understand and value themselves and others, in terms of their differences as well as their similarities. It is well researched and non-threatening when used appropriately.

The four MBTI preference scales, which are based on Jung's theories of psychological types, represent two opposite preferences:

Extroversion – Introversion	– how we prefer to give/receive energy or focus our attention
Sensing – Intuition	– how we prefer to gather information
Thinking – Feeling	– how we prefer to make decisions
Judgement – Perception	– how we prefer to handle the outer world.

To understand what is meant by preferences, the analogy of left- and right-handedness is useful. Most people have a preference to write with either their left or their right hand. When using the preferred hand, they tend not to think about it, it is done naturally. When writing with the other hand, however, it takes longer, needs careful concentration, seems more difficult, but with practice would no doubt become easier. Most people *can* write with and use both hands, but tend to prefer one over the other. This is similar to the MBTI psychological preferences: most people are able to use both preferences at different times, but will indicate a preference on each of the scales.

In all, there are eight possible preferences – E or I, S or N, T or F, J or P, i.e. two opposites for each of the four scales. An individual's *type* is the combination and interaction of the four preferences. It can be assessed initially by completion of a simple questionnaire. Hence, if each preference is represented by its letter, a person's type may be shown by a four-letter code – there are sixteen in all. For example, ESTJ represents an *extrovert* (E) who prefers to gather information with *sensing* (S), prefers to make decisions by *thinking* (T) and has a *judging* (J) attitude towards the world, i.e. prefers to make decisions rather than continue to collect information. The person with opposite preferences on all four scales would be an INFP, an introvert who prefers intuition for perceiving, feelings or values for making decisions, and likes to maintain a perceiving attitude towards the outer world.

The questionnaire, its analysis and feedback must be administered by a qualified MBTI practitioner, who may also act as external facilitator to the team in its forming and storming stages.

Type and teamwork

With regard to teamwork, the preference types and their interpretation are extremely powerful. The *extrovert* prefers action and the outer world, whilst the *introvert* prefers ideas and the inner world.

Sensing–thinking types are interested in facts, analyse facts impersonally, and use a step-by-step process from cause to effect, premise to conclusion. The *sensing–feeling* combinations, however, are interested in facts, analyse facts personally, and are concerned about how things matter to themselves and others.

Intuition–thinking types are interested in possibilities, analyse possibilities impersonally, and have theoretical, technical, or executive abilities. On the other hand, the *intuition–feeling* combinations are interested in possibilities, analyse possibilities personally, and prefer new projects, new truths, things not yet apparent.

ISTJ	ISFJ	INFJ	INTJ
ISTP	ISFP	INFP	INTP
ESTP	ESFP	ENFP	ENTP
ESTJ	ESFJ	ENFJ	ENTJ

Figure 11.7 *MBTI type table form. (Source: Isabel Myers–Briggs, Introduction to Type[2])*

Judging types are decisive and are planners, they live in orderly fashion, and like to regulate and control. *Perceivers*, on the other hand, are flexible, live spontaneously, and understand and adapt readily.

As we have seen, an individual's type is the combination of four preferences on each of the scales. There are sixteen combinations of the preference scales and these may be displayed on a *type table* (Figure 11.7). If the individuals within a team are prepared to share with each other their MBTI preferences, this can dramatically increase understanding and frequently is of great assistance in team development and good teamworking. The similarities and differences in behaviour and personality can be identified. The assistance of a qualified MBTI practitioner is absolutely essential in the initial stages of this work.

Interpersonal relations – FIRO-B and the Elements

The FIRO-B (Fundamental Interpersonal Relations Orientation – Behaviour) is a powerful psychological instrument which can be used to give valuable insights into the needs individuals bring to their relationships with other people. The instrument assesses needs for inclusion, control and openness and therefore offers a framework for understanding the dynamics of interpersonal relationships.

Use of the FIRO instrument helps individuals to be more aware of how they relate to others and to become more flexible in this behaviour. Consequently it enables people to build more productive teams through better working relationships.

Since its creation by William Schutz in the 1950s, to predict how military personnel would work together in groups, the FIRO-B instrument has been used throughout the world by managers and professionals to look at management and decision-making styles. Through its ability to predict areas of probable tension and compatibility between individuals, the FIRO-B is a highly effective team-building tool which can aid in the creation of the positive environment in which people thrive and achieve improvements in performance.

The theory underlying the FIRO-B incorporates ideas from the work of Adomo, Fromm and Bion and it was first fully described in Schutz's book, *FIRO: A Three Dimensional Theory of Personal Behaviour* (1958). In his more recent book *The Human Element*, Schutz developed the instrument into a series of 'elements', B, F, S, etc., and offers strategies for heightening our awareness of ourselves and others.

The FIRO-B takes the form of a simple-to-complete questionnaire, the analysis of which provides scores that estimate the levels of behaviour with which the individual is comfortable, with regard to his/her needs for inclusion, control and openness. Schutz described these three dimensions in the form of the decision we make in our relationships regarding whether we want to be:

- 'in' or 'out' – inclusion
- 'up' or 'down' – control
- 'close' or 'distant' – openness.

The FIRO-B estimates our unique level of needs for each of these dimensions of interpersonal interaction.

The instrument further divides each of these dimensions into:

i) the behaviour we feel most comfortable exhibiting towards other people – expressed behaviours, and
ii) the behaviour we want from others – wanted behaviours.

Hence, the FIRO-B 'measures', on a scale of 0–9, each of the three interpersonal dimensions in two aspects (Table 11.1).

Table 11.1 *The FIRO-B interpersonal dimensions and aspects*

	Inclusion	*Control*	*Openness*
Expressed behaviour	Expressed inclusion	Expressed control	Expressed openness
Wanted behaviour	Wanted inclusion	Wanted control	Wanted openness

Modified from: W. Schutz (1978) *FIRO Awareness Scales Manual,* Palo Alto, CA, Consulting Psychologists Press.

The *expressed* aspect of each dimension indicates the level of behaviour the individual is most comfortable with towards others, so high scores for the expressed dimensions would be associated with:

High scored expressed behaviours

Inclusion   Makes efforts to include other people in his/her activities – tries to belong to or join groups and to be with people as much as possible.

Control   Tries to exert control and influence over people and tell them what to do.

Openness   Makes efforts to become close to people – expresses friendly open feelings, tries to be personal and even intimate.

Low scores would be associated with the opposite expressed behaviour.

The *wanted* aspect of each dimension indicates the behaviour the individual prefers others to adopt towards him/her, so high scores for the wanted dimensions would be associated with:

High scored wanted behaviours

Inclusion   Wants other people to include him/her in their activities – to be invited to belong to or join groups (even if no effort is made by the individual to be included).

Control   Wants others to control and influence him/her and be told what to do.

Openness   Wants others to become close to him/her and express friendly, open, even affectionate feelings.

Low scores would be associated with the opposite wanted behaviours.

It is interesting to look at typical manager FIRO-B profiles, based on their scores for the six dimensions/aspects in Table 11.1. Figure 11.8 shows the average of a sample of 700 middle and senior managers in the UK with boundaries at one sigma, plotted on expressed/wanted scales for the three dimensions.

On average, the managers show a higher level of expressed inclusion – including people in his/her activities – than wanted inclusion. Similarly, and not surprisingly perhaps, expressed control – trying to exert influence and control over others – is higher in managers than wanted control. When it comes to openness, the managers tend to want others to be open, rather than be open themselves.

It is even more interesting to contemplate these results when one considers the demands of some of the recent popular management programmes, such as total quality management, employment involvement and self-directed teams. These tend to require from managers certain behaviours, for example lower levels of expressed control and higher levels of wanted control, so that the people feel empowered. Similarly, managers are encouraged to be more open. These, however, are opposite to the apparent behaviours of the sample of managers shown graphically in Figure 11.8. It is not surprising then that TQM has failed in some organizations where managers were being

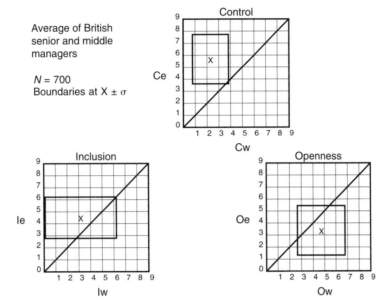

Figure 11.8 *Typical manager profiles (FIRO-B)*

asked to empower employees and be more open – and who can argue against that – yet their basic underlying needs caused them to behave in the opposite way.

Understanding what drives these behaviours is outside the scope of this book but other FIRO and Element instruments can help individuals to further develop understanding of themselves and others. FIRO and Schutz's elements instruments for measuring *feelings* (F) and *self-concept* (S) can deepen the awareness of what lies behind our behaviours with respect to inclusion, control and openness. The reader is advised to undertake further reading and seek guidance from a trained administrator of these instruments, but the overall relationship between the B and F instruments is:

Behaviours related to:	**Feelings related to:**
Inclusion	Significance
Control	Competence
Openness	Likeability

Issues around control behaviour then may arise because of underlying feelings about competence. Similarly, underlying feelings concerning significance may lead to certain inclusion behaviours.

FIRO-B in the workplace

The inclusion, control and openness dimensions form a cycle (Figure 11.9) which can help groups of people to understand how their individual and joint behaviour develops as teams are formed. Given in Table 11.2 are the considerations, questions and outcomes under each dimension. If inclusion issues are resolved first it is possible to

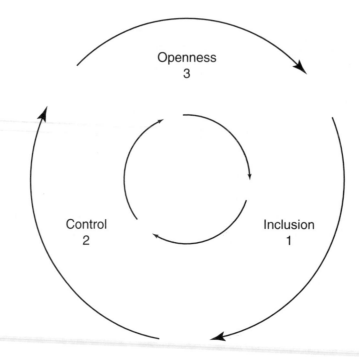

Figure 11.9 *The inclusion, control and openness cycle*

progress to dealing with the control issues, which in turn must be resolved if the openness issues are to be dealt with successfully. As a team develops, it travels around the inclusion, control and openness cycle time and time again. If the issues are not resolved in each dimension, further progress in the next dimension will be hindered – it is difficult to deal with issues of control if unresolved inclusion issues are still around and people do not know whether they are 'in' or 'out' of the group. Similarly it is difficult to be open if it is not clear where the power base is in the group.

This I-C-O cycle has led to the development by the author and his colleagues of an 'openness model' which is in three parts. Part 1 is based on the premise that to participate productively in a team individuals must firstly be involved and then committed. Figure 11.10 shows some of the questions which need to be answered and the outcomes from this stage. Part 2 deals with the control aspects of empowerment and management and Figure 11.11 summarizes the questions and outcomes. Finally Part 3, summarized in Figure 11.12, ensures openness through acknowledgement and trust. The full openness cycle (Figure 11.13) operates in a clockwise direction so that trust leads to more involvement, further commitment, increased empowerment, etc. Of course, if progress is not made round the cycle and trust is replaced by fear, it is possible to send the whole process into reverse – a negative cycle of suspicion, fault-finding, abdication and confusion (Figure 11.14). Unfortunately this will be recognized as the culture in some organizations where the focus of enquiry is 'what has gone wrong' leading to 'whose fault was it?'

Table 11.2 *Considerations, questions and outcomes for the FIRO-B dimensions*

Dimension	Considerations	Some typical questions	If resolved we get:	If not resolved we get:
Inclusion	Involvement – how much you want to include other people in your life and how much attention and recognition you want	Do I care about this? Do I want to be involved? Does this fit with my values? Do I matter to this group? Can I be committed? . . . leading to . . . Am I 'in' or 'out'?	A feeling of belonging A sense of being recognized and valued Willingness to become committed	A feeling of alienation A sense of personal insignificance No desire for commitment or involvement
Control	Authority, responsibility, decision making, influence	Who is in charge here? Do I have power to make decisions? What is the plan? When do we start? What support do I have? What resources do I have? . . . leading to . . . Am I 'up' or 'down'?	Confidence in self and others Comfort with level of responsibility Willingness to belong	Lack of confidence in leadership Discomfort with level of responsibility – fear of too much – frustration with too little 'Griping' between individuals
Openness	How much are we prepared to express our true thoughts and feelings with other individuals	Does she like me? Will my work be recognized? Is he being honest with me? How should I show appreciation? Do I appear aloof? . .leading to . . . Am I 'open' or 'closed'?	Lively and relaxed atmosphere Good-humoured interactions Open and trusting relationships	Tense and suspicious atmosphere Flippant or malicious humour Individuals isolated

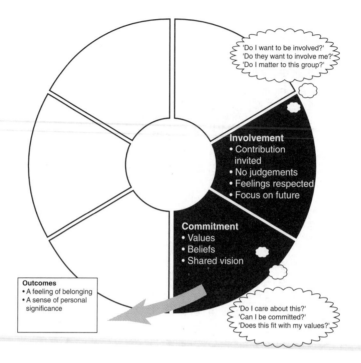

Figure 11.10 *The openness model, Part 1 Inclusion: involvement, inviting contribution, responding*

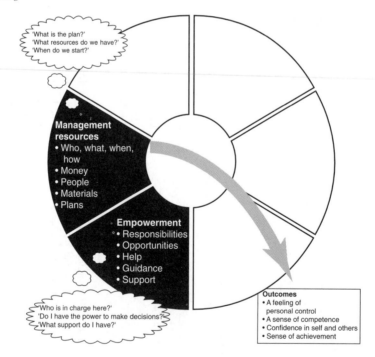

Figure 11.11 *The openness model, Part 2 Control: choice, influence, power*

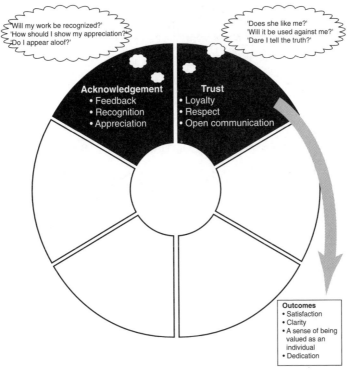

Figure 11.12 *The openness model, Part 3 Openness: expression of true thoughts and feelings with respect for self and others*

Figure 11.13 *The full openness model*

Figure 11.14 *The negative cycle*

Fortunately, organizations and individuals seem keen to learn ways to change these negative communications that sour relationships, dampen personal satisfaction and reduce productivity. The inclusion, control, openness cycle is a useful framework for helping teams to pass successfully through the forming and storming stages of team development. As teams are disbanded for whatever reason, the process reverses and the first thing which goes is the openness.

The five 'A' stages for teamwork

The awareness provided by the use of the MBTI and FIRO-B instruments helps people to appreciate their own uniqueness and the uniqueness of others – the foundation of mutual respect and for building positive, productive and high-performing teams.

For any of these models or theories to benefit a team, however, the individuals within it need to become aware of the theory, e.g. the MBTI or FIRO-B. They then need to accept the principles as valid, adopt them for themselves in order to *adapt* their behaviour accordingly. This will lead to individual and team *action* (Figure 11.15).

In the early stages of team development particularly, the assistance of a skilled facilitator to aid progress through these stages is necessary. This is often neglected, causing failure in so many team initiatives. In such cases the net output turns out to be lots of nice warm feelings about 'how good that team workshop was a year ago', but the nagging reality that no action came out and nothing has really changed.

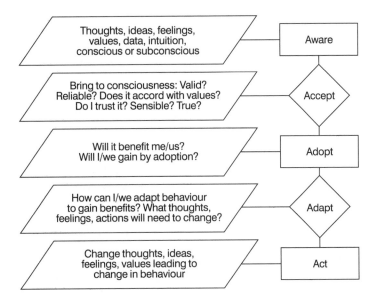

Figure 11.15 *The five 'A' stages for teamwork*

Implementing teamwork for quality improvement – the 'DRIVE' model

The author and his colleagues have developed a model for a structured approach to problem solving in teams, the *DRIVE* model. The mnemonic provides landmarks to keep the team on track and in the right direction:

Define	– the problem. *Output*: written definition of the task and its success criteria.
Review	– the information. *Output*: presentation of known data and action plan for further data.
Investigate	– the problem. *Output*: documented proposals for improvement and action plans.
Verify	– the solution. *Output*: proposed improvements that meet success criteria.
Execute	– the change. *Output*: task achieved and improved process documented.

The DRIVE model fits well with the MBTI Z-shaped problem-solving approach. Figure 11.16 shows how the states relate to the S-N-T-F path.

The various stages are discussed in detail in Oakland (1999).[2]

Steps in the introductions of teams

The idea of introducing problem-solving groups, quality circles or quality improvement teams often makes its way into an organization through the awareness of successful

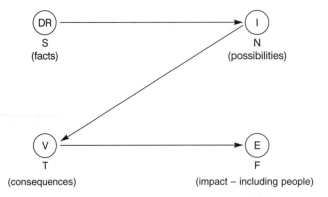

Figure 11.16 *The DRIVE model and MBTI-based problem solving*

results in other organizations or companies. There is no fixed methodology for starting a teamwork programme, but there are certain key points that must be considered:

1 The concept should be presented to (or come from) management and supervision, and their commitment and support enlisted. It should be possible at this stage to engage the interest and support of potential team leaders.
2 Projects should be started slowly and on a small scale. Ideally a pilot scheme, run by the most enthusiastic candidates and in the most promising areas, should be launched. Early teething troubles, doubts and worries may then be identified and resolved.
3 Selected or volunteer team or circle leaders must be trained in all aspects of group leadership, and the appropriate techniques, and they should subsequently help train the team members in the techniques required in effective problem solving. The techniques of statistical process control (SPC) should be introduced, particularly brainstorming, cause and effect analysis, Pareto analysis and charting. These concepts lay the groundwork for analysing problems in a systematic fashion, and show that the majority of the problems are concentrated into a few areas.
4 Once the causes have been determined, a solution can be proposed. This solution may affect any of the components of the process: equipment, procedures, training, input requirements or output requirements. The proposed solution should be tested by the team or circle, particularly if procedures are affected.
5 If the test of a solution proves successful, full-scale implementation can then be carried out. In the case of procedures, full documentation of the solution and management approval should be obtained. The procedure can then be communicated to all personnel concerned. Full-scale changes in equipment and other processes should occur in the same manner. The team should monitor implementation of the solution, plotting the appropriate data until the criteria for solution are met.

With the initial problems declared solved, the circle or team may then tackle another problem, and another, or be disbanded and new teams formed. The record of successful solutions will motivate other teams within the organization, and ideas should spread. As the number of teams in a company grows, new opportunities arise for stimulating interest. Some large companies organize in-house conferences of their quality/process improvement teams and quality circles, providing the opportunity for the publication of results and for recognition. Experience has shown that very significant improvements in areas such as energy reduction, productivity and cost-effectiveness, in addition to quality, may be achieved by the project team approach.

One of the problems of the team approach to problem identification and solving is that sometimes the teams are organized because it is the fashionable thing to do. They either exist on paper only, or the meetings are social gatherings where nothing is learned, no projects are initiated, and people do not grow. Another common problem is that the teams attempt to solve problems without first learning the necessary techniques: enthusiasm outruns ability. Teams have enormous potential for helping to solve an organization's problems, but for them to be successful, they must follow a disciplined approach to problem solving, using proven techniques.

The team approach to problem solving works. It taps the skills and initiative of all personnel engaged in a process. This may mean a change in culture, which must be supported by management through its own activities and behaviour.

Adding the teams to the TQM model

In Part 1 of this book the foundations for TQM were set down. The core of customer–supplier chains and, at every interface, a process were surrounded by the 'soft' outcomes of culture, communications and commitment. In Parts 2 and 3 were added the hard management necessities of systems and tools. We are now ready to complete the model with the necessity of teams – the committees/councils, the PQTs, QITs, quality circles, DPA groups, etc., which work on the processes – using the tools – to bring about continuous improvements in the systems that manage them (Figure 11.17).

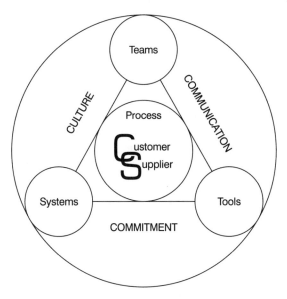

Figure 11.17 *Total quality management – teamwork added to complete the model*

Chapter highlights

The need for teamwork

- The only efficient way to tackle process improvement or complex problems is through teamwork. The team approach allows individuals and organizations to grow.
- Employees will not engage continual improvement without commitment from the top, a quality 'climate', and an effective mechanism for capturing individual contributions.
- Teamwork for quality improvement is driven by a strategy, needs a structure, and must be implemented thoughtfully and effectively.

Teamwork and action-centred leadership

- Early work in the field of human relations by McGregor, Maslow and Hertzberg was useful to John Adair in the development of his model for teamwork and action-centred leadership.
- Adair's model addresses the needs of the task, the team, and the individuals in the team, in the form of three overlapping circles. There are specific task, team and individual functions for the leader, but he or she must concentrate on the small central overlap area of the three circles.
- The team process has inputs and outputs. Good teams have three main attributes: high task fulfilment, high team maintenance and low self-orientation.
- In dealing with the task, the team and its individuals, a situational style of leadership must be adopted. This may follow the Tannenbaum and Schmidt and the Blanchard models through directing, coaching and supporting to delegating.

Stages of team development

- When teams are put together, they pass through Tuckman's forming (awareness), storming (conflict), norming (co-operation), and performing (productivity) stages of development.
- Teams that go through these stages successfully become effective and display clear objectives and agreed goals, openness and confrontation, support and trust, co-operation and conflict, good decision-making, appropriate leadership, review of the team processes, sound relationships, and individual development opportunities.

Personality types and the MBTI

- A powerful aid to team development is provided by the Myers–Briggs Type Indicator (MBTI).
- The MBTI is based on individuals' preferences on four scales for giving and receiving 'energy' (extroversion – E or introversion – I), gathering information (sensing – S or intuition – N), making decisions (thinking – T or feeling – F) and handling the outer world (judging – J or perceiving – P).

- An individual's type is the combination and interaction of the four scales and can be assessed initially by completion of a simple questionnaire. There are sixteen types in all, which may be displayed for a team on a type table.

Interpersonal relations – FIRO-B and the Elements

- The FIRO-B (Fundamental Interpersonal Relations Orientation – Behaviour) instrument gives insights into the needs individuals bring to their relationships with other people.
- The FIRO-B questionnaire assesses needs for inclusion, control and openness, in terms of expressed and wanted behaviour.
- Typical manager FIRO-B profiles conflict with some of the demands of TQM and can, therefore, indicate where particular attention is needed to achieve successful TQM implementation.
- The inclusion, control and openness dimensions form an 'openness' cycle which can help groups to understand how to develop their individual and joint behaviours as the team is formed. An alternative negative cycle may develop if the understanding of some of these behaviours is absent.
- The five As: for any of the teamwork models and theories, the individuals must become aware, need to accept, adopt and adapt, in order to act. A skilled facilitator is always necessary.

Implementing teamwork for quality – the 'DRIVE' model

- A structured approach to problem solving is provided by the DRIVE model: define the problem, review the information, investigate the problem, verify the solution, and execute the change; this is similar to the Z-shaped MBTI stepwise problem-solving process S-N-T-F.
- After initial problems are solved, others should be tackled – successful solutions motivating new teams. In all cases teams should follow a disciplined approach to problem solving, using proven techniques.
- Teamwork may mean a change in culture, which must be supported by management through its activities and behaviour.

Adding the teams to the TQM model

- The third and final hard management necessity – the teams – are added to the tools and systems to complete the TQM model.

References

1. See references under *TQM through people and teamwork* heading in the Bibliography.
2. Oakland, J., *Total Organizational Excellence*, Butterworth-Heinemann, 1999.

Discussion questions

1 The so-called process approach has certain implications for organizational structures. Discuss the main organizational issues influencing the involvement of people in process improvement.

2 Various TQM teamwork structures are advocated by many writers. Describe the role of the various 'quality teams' in the continuous improvement process. How can an organization ensure that the outcome of teamwork is consistent with its mission?

3 Describe the various types of quality teams which should be part of a total quality programme. Explain the organizational requirements associated with these and give some indication of how the teams operate.

4 A large insurance company has decided that teamwork is to be the initial focus of its TQM programme. Describe the role of a Quality Council or Steering Group and Process Quality Teams in managing teamwork initiatives in quality improvement.

5 Explain the difference between Quality Improvement Teams and Quality Circles. What is their role in quality improvement activities?

6 Discuss some of the factors that may inhibit teamwork activities in a TQM programme.

7 Suggest an organization for teamwork in a quality improvement programme and discuss how the important aspects must be managed, in order to achieve the best results from the use of teams. Describe briefly how the teams would proceed, including the tools they would use in their work.

8 Describe in full the various types of quality teams which are necessary in a total quality programme. Give some indication of how the teams operate at each level and, using the 'DRIVE' model, discuss the problem-solving approach that may be adopted.

9 Discuss the various models for teamwork within a total quality approach to business performance improvement. Explain through these models the role of the individual in TQM, and what work can be carried out in this area to help teams through the 'storming' stage of their development.

10 Teamwork is one of the key 'necessities' for TQM. John Adair's 'Action-Centred Leadership' model is useful to explain the areas which require attention for successful teamwork. Explain the model in detail, showing your understanding of each of the areas of 'needs'. Pay particular attention to the needs of the individual, showing how a psychometric instrument, such as the Myers–Briggs Type Indicator (MBTI) or FIRO-B, may be useful here.

Part Five

TQM – The Implementation

All words, and no performance!
Philip Massinger, 1583–1640, from 'Parliament of Love', ca 1619

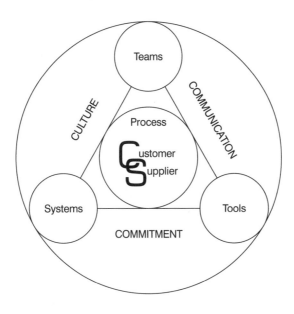

Chapter 12

Communications and training for quality

Communicating the total quality strategy

People's attitudes and behaviour clearly can be influenced by communications; one has only to look at the media or advertising to understand this. The essence of changing attitudes to quality is to gain acceptance for the need to change, and for this to happen it is essential to provide relevant information, convey good practices, and generate interest, ideas and awareness through excellent communication processes. This is possibly the most neglected part of many organizations' operations, yet failure to communicate effectively creates unnecessary problems, resulting in confusion, loss of interest and eventually in declining quality through apparent lack of guidance and stimulus.

Total quality management will significantly change the way many organizations operate and 'do business'. This change will require direct and clear communication from the top management to all staff and employees, to explain the need to focus on processes. Everyone will need to know their roles in understanding processes and improving their performance.

Whether a strategy is developed by top management for the direction of the business/ organization as a whole, or specifically for the introduction of TQM, that is only half the battle. An early implementation step must be the clear widespread communication of the strategy.

An excellent way to accomplish this first step is to issue a total quality message that clearly states top management's commitment to TQM and outlines the role everyone must play. This can be in the form of a quality policy (see Chapter 2) or a specific statement about the organization's intention to integrate TQM into the business operations. Such a statement might read:

The Board of Directors (or appropriate title) believe that the successful implementation of Total Quality Management is critical to achieving and maintaining our business goals of leadership in quality, delivery and price competitiveness.

We wish to convey to everyone our enthusiasm and personal commitment to the Total Quality approach, and how much we need your support in our mission of process improvement. We hope that you will become as convinced as we are that process improvement is critical for our survival and continued success.

We can become a Total Quality organization only with your commitment and dedication to improving the processes in which you work. We will help you by putting in place a programme of education, training, and teamwork development, based on process improvement, to ensure that we move forward together to achieve our business goals.

The quality director or TQM co-ordinator should then assist the quality council to prepare a directive. This must be signed by all business unit, division or process leaders, and distributed to everyone in the organization. The directive should include the following:

- Need for improvement.
- Concept for total quality.
- Importance of understanding business processes.
- Approach that will be taken.
- Individual and process group responsibilities.
- Principles of process measurement.

The systems for disseminating the message should include all the conventional communication methods of seminars, departmental meetings, posters, newsletters, intranet, etc. First-line supervision will need to review the directive with all the staff, and a set of questions and answers may be suitably pre-prepared in support.

Once people understand the strategy, the management must establish the infrastructure (see Chapter 10). The required level of individual commitment is likely to be achieved, however, only if everyone understands the aims and benefits of TQM, the role they must play, and how they can implement process improvements. For this understanding, a constant flow of information is necessary, including:

1 When and how individuals will be involved.
2 What the process requires.
3 The successes and benefits achieved.

The most effective means of developing the personnel commitment required is to ensure people know what is going on. Otherwise they will feel left out and begin to believe that TQM is not for them, which will lead to resentment and undermining of the whole process. The first line of supervision again has an important part to play in ensuring key messages are communicated and in building teams by demonstrating everyone's participation and commitment.

In the Larkins' excellent book *Communicating Change*, McGraw-Hill, 1994, the authors refer to three 'facts' regarding the best ways to communicate change to employees:

1 Communicate directly to supervisors (first-line).
2 Use face-to-face communication.
3 Communicate relative performance of the local work area.

The language used at the 'coal face' will need attention in many organizations. Reducing the complexity and jargon in written and spoken communications will facilitate comprehension. When written business communications cannot be read or understood easily, they receive only cursory glances, rather than the detailed study they require. *Simplify and shorten* must be the guiding principles. The communication model illustrated in Figure 12.1 indicates the potential for problems through environmental distractions, mismatches between sender and receiver (or more correctly, decoder) in terms of attitudes – towards the information and each other – vocabulary, time pressures, etc.

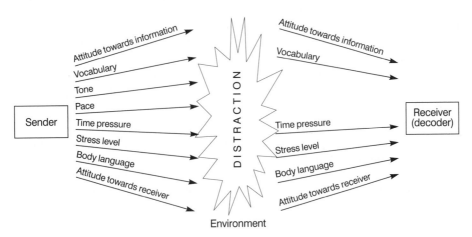

Figure 12.1 *Communication model*

All levels of management should introduce and stress 'open' methods of communication, by maintaining open offices, being accessible to staff/employees and taking part in day-to-day interactions and the detailed processes. This will lay the foundation for improved interactions *between* staff and employees, which is essential for information flow and process improvement. Opening these lines of communication may lead to confrontation with many barriers and much resistance. Training and the behaviour of supervisors/managements should be geared to helping people accept responsibility for their own behaviour, which often creates the barriers, and for breaking the barriers down by concentrating on the process rather than 'departmental' needs.

Resistance to change will always occur and is to be expected. Again first-line management should be trained to help people deal with it. This requires an understanding of the dynamics of change and the support necessary – not an obsession with forcing people to change. Opening up lines of communication through a previously closed system, and publicizing people's efforts to change and their results, will aid the process. Change can be – even should be – exciting if employees start to share their development, growth, suggestions and questions. Management needs to encourage and participate in this by creating the most appropriate communication systems.

Communicating the quality message

The people in most organizations fall into one of four 'audience' groups, each with particular general attitudes towards TQM:

- *Senior managers*, who should see TQM as an opportunity, both for the organization and themselves.
- *Middle managers*, who may see TQM as another burden without any benefits, and may perceive a vested interest in the status quo.
- *Supervisors* (first-line or junior managers), who may see TQM as another 'flavour of the period' or campaign, and who may respond by trying to keep heads down so that it will pass over.
- *Other employees*, who may not care, so long as they still have jobs and get paid, though these people must be the custodians of the delivery of quality to the customer and own that responsibility.

Senior management needs to ensure that each group sees TQM as being beneficial to them. Total quality training material and support (whether internal from a quality director and team or from external consultants) will be of real value only if the employees are motivated to respond positively to them. The implementation strategy must then be based on two mutually supporting aspects:

1 'Marketing' any TQM initiatives.
2 A positive, logical process of communication designed to motivate.

There are of course a wide variety of approaches to, and methods of, TQM. Any individual organization's TQ strategy must be designed to meet the needs of its own structure and business, and the state of commitment to continuous improvement activities. These days very few organizations are starting from a green-field site. The key is that groups of people must feel able to 'join' the TQM process at the most appropriate point for them. For middle managers to be convinced that they must participate, TQM must be presented as the key to help them turn the people who work for them into total quality employees.

The noisy, showy, hype-type activity is not appropriate to any aspect of TQM. TQM 'events' should of course be fun, because this is often the best way to persuade and motivate, but the value of any event should be judged by its ability to contribute to understanding and the change to TQM. Key words in successful exercises include 'discovery', affirmation, participation and team-based learning. In the difficult area of dealing with middle and junior managers, who can and will prevent change with ease and invisibility, the recognition that progress must change from being a threat to a promise will help. In any workshops designed for them, managers and supervisors should be made to feel recognized, not victimized, and the programmes should be delivered by specially trained people. The environment and conduct of the workshops must also demonstrate the organization's concern for quality.

The key medium for motivating the employees and gaining their commitment to TQM is face-to-face communication and *visible* management commitment. Much is written and spoken about leadership, but it is mainly about communication. If people are good leaders, they are invariably good communicators. Leadership is a human interaction depending on the communications between the leaders and the followers. It calls for many skills that can be *learned* from education and training, but must be *acquired* through practice.

Types of communication

It may be useful to consider why people learn. They do so for several reasons, some of which are:

a) Self-betterment
b) Self-preservation
c) Need for responsibility
d) Saving time or effort
e) Sense of achievement
f) Pride of work
g) Curiosity.

So communication and training can be a powerful stimulus to personal development at the workplace, as well as achieving improvements for the organization. This may be useful in the selection of the appropriate method(s) of communication, the principal ones being:

- *Verbal communication* either between individuals or groups, using direct or indirect methods, such as public address and other broadcasting systems and recordings.
- *Written communication* in the form of notices, bulletins, information sheets, reports, e-mail and recommendations.
- *Visual communication* such as posters, films, video, internet/intranet, exhibitions, demonstrations, displays and other promotional features. Some of these also call for verbal and written communication.
- *Example*, through the way people conduct themselves and adhere to established working codes and procedures, through their effectiveness as communicators and ability to 'sell' good-quality practices.

The characteristics of each of these methods should be carefully examined before they are used in communicating the quality message.

It's Monday – it must be training

It is the author's belief that training is the single most important factor in actually improving quality, once there has been commitment to do so. For training to be effective, however, it must be planned in a systematic and objective manner. Quality training must be continuous to meet not only changes in technology but also changes in the environment in which an organization operates, its structure, and perhaps most important of all the people who work there.

Training cycle of improvement

Quality training activities can be considered in the form of a cycle of improvement (Figure 12.2), the elements of which are the following.

Ensure training is part of the quality policy

Every organization should define its policy in relation to quality (see Chapter 2). The policy should contain principles and goals to provide a framework within which training activities may be planned and operated. This policy should be communicated to all levels.

Allocate responsibilities for training

Quality training must be the responsibility of line management, but there are also important roles for the quality manager and his function.

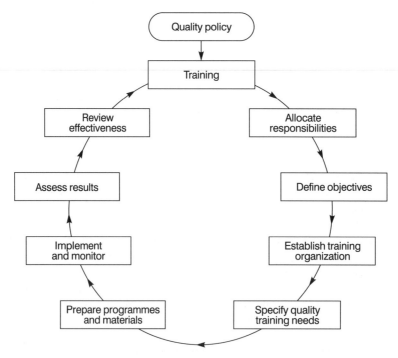

Figure 12.2 *The quality training circle*

Define training objectives

The following questions are useful first steps when identifying training objectives:

- How are the customer requirements transmitted through the organization?
- Which areas need improved performance?
- What changes are planned for the future?
- What new procedures and provisions need to be drawn up?

When attempting to set training objectives, three essential requirements must be met:

1 Senior management must ensure that objectives are clarified and priorities set.
2 Defined objectives must be realized and attainable.
3 The main problems should be identified for all functional areas in the organization. Large organizations may find it necessary to promote a phased plan to identify these problems.

Establish training organization

The overall responsibility for seeing that quality training is properly organized must be assumed by one or more designated senior executives. All managers have a responsibility for ensuring that personnel reporting to them are properly trained and competent in their jobs. This responsibility should be written into every manager's job description. The question of whether line management requires specialized help should be answered when objectives have been identified. It is often necessary to use specialists, who may be internal or external to the organization.

Specify quality training needs.

The next step in the cycle is to assess and clarify specific quality training needs. The following questions need to be answered:

a) Who needs to be trained?
b) What competencies are required?
c) How long will training take?
d) What are the expected benefits?
e) Is the training need urgent?
f) How many people are to be trained?
g) Who will undertake the actual training?
h) What resources are needed, e.g. money, people, equipment, accommodation, outside resources?

Prepare training programmes and materials

Quality management should participate in the creation of draft programmes, although line managers should retain the final responsibility for what is implemented, and they will often need to create the training programmes themselves.

Quality training programmes should include:

- The training objectives expressed in terms of the desired behaviour.
- The actual training content.

- The methods to be adopted.
- Who is responsible for the various sections of the programme.

Implement and monitor training

The effective implementation of quality training programmes demands considerable commitment and adjustment by the trainers and trainees alike. Training is a progressive process, which must take into account the learning problems of the trainees.

Assess the results

In order to determine whether further training is required, line management should themselves review performance when training is completed. However good the quality training may be, if it is not valued and built upon by managers and supervisors, its effect can be severely reduced.

Review effectiveness of training

Senior management will require a system whereby decisions are taken at regular fixed intervals on:

- The quality policy.
- The quality training objectives.
- The training organization.

Even if the quality policy remains constant, there is a continuing need to ensure that new quality training objectives are set either to promote work changes or to raise the standards already achieved.

The purpose of management system audits and reviews is to assess the effectiveness of an organization's quality effort. Clearly, adequate and refresher training in these methods is essential if such checks are to be realistic and effective. Audits and reviews can provide useful information for the identification of changing quality training needs.

The training organization should similarly be reviewed in the light of the new objectives, and here again it is essential to aim at continuous improvement. Training must never be allowed to become static, and the effectiveness of the organization's quality training programmes and methods must be assessed systematically.

A systematic approach to quality training

Training for quality should have, as its first objective, an appreciation of the personal responsibility for meeting the 'customer' requirements by everyone from the most senior executive to the newest and most junior employee. Responsibility for the training of employees in quality rests with management at all levels and, in particular, the person nominated for the co-ordination of the organization's quality effort. Quality training will not be fully effective, however, unless responsibility for the quality policy rests clearly with the Chief Executive. One objective of this policy should be to develop a *climate* in which everyone is quality conscious and acts with the needs of the activities and the place of training in their achievement.

The main elements of effective and systematic quality training may be considered under four broad headings:

- Error/defect/problem prevention
- Error/defect/problem reporting and analysis
- Error/defect/problem investigation
- Review.

The emphasis should obviously be on error, defect or problem prevention, and hopefully what is said under the other headings maintains this objective.

Error/defect/problem prevention

The following contribute to effective and systematic training for prevention of problems in the organization:

1 An issued quality policy.
2 A written management system.
3 Job specifications that include quality requirements.
4 Effective steering committees, including representatives of both management and employees.
5 Efficient housekeeping standards.
6 Preparation and display of maps, flow diagrams and charts for all processes.

Error/defect/problem reporting and analysis

It will be necessary for management to arrange the necessary reporting procedures, and ensure that those concerned are adequately trained in these procedures. All errors, rejects, defects, defectives, problems, waste, etc. should be recorded and analysed in a way that is meaningful for each organization, bearing in mind the corrective action programmes that should be initiated at appropriate times.

Error/defect/problem investigation

The investigation of errors, defects and problems can provide valuable information that can be used in their prevention. Participating in investigations offers an opportunity for training. The following information is useful for the investigation:

a) Nature of problem
b) Date, time and place
c) Product/service with problem
d) Description of problem
e) Causes and reasons behind causes
f) Action advised
g) Action taken to prevent recurrence.

Review of quality training

Review of the effectiveness of quality training programmes should be a continuous process. However, the measurement of effectiveness is a complex problem. One way of reviewing the content and assimilation of a training course or programme is to monitor behaviour during quality audits. This review can be taken a stage further by comparing employees' behaviour with the objectives of the quality training programme. Other measures of the training processes should be found to establish the benefits derived.

Training records

All organizations should establish and maintain procedures for the identification of training needs and the provision of the actual training itself. These procedures should be designed (and documented) to include all personnel. In many situations it is necessary to employ professionally qualified people to carry out specific tasks, e.g. accountants, lawyers, engineers, chemists, etc., but it must be recognized that all other employees, including managers, must have or receive from the company the appropriate education, training and/or experience to perform their jobs. This leads to the establishment of training records.

Once an organization has identified the special skills required for each task, and developed suitable training programmes to provide competence for the tasks to be undertaken, it should prescribe how the competence is to be demonstrated. This can be by some form of examination, test or certification, which may be carried out in-house or by a recognized external body. In every case, records of personnel qualifications, training and experience should be developed and maintained. National vocational qualifications (NVQs) have an important role to play here.

At the simplest level this may be a record of tasks and a date placed against each employee's name as he/she acquires the appropriate skill through training. Details of attendance on external short courses, in-house induction or training schemes complete such records. What must be clear and easily retrievable is the status of training and development of any single individual, related to the tasks that he/she is likely to encounter. For example, in a factory producing contact lenses that has developed a series of well-defined tasks for each stage of the manufacturing process, it would be possible, by turning up the appropriate records, to decide whether a certain operator is competent to carry out a lathe-turning process. Clearly, as the complexity of jobs increases and managerial activity replaces direct manual skill, it becomes more difficult to make decisions on the basis of such records alone. Nevertheless, they should document the basic competency requirements and assist the selection procedure.

Starting where and for whom?

Training needs occur at four levels of an organization:

- *Very senior management* (strategic decision makers)
- *Middle management* (tactical decision makers or implementers of policy)

- *First-level supervision and quality team leaders* (on-the-spot decision makers)
- *All other employees* (the doers).

Neglect of training in any of these areas will, at best, delay the implementation of TQM. The provision of training for each group will be considered in turn, but it is important to realize that an integrated training programme is required, one that includes follow-up activities and encourages exchange of ideas and experience, to allow each transformation process to achieve quality at the supplier–customer interface.

Very senior management

The Chief Executive and his team of strategic policy makers are of primary importance, and the role of training here is to provide awareness and instil commitment to quality. The importance of developing real commitment must be established; and often this can only be done by a free and frank exchange of views between trainers and trainees. This has implications for the choice of the trainers themselves, and the fresh-faced graduate, sent by the 'package consultancy' operator into the lion's den of a boardroom will not make much impression with the theoretical approach that he or she is obliged to bring to bear. The author recalls thumping many a boardroom table, and using all his experience and whatever presentation skills he could muster, to convince senior managers that without the TQM approach they would fail. It is a sobering fact that the pressure from competition and customers has a much greater record of success than enlightenment, although dragging a team of senior managers down to the shop floor to show them the results of poor management was successful on one occasion.

Executives responsible for marketing, sales, finance, design, operations, purchasing, personnel, distribution, etc., all need to understand quality. They must be shown how to define the quality policy and objectives, how to establish the appropriate organization for quality, how to clarify authority, and generally how to create the atmosphere in which total quality will thrive. This is the only group of people in the organization that can ensure that adequate resources are provided and directed at:

1 Meeting customer requirements – internally and externally.
2 Setting standards to be achieved – zero failure.
3 Monitoring quality performance – quality costs.
4 Introducing a good-quality management system – prevention.
5 Implementing process control methods – SPC.
6 Spreading the idea of quality throughout the whole workforce – TQM.

Middle management

The basic objectives of management quality training should be to make managers conscious of and anxious to secure the benefits of the total quality effort. One particular 'staff' manager will require special training – the quality manager, who will carry the responsibility for management of the quality management system, including its design, operation and review.

The middle managers should be provided with the technical skills required to design, implement, review and change the parts of the quality management system that will be under their direct operational control. It will be useful throughout the training programmes to ensure that the responsibilities for the various activities in each of the functional areas are clarified. The presence of a highly qualified and experienced quality manager should not allow abdication of these responsibilities, for the internal 'consultant' can easily create not-invented-here feelings by writing out procedures without adequate consultation of those charged with implementation.

Middle management should receive comprehensive training on the philosophy and concepts of teamwork, and the techniques and applications of statistical process control (SPC). Without the teams and tools, the quality management system will lie dormant and lifeless. It will relapse into a paper-generating system, fulfilling the needs of only those who thrive on bureaucracy.

First-level supervision

There is a layer of personnel in many organizations which plays a vital role in their inadequate performance – foremen and supervisors, the forgotten men and women of industry and commerce. Frequently promoted from the 'shop floor' (or recruited as graduates in a flush of conscience and wealth!), these people occupy one of the most crucial managerial roles, often with no idea of what they are supposed to be doing, without an identity, and without training. If this behaviour pattern is familiar and is continued, then TQM is doomed.

The first level of supervision is where the implementation of total quality is actually 'managed'. Supervisors' training should include an explanation of the principles of TQM, a convincing exposition on the commitment to quality of the senior management, and an explanation of what the quality policy means for them. The remainder of their training needs to be devoted to explaining their role in the operation of the quality management system, teamwork, SPC, etc., and to gaining *their* commitment to the concepts and techniques of total quality.

It is often desirable to involve the middle managers in the training of first-level supervision in order to:

- Ensure that the message they wish to convey through their tactical manoeuvres is not distorted.
- Indicate to the first-level supervision that the organization's whole management structure is serious about quality, and intends that everyone is suitably trained and concerned about it too. One display of arrogance towards the training of supervisors and the workforce can destroy such careful planning, and will certainly undermine the educational effort.

All other employees

Awareness and commitment at the point of production or operation is just as vital as at the very senior level. If it is absent from the latter, the TQM programme will not begin; if it is absent from the shop floor, total quality will not be implemented. The training here should include the basics of quality, and particular care should be given to using easy reference points for the explanation of the terms and concepts. Most people can relate to quality and how it should be managed, if they can think about the applications in their own lives and at home. Quality is really such common sense that, with sensitivity and regard to various levels of intellect and experience, little resistance should be experienced.

All employees should receive detailed training processes and procedures relevant to their own work. Obviously they must have appropriate technical or 'job' training, but they must also understand the requirements of their customers. This is frequently a difficult concept to introduce, particularly in the non-manufacturing areas, and time and follow-up assistance needs to be given if TQM is to take hold. It is always bad management to ask people to follow instructions without understanding why and where they fit into their own scheme of things.

Follow-up

For the successful implementation of TQM, training must be followed up during the early stages. Follow-up can take many forms, but the managers need to provide the lead through the design of improvement projects and 'surgery' workshops.

In introducing statistical methods of process control, for example, the most satisfactory strategy is to start small and build up a bank of knowledge and experience. Sometimes it is necessary to introduce SPC techniques alongside existing methods of control (if they exist), thus allowing comparisons to be made between the new and old methods. When confidence has been established from these comparisons, the SPC methods will almost take over the control of the processes themselves. Improvements in one or two areas of the organization's operations, by means of this approach, will quickly establish the techniques as reliable methods of controlling quality.

The author and his colleagues have found that a successful formula is the in-company training course plus follow-up workshops. Usually a workshop or seminar on TQM is followed within a few weeks by a 'surgery' workshop at which participants on the initial training course present the results of their efforts to improve processes, and use the various methods. The presentations and specific implementation problems are discussed. A series of such workshops will add continually to the follow-up, and can be used to initiate process or quality improvement teams. Wider organizational presence and activities are then encouraged by the follow-up activities.

Chapter highlights

Communicating the total quality strategy

- People's attitudes and behaviour can be influenced by communication, and the essence of changing attitudes is to gain acceptance through excellent communication processes.
- The strategy and changes to be brought about through TQM should be clearly and directly communicated from top management to all staff/employees. The first step is to issue a 'total quality message'. This should be followed by a signed TQM directive.

- People must know when and how they will be brought into the TQM process, what the process is, and the successes and benefits achieved. First-level supervision has an important role in communicating the key messages and overcoming resistance to change.
- The complexity and jargon in the language used between functional groups needs to be reduced in many organizations. Simplify and shorten are the guiding principles.
- 'Open' methods of communication and participation should be used at all levels. Barriers may need to be broken down by concentrating on process rather than 'departmental' issues.
- There are four audience groups in most organizations – senior managers, middle managers, supervisors and employees – each with different general attitudes towards TQM. The senior management must ensure that each group sees TQM as being beneficial.
- Good leadership is mostly about good communications, the skills of which can be learned through training but must be acquired through practice.
- There are four principal types of communication: verbal (direct and indirect), written, visual and by example. Each has its own requirements, strengths and weaknesses.

It's Monday – it must be training

- Training is the single most important factor in improving quality, once commitment is present. Quality training must be objectively, systematically and continuously performed.
- All training should occur in an improvement cycle of ensuring training is part of quality policy, allocating responsibilities, defining objectives, establishing training organizations, specifying needs, preparing programmes and materials, implementing and monitoring, assessing results and reviewing effectiveness.

A systematic approach to quality training

- Responsibility for quality training of employees rests with management at all levels. The main elements should include error/defect/problem prevention, reporting and analysis, investigation and review.
- Training procedures and records should be established to show how job competence is demonstrated.

Starting where and for whom?

- Needs for integrating quality training occur at four levels of the organization: very senior management, middle management, first-level supervision and quality team leaders, and all other employees.

Follow-up

- All quality training should be followed up with improvement projects and 'surgery' workshops.

Chapter 13

Implementation of TQM and the management of change

TQM and the management of change

The author recalls the managing director of a large transportation company who decided that a major change was required in the way the company operated if serious competitive challenges were to be met. The Board of Directors went away for a weekend and developed a new vision for the company and its 'culture'. A human resources director was recruited and given the task of managing the change in the people and their 'attitudes'. After several 'programmes' aimed at achieving the required change, including a new structure for the organization, a staff appraisal system linked to pay, and seminars to change attitudes, very little change in actual organizational behaviour had occurred.

Clearly something had gone wrong somewhere. But what, who, where? Everything was wrong, including what needed changing, who should lead the changes and, in particular, how the change should be brought about. This type of problem is very common in organizations which desire to change the way they operate to deal with increased competition, a changing market place, and different business rules. In this situation many companies recognize the need to move away from an autocratic management style, with formal rules and hierarchical procedures, and narrow work demarcations. Some have tried to create teams, to delegate (perhaps for the first time) and to improve communications.

Some of the senior managers in such organizations recognize the need for change to deal with the new realities of competitiveness, but they lack an understanding of how the change should be implemented. They often believe that changing the formal organizational structure, having 'culture change' programmes and new payment systems will, by themselves, make the transformations. In much research work carried out by the European Centre for Business Excellence, the research and education division of Oakland Consulting plc, it has been shown that there is almost an inverse relationship between successful change and having formal organization-wide 'change programmes'. This is particularly true if one functional group, such as HR, 'owns' the programme.

In several large organizations in which total quality management has been used successfully to effect change, the senior management did not focus on formal structures and systems, but set up *process-management* teams to solve real business or organization problems. The key to success in this area is to align the employees of the business, their roles and responsibilities with the organization and its *process*. This is the core of process mapping or alignment. When an organization focuses on its key processes, that is the activities and tasks themselves, rather than on abstract issues such as 'culture' and 'participation', then the change process can begin in earnest.

An approach to change based on process alignment, and starting with the vision and mission statements, analysing the critical success factors, *and* moving on to the core processes, is the most effective way to engage the staff in an enduring change process. Many change programmes do not work because they begin trying to change the knowledge, attitudes and beliefs of individuals. The theory is that changes in these areas will lead to changes in behaviour throughout the organization. It relies on a form of religion spreading through the people in the business.

What is often required, however, is virtually the opposite process, based on the recognition that people's behaviour is determined largely by the roles they have to take up. If we create for them new responsibilities, team roles and a process-driven environment, a new situation will develop, one that will force their attention and work on the processes. This will change the culture. *Teamwork* is an especially important part of the TQM model in terms of bringing about change. If changes are to be made in quality, costs, market, product or service development, close co-ordination among the marketing, design, production/operations and distribution groups is essential. This can be brought about effectively only by multifunctional teams working on the processes and understanding their interrelationships. *Commitment* is a key element of support for the high levels of co-operation, initiative and effort that will be required to understand and work on the labyrinth of processes existing in most organizations. In addition to the knowledge of the business as a whole, which will be brought about by an understanding of the mission, CSF, process breakdown links, certain *tools*, *techniques* and *interpersonal skills* will be required for good *communication* around the processes. These are essential if people are to identify and solve problems as teams.

If any of these elements are missing the total quality underpinned change process will collapse. The difficulties experienced by many organizations' formal change processes are caused by the fact that they tackle only one or two of these necessities. Many organizations trying to create a new philosophy based on teamwork fail to recognize that the employees do not know which teams need to be formed round their *process*, which they begin to understand together – perhaps for the first time – and further recognition that they then need to be helped as individuals through the forming-storming-norming-performing sequence, will generate the interpersonal skills and attitude changes necessary to make the new 'structure' work.

Integrating TQM into the strategy of the business

Organizations will avoid the problems of 'change programmes' by concentrating on 'process alignment' – recognizing that people's roles and responsibilities must be related to the processes in which they work. Senior managers may begin the task of process alignment by a series of seven distinct but clearly overlapping steps. This recommended path develops a self-reinforcing cycle of *commitment, communication* and *culture* change. The order of the steps is important because some of the activities will be inappropriate if started too early. In the introduction of total quality for managing change, timing can be critical.

Step 1 Gain commitment to change through the organization of the top team

Process alignment requires the starting point to be a broad review of the organization and the changes required by the top management team. By gaining this shared diagnosis of what changes are required, what the 'business' problems are, and/or what must be improved, the most senior executive mobilizes the initial commitment that is vital to begin the change process. An important element here is to get the top team working as a team, and techniques such as MBTI and/or FIRO-B will play an important part (see Chapter 11).

Step 2 Develop a shared vision and mission for the business or of what change is required

Once the top team is committed to the analysis of the changes required, it can develop vision and mission statements that will help to define the new process-alignment, roles and responsibilities. This will lead to a co-ordinated flow of analysis of processes that cross the traditional functional areas at all levels of the organization, without changing formal structures, titles and systems which can create resistance (Figure 13.1).

The mission statement gives a purpose to the organization or unit. It should answer the questions, 'What are we here for?' or 'What is our basic purpose?' and 'What have we got to achieve?' It therefore defines the boundaries of the business in which the organization operates. This will help to focus on the 'distinctive competence' of the organization, and to orient everyone in the same direction of what has to be done. The mission must be documented, agreed by the top management team, sufficiently explicit to enable its eventual accomplishment to be verified, and ideally be no more than four sentences. The statement must be understandable, communicable, believable and usable.

The mission statement is:

- An expression of the aspiration of the organization.
- The touchstone against which all actions or proposed actions can be judged.
- Usually long term.
- Short term if the mission is survival.

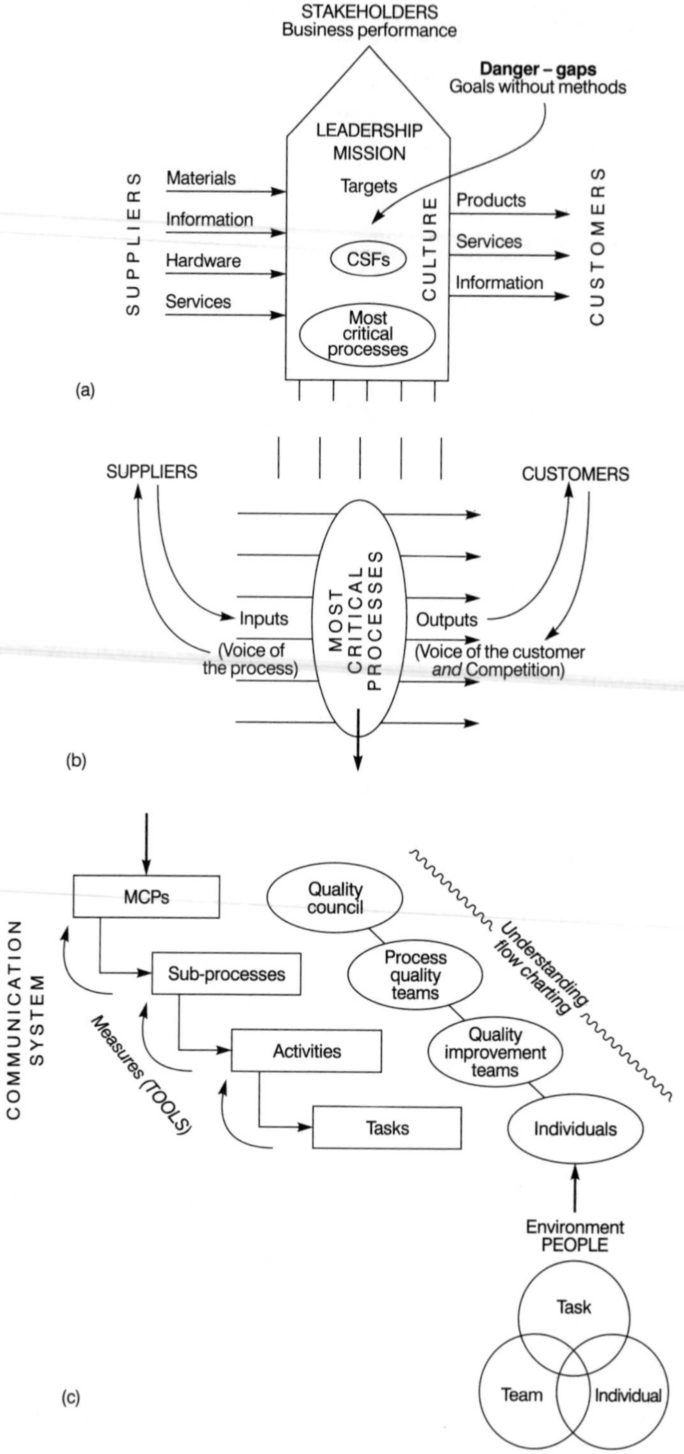

Figure 13.1 *From mission to process breakdown*

Typical content includes a statement of:

- The role or contribution of the business or unit – for example, profit generator, service department, opportunity seeker.
- The definition of the business – for example, the needs you satisfy or the benefits you provide. Do not be too specific or too general.
- Your distinctive competence – this should be a brief statement that applies to only your specific unit. A statement which could apply equally to any organization is unsatisfactory.
- Indications for future direction – a brief statement of the principal things you would give serious consideration to.

Some questions that may be asked of a mission statement are:

- Does it define the organization's role?
- Does it contain the need to be fulfilled:
  - Is it worthwhile/admirable?
  - Will employees identify with it?
  - How will it be viewed externally?
- Does it take a long-term view, leading to, for example, commitment to new product or service development, or training of personnel?
- Does it take into account all the 'stakeholders' of the organization?
- Does it ensure the purpose remains constant despite changes in top management?

It is important to establish in some organizations whether or not the mission is survival. This does not preclude a longer-term mission, but the short-term survival mission must be expressed, if it is relevant. The management team can then decide whether they wish to continue long-term strategic thinking. If survival is a real issue the author and his colleagues would advise against concentrating on the long-term planning initially.

There must be open and spontaneous discussion during generation of the mission, but there must in the end be convergence on one statement. If the mission statement is wrong, everything that follows will be wrong too, so a clear understanding is vital.

Step 3 Develop the 'mission' into its critical success factors (CSFs) to coerce and move it forward

The development of the mission is clearly not enough to ensure its implementation. This is the 'danger gap' which many organizations fall into because they do not foster the skills needed to translate the mission through its CSFs into the core processes. Hence, they have 'goals without methods' and change is not integrated properly into the business.

Once the top managers begin to list the CSFs they will gain some understanding of what the mission or the change requires. The first step in going from mission to CSFs is to brainstorm all the possible impacts on the mission. In this way 30 to 50 items ranging from politics to costs, from national cultures to regional market peculiarities, may be derived.

The CSFs may now be defined – *what* the organization must accomplish to achieve the mission – by examination and categorization of the impacts. This should lead to a balanced set of deliverables for the organization in terms of:

- financial and non-financial performance
- customer/market satisfaction
- people/internal organization satisfaction
- environmental/societal satisfaction.

There should be no more than eight CSFs, and no more than four if the mission is survival. They are the building blocks of the mission – minimum key factors or subgoals that the organization must have or needs and which together will achieve the mission. They are the *whats* not the *hows*, and are not directly manageable – they may be in some cases statements of hope or fear. But they provide direction and the success criteria, and are the end product of applying the processes. In CSF determination, a management team should follow the rule that each CSF is necessary and together they are sufficient for the mission to be achieved.

Some examples of CSFs may clarify their understanding:

- We must have right-first-time suppliers.
- We must have motivated, skilled workers.
- We need new products that satisfy market needs.
- We need new business opportunities.
- We must have best-in-the-field product quality.

The list of CSFs should be an agreed balance of strategic and tactical issues, each of which deals with a 'pure' factor, the use of 'and' being forbidden. It will be important to know when the CSFs have been achieved, but an equally important step is to use the CSFs to enable the identification of the processes.

Step 4 Define the key performance indicators as being the quantifiable indicators of success in terms of the mission and CSFs

The mission and CSFs provide the 'what' of the organization, but they must be supported by measurable key performance indicators (KPIs) that are tightly and inarguably linked. These will help to translate the directional and sometimes 'loose' statements of the mission into clear targets, and in turn to simplify management's thinking. The KPIs will be used to monitor progress and as evidence of success for the organization, in every direction, internally and externally.

Each CSF should have an 'owner' who is a member of the management team that agreed the mission and CSFs. The task of an owner is to:

- Define and agree the KPIs and associated *targets*.
- Ensure that appropriate data is collected and recorded.
- Monitor and report progress towards achieving the CSF (KPIs and targets) on a regular basis.
- Review and modify the KPIs and targets where appropriate.

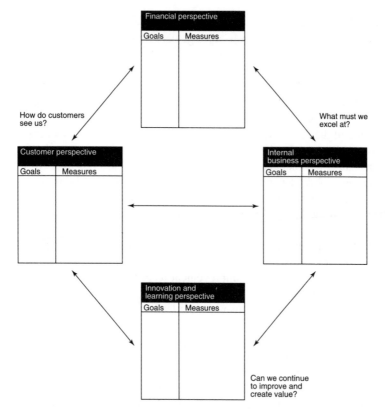

Figure 13.2 *The balanced scorecard linking performance measures*

The derivation of KPIs may follow the 'balanced scorecard' model, proposed by Kaplan and Norton, which divides measures into financial, customer, internal business and innovation and learning perspectives (Figure 13.2).

A balanced scorecard derived from the excellence model described in Chapter 6 would include financial and non-financial results, customer results (measured via the use of customer satisfaction surveys and other measures, including quality and delivery), employee results (employee development and satisfaction) and societal results (including community perceptions and environmental performance).

Financial performance for external reporting purposes may be seen as a result of performance across the other KPIs, the non-financial KPIs assumed to be the leading indicators of performance. The only aspect of financial performance that is cascaded throughout the organization is the budgetary process, which acts as a constraint rather than a performance improvement measure.

In summary then, organizational KPIs should be derived from the balancing of internal capabilities against the requirements of identified stakeholder groups. This has implications for both the choice of KPIs and the setting of appropriate targets. There is a need to develop appropriate action plans and clearly define responsibility for meeting targets if the KPIs and targets are to be taken seriously.

Step 5 Understand the core processes and gain process sponsorship

This is the point when the top management team have to consider how to institutionalize the mission or the change in the form of processes that will continue to be in place, after any changes have been effected (Figure 13.1b).

The core business processes describe what actually is or needs to be done so that the organization meets its CSFs. As with the CSFs and the mission, each process which is necessary for a given CSF must be identified, and together the processes listed must be sufficient for all the CSFs to be accomplished. To ensure that processes are listed, they should be in the form of verb plus object, such as 'research the market', 'recruit competent staff' or 'manage supplier performance'. The core processes identified frequently run across 'departments' or functions, yet they must be measurable.

Each core process should have a sponsor, preferably a member of the management team that agreed the CSFs. The task of a sponsor is to:

- Ensure that appropriate resources are made available to map, investigate and improve the process.
- Assist in selecting the process improvement team leader and members.
- Remove blocks to the teams' progress.
- Report progress to the senior management team.

The first stage in understanding the core processes is to produce a set of processes of a common order of magnitude. Some smaller processes identified may combine into core processes; others may be already at the appropriate level. This will ensure that the change becomes entrenched, the core processes are identified and that the right people are in place to sponsor or take responsibility for them. This will be the start of getting the process team organization up and running.

The questions will now come thick and fast. Is the process currently carried out? By whom? When? How frequently? With what performance and how well compared with competitors? The answering of these questions will force process ownership into the business. The process sponsor may form a process team which takes quality improvement into the next steps. Some form of prioritization using process performance measures is necessary at this stage to enable effort to be focused on the key areas for improvement.[1] This may be carried out by a form of impact matrix analysis (see Figure 13.3). The outcome should be a set of 'most critical processes' (MCPs) which receive priority attention for improvement, based on the number of CSFs impacted by each process and its performance on a scale A to E.

Step 6 Break down the core processes into subprocesses, activities and tasks and form improvement teams around these

Once an organization has defined and mapped out the core processes, people need to develop the skills to understand how the new process structure will be analysed and made to work. The very existence of new process teams with new goals and responsibilities will force the organization into a learning phase. The changes should foster new attitudes and behaviours.

No.	Process	CSF No.																	Number of CSF impacts	A–E ranking

A–E process ranking: A-Excellent; B-Good; C-Average; D-Poor; E-Embryonic

Figure 13.3 *Process/CSF matrix*

An illustration of the breakdown from mission through CSFs and core processes to individual tasks may assist in understanding the process required (Figure 13.1c).

Mission

Two of the statements in a well-known management consultancy's mission statement are:

> Gain and maintain a position as Europe's foremost management consultancy in the development of organizations through management of change.
> Provide the consultancy, training and facilitation necessary to assist with making continuous improvement an integral part of our customers' business strategy.

↓

Critical success factor

One of the CSFs which clearly relates to this is:

> We need a high level of awareness.

↓

Core process

One of the core processes which clearly must be done particularly well to achieve this CSF is:

> Promote, advertise and communicate the company's business capability.

↓

Subprocess

One of the subprocesses which results from a breakdown of this core process is:

> Prepare the company's information pack.

↓

Activity

One of the activities which contributes to this subprocess is:

> Prepare *one* of the subject booklets, i.e. 'Business Excellence and Self-Assessment'.

↓

Task

One of the tasks which contributes to this is:

> Write the detailed leaflet for a particular seminar, e.g. one-day or three-day seminar on self-assessment.

Individuals, tasks and teams

Having broken down the processes into subprocesses, activities and tasks in this way, it is now possible to link them with the Adair model of action-centred leadership and teamwork (see Chapter 11).

The tasks are clearly performed, at least initially, by individuals. For example, somebody has to sit down and draft out the first version of a seminar leaflet. There has to be an understanding by the individual of the task and its position in the hierarchy of processes. Once the initial task has been performed, the results must be checked against the activity of co-ordinating the promotional booklet – say for TQM. This clearly brings in the team, and there must be interfaces between the needs of the *tasks*, the *individuals* who performed them and the *team* concerned with the *activities*.

Using the hierarchy of processes, it is possible to link this with the hierarchy of quality teams. Hence:

- Senior steering committee/council – mission – CSFs – core processes.
- Process quality teams – core processes.
- Processor quality improvement teams (PQTs/QITs) – subprocesses.
- QITs – activities.
- QITs and quality circles/Kaizen teams/individuals – tasks.

Performance measurement and metrics

Once the processes have been analysed in this way, it should be possible to develop metrics for measuring the performance of the processes, subprocesses, activities and tasks. These must be meaningful in terms of the *inputs* and *outputs* of the processes, and in terms of the *customers* and of *suppliers* to the processes (Figure 13.1c).

At first thought, this form of measurement can seem difficult for processes such as preparing a sales brochure or writing leaflets advertising seminars. However, if we think carefully about the *customers* for the leaflet-writing tasks, these will include the *internal* ones, i.e. the consultants, and we can ask whether the output meets their requirements. Does it really say what the seminar is about, what its objectives are and what the programme will be? Clearly, one of the 'measures' of the seminar leaflet-writing task could be the number of typing errors in it, but is this a *key* measure of the performance of the process? Only in the context of office management is this an important measure. Elsewhere it is not.

The same goes for the *activity* of preparing the subject booklet. Does it tell the 'customer' what TQM or SPC is and how the consultancy can help? For the *subprocess* of preparing the company brochure, does it inform people about the company and does it bring in enquiries from which customers can be developed? Clearly, some of these measures require *external market research*, and some of them *internal research*. The main point is that metrics must be developed and used to reflect the *true performance* of the processes, subprocesses, activities and tasks. These must involve good contact with external and internal customers of the processes. The metrics may be quoted as *ratios*, e.g. numbers of customers derived per number of brochures mailed out. Good data-collection, record-keeping and analysis are clearly required.

It is hoped that this illustration will help the reader to:

- Understand the breakdown of processes into subprocesses, activities and tasks.
- Understand the links between the process breakdowns and the task, individual and team concepts.
- Link the hierarchy of processes with the hierarchy of quality teams.
- Begin to assemble a cascade of flowcharts representing the process breakdowns, which can form the basis of the quality management system and communicate what is going on throughout the business.
- Understand the way in which metrics must be developed to measure the true performance of the process, and their links with the customers, suppliers, inputs and outputs of the processes.

This whole concept/structure is represented in Figure 13.1. The changed patterns of co-ordination, driven by the process maps, should increase collaboration and information sharing. Clearly the senior and middle managers need to provide the right support. Once employees, at all levels, identify what kinds of new skill are needed, they will ask for the formal training programmes in order to develop those skills further. This is a key area, because teamwork around the processes will ask more of employees, so they will need increasing support from their managers.

This has been called 'just-in-time' training, which describes very well the nature of the training process required. This contrasts with the blanket or carpet bombing training associated with many unsuccessful change programmes, which targets competencies or skills but does not change the organization's patterns of collaboration and co-ordination.

Step 7 Ensure process and people alignment through a policy deployment or goal translation process

One of the keys to integrating excellence into the business strategy is a formal 'goal translation' or 'policy deployment' process. If the mission and measurable goals have been analysed in terms of critical success factors and core processes, then the organization has begun to understand how to achieve the mission. Goal translation ensures that the 'whats' are converted into 'hows', passing this right down through the organization, using a quality function deployment (QFD) type process as shown in Figure 13.4. The method is best described by an example.

At the top of an organization in the chemical process industries, five measurable goals have been identified. These are listed under the heading 'What' in Figure 13.4. The top team listens to the 'voice of the customer' and tries to understand *how* these business goals will be achieved. They realize that product consistency, on-time delivery, and speed or quality of response are the keys. These CSFs are placed along the first row of the matrix and the relationships between the *what* and the *how* estimated as strong, medium or weak. A measurement target for the *hows* is then specified.

The *how* becomes the *what* for the next layer of management. The top team share their goals with their immediate reports and ask them to determine their *hows*, indicate the relationship and set measurement targets. This continues down the organization through a 'catch-ball' process until the senior management goals have been translated through the

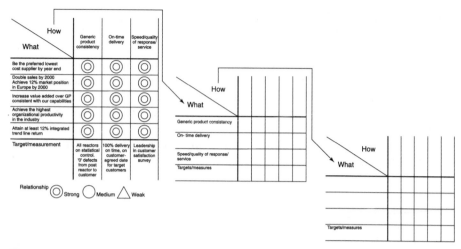

Figure 13.4 *The goal translation process*

what/how → *what/how* → *what/how* matrices to the individual tasks within the organization. This provides a good discipline to support the breakdown and understanding of the business process mapping described in Chapter 4.

It is important to get clarity at the corporate and business unit management levels about the *whats/hows* relationships, but the ethos of the whole process is one of involvement and participation in goal/target setting, based on good understanding of processes – so that it is known and agreed what can be achieved and what needs measuring and targeting at the business unit level.

Strategic planning for TQM needs itself to be done within the continuous improvement cycle to avoid the 'danger gaps' shown in Figure 13.5.

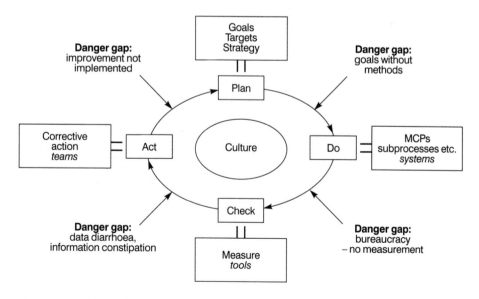

Figure 13.5 *TQM implementation – all done with the Deming continuous improvement cycle*

Continuous improvement

Never-ending or continuous improvement is probably the most powerful concept to guide management. It is a term not well understood in many organizations, although that must begin to change if those organizations are to survive. To maintain a wave of interest in quality, it is necessary to develop generations of managers who not only understand but are dedicated to the pursuit of never-ending improvement in meeting external and internal customer needs.

The concept requires a systematic approach to quality management that has the following components:

- *Planning* the processes and their inputs.
- *Providing* the inputs.
- *Operating* the processes.
- *Evaluating* the outputs.
- *Examining* the performance of the processes.
- *Modifying* the processes and their inputs.

This system must be firmly tied to a continuous assessment of customer needs, and depends on a flow of ideas on how to make improvements, reduce variation and generate greater customer satisfaction. It also requires a high level of commitment and a sense of personal responsibility in those operating the processes.

The never-ending improvement cycle ensures that the organization learns from results, standardizes what it does well in a documented quality management system, and improves operations and outputs from what it learns. But the emphasis must be that this is done in a planned, systematic and conscientious way to create a climate – a way of life – that permeates the whole organization.

There are three basic principles of never-ending improvement:

- Focusing on the *customer*.
- Understanding the *process*.
- All *employees* committed to quality.

Focusing on the customer

An organization must recognize, throughout its ranks, that the purpose of all work and all efforts to make improvements is to serve the customers better. This means that it must always know how well its outputs are performing, in the eyes of the customer, through measurement and feedback. The most important customers are the external ones, but the quality chains can break down at any point in the flows of work. Internal customers therefore must also be well served if the external ones are to be satisfied.

Understanding the process

In the successful operation of any process it is essential to understand what determines its performance and outputs. This means intense focus on the design and control of the inputs, working closely with suppliers, and understanding process flows to eliminate bottlenecks and reduce waste. If there is one difference between management/ supervision in the Far East and the West, it is that in the former management is closer to, and more involved in, the processes. It is not possible to stand aside and manage in never-ending improvement. TQM in an organization means that everyone has the determination to use their detailed knowledge of the processes and make improvements, and use appropriate statistical methods to analyse and create action plans.

All employees committed to quality

Everyone in the organization, from top to bottom, from offices to technical service, from headquarters to local sites, must play their part. People are the source of ideas and innovation, and their expertise, experience, knowledge and co-operation have to be harnessed to get those ideas implemented.

When people are treated like machines, work becomes uninteresting and unsatisfying. Under such conditions it is not possible to expect quality services and reliable products. The rates of absenteeism and of staff turnover are measures that can be used in determining the strengths and weaknesses, or management style and people's morale, in any company.

The first step is to convince everyone of their own role in total quality. Employers and managers must of course take the lead, and the most senior executive has a personal responsibility for quality. The degree of management's enthusiasm and drive will determine the ease with which the whole workforce is motivated.

Most of the work in any organization is done away from the immediate view of management and supervision, and often with individual discretion. If the co-operation of some or all of the people is absent, there is no way that managers will be able to cope with the chaos that will result. This principle is extremely important at the points where the processes 'touch' the outside customer. Every phase of these operations must be subject to continuous improvement, and for that everyone's co-operation is required.

Never-ending improvement is the process by which greater customer satisfaction is achieved. Its adoption recognizes that quality is a moving target, but its operation actually results in quality.

A model for total quality management

The concept of total quality management is basically very simple. Each part of an organization has customers, whether within or without, and the need to identify what the customer requirements are, and then set about meeting them, forms the core of a total quality approach. This requires the three hard management necessities: a good quality management system, tools such as statistical process control (SPC) and teamwork. These are complementary in many ways, and they share the same requirement for an uncompromising commitment to quality. This must start with the most senior management and flow down through the organization. Having said that, teamwork, SPC or the quality system, or all three, may be used as a spearhead to drive TQM through an organization. The attention to many aspects of a company's operations – from purchasing through to distribution, from data recording to control

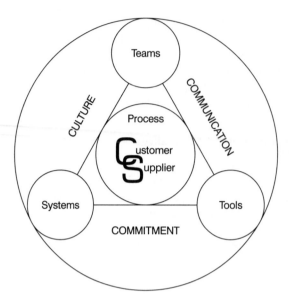

Figure 13.6 *Total quality management model*

chart plotting – which are required for the successful introduction of a good-quality system, or the implementation of SPC, will have a 'Hawthorne effect', concentrating everyone's attention on the customer–supplier interface, both inside and outside the organization.

Total quality management calls for consideration of processes in all the major areas: marketing, design, procurement, operations, distribution, etc. Clearly, these each require considerable expansion and thought, but if attention is given to all areas, using the concepts of TQM, then very little will be left to chance. Much of industry and commerce would benefit from the improvements in quality brought about by the approach represented in Figures 13.1 and 13.6. This approach will ensure the implementation of the management commitment represented in the quality policy, and provide the environment and information base on which teamwork thrives.

Chapter highlights

TQM and the management of change

- Senior managers in some organizations recognize the need for change to deal with increasing competitiveness, but lack an understanding of how to implement the changes.
- Successful change is effected not by focusing on formal structures and systems, but by aligning process management teams. This starts with writing the mission statement, analysis of the critical success factors (CSFs) and understanding the critical or key processes.

Integrating TQM into the strategy of the business

- Senior management may begin the task of process alignment through seven steps to a self-reinforcing cycle of commitment, communication and culture change.
- The first three steps are: gain commitment to change; develop a shared vision and mission for the business or desired change; and develop the critical success factors.
- The remaining four steps comprise: defining the key performance indicators (balanced scorecard); understanding the core processes and gaining ownership; breaking down the core processes into subprocesses, activities and tasks; and ensuring process and people alignment through a policy deployment or goal translation process.

Continuous improvement

- Managers must understand and pursue never-ending improvement. This should cover planning and operating processes, providing inputs, evaluating outputs, examining performance, and modifying processes and their inputs.
- There are three basic principles of continuous improvement: focusing on the customer, understanding the process, and seeing that all employees are committed to quality.

A model for total quality management

- In the model for TQM the customer–supplier chains form the core, which is surrounded by the hard management necessities of a good-quality system, tools and teamwork.

Reference

1. See, for example, Hardaker, M. and Ward, B.K., 'Getting Things Done – how to make a team work', *Harvard Business Review,* Nov./Dec. 1987, pp. 112–119.

Part Five

Discussion questions

1 You have just been appointed the Production Manager of a small chemical company. You are shocked at the apparent disregard for procedures which have been laid down. This is particularly noticeable amongst the younger/newer members of the workforce. Briefly outline your responsibility in the area of quality and describe how you could proceed to improve the situation.

2 You have just joined a company as the Quality Executive. The method of quality control is based on the use of inspectors who return about 15% of all goods inspected for modification, rework or repair. The monthly cost accounts suggest that the scrap rate of raw materials is equivalent to about 10% of the company's turnover and that the total cost of employing the inspectors is equal to about 15% of the direct labour costs.

Outline your plan of action over the first 12 months.

3 You have recently been appointed as Transport Manager of the haulage division of an expanding company and have been alarmed to find that maintenance costs seem to be higher than you would have expected in an efficient organization.

Outline some of the measures that you would take to bring the situation under control.

4 TQM has been referred to as 'a rain dance to make people feel good without impacting on bottom line results'. It was also described as 'flawed logic that confuses ends with means, processes with outcomes'. The arguments on whether to focus on budget control through financial management or quality improvement through process management clearly will continue in the future.

Discuss the problems associated with taking a financial management approach which has been the traditional method used in the West.

5 a) Discuss what is meant by taking a process management approach. What are the key advantages of focusing on process improvement?
   b) Discuss how TQM can impact on bottom line results.

6 You are a Management Consultant who has been invited to make a presentation on Total Quality Management to the board of directors of a company employing around 200 people. They are manufacturers of injection-moulded polypropylene components for the automotive and electronics industries, and they also produce some lower technology products, such as beverage bottle crates.

   As they supply Ford Motor Company and have achieved their Q1 approval, the board have asked you to stress the role of quality systems and statistical process control (SPC) in TQM.

   Prepare your presentation, including references to appropriate models as visual aids.

7 Describe the key stages in integrating total quality management into the strategy of an organization. Illustrate your answer by reference to one of the following types of organization: a large national automotive manufacturer, an international petro-chemical company, a national military service, a large bank.

8 What are the critical elements of integrating total quality management or business improvement into the strategy of an organization? Illustrate your approach with reference to an organization with which you are familiar, or which you have heard about and studied.

9 You are the new Quality Director of part of a large electrical component manufacturing assembly and service company. Some members of the top management team have had some brief exposure to TQM, and you have been appointed to lay down plans for its implementation.

   Set down plans for the process which you would initiate to achieve this. Your plans should include reference to any training needs, outside help and additional internal appointments required, with timescales.

10 You have been appointed as an external personal adviser to the Chief Executive of ONE of the following:

   National Westminster Bank
   Portsmouth Royal Infirmary
   University of Leeds.

   The members of the top management have had some brief exposure to TQM/ Business Excellence and you have been appointed to help the Chief Executive lay down plans for its implementation.

Choose any of the above organizations and set down plans for the process which you would initiate to help the Chief Executive achieve this. Your plans should be as fully developed as possible and include reference to any training needs, further outside help and any internal appointments required, with a realistic timescale.

Case Studies

Case Studies

Part One

Foundations

Ardmac Performance Contracting Ltd
The team approach to interior contracting

Company background

Ardmac specializes in interiors and clean room construction. The company has grown from a small subcontractor with a turnover of under £5m at the start of the 1990s to a group achieving over £25m.

Ardmac serves four main market sectors:

- Commercial interiors
- Industrial interiors
- Cleanrooms
- Sterile rooms.

The company's business is divided roughly equally between Britain and Ireland: about half is concerned with clean rooms and half with commercial and industrial interiors.

Ardmac is focused exclusively on the architectural envelope – floors, walls, ceilings and interior fittings – and generally acts as a subcontractor. Offices are located in London, Manchester, Hamilton and Dublin, with satellite offices in Craigavon and Cork.

Total quality

Ardmac has made its own commitment to quality, and this is expressed in a company statement. Ardmac strives to be a learning organization, and recognizes that this demands continuity of key staff.

Ardmac sees its business as being a partnership with customers and suppliers. The company recognizes the need for continuous improvement and strives to achieve it through a multi-pronged strategy. This covers:

- Safety commitment
- Total quality management
- Teamwork
- Directly employed workforce: there is only limited use of subcontract labour
- Empowered site management
- Information systems
- Local presence.

Ardmac has had to face the problems of rapid growth. In 1992, turnover was just over £5m at five locations, but has now reached £25m at six locations. There is now sufficient critical mass in each location to allow quality systems to be operated successfully. A key indicator is the number of PCs: in 1992, there were 0.32 per member of staff, mostly in the finance function; there are now 0.63 per member of staff, with the entire growth having taken place outside the finance function.

Ardmac has worked to apply the EFQM Business Excellence Model, focusing initially on processes and structure. A key initiative in this context has been a 'MAPS' programme, which covers:

- Marketing – getting the business.
- Administration – support to production and marketing.
- Production – getting the work done.
- Strategy – setting vision and objectives.

The company recognizes that, while it has made progress in each of these areas, more is needed, particularly in articulating and communicating strategy.

Dominant activity and growth

Since 1992, key issues addressed (in sequence) have been:

- Organization and structure
- Job definition procedures
- Management information systems
- Management development
- Leadership development.

Information systems progression

Ardmac has developed an association with a US company, which has greatly stimulated its application of information systems (IS). Ardmac's IS in 1992 consisted of little more than spreadsheets on free-standing PCs. ISDN connections were introduced from 1994, and a database, AJACS (Ardmac Job Administration Control System), was established at the same time. This focused initially on financial issues, but developed into a powerful tool for business management.

Local area networks were phased in from 1995. A full wide area network followed in 1996, along with LIMITS (Labour and Material Tracking System). Full connectivity has now been achieved, covering all offices and major sites and allowing instantaneous data transfer.

Staff issues

Ardmac recognizes that, if it is to remain a learning organization, continuity of key staff is essential. This has entailed moving away from a culture of the generalist to one of depth of expertise.

The future

The Business Excellence Model is crucial to Ardmac's future development. The company has learnt much about the model and its potential from the experience over recent years and is now in a strong position to apply it more extensively and productively. TQM offers great potential for growth and empowerment in Ardmac. Ardmac's core organization will retain the flexibility to respond to market development. To complement this, centres of excellence are being developed for particular areas of expertise.

Contractors

Ardmac's history was as a product-led company. The 1980s recession in Ireland led it to market direct inward-investing clients, principally in the electronics and pharmaceuticals sectors, leading to a diminishing reliance on main contractors. Ardmac's experience is that, among those main contractors with whom it still does business, not all are fully committed to TQM. However, most construction managers are strongly supportive.

Questions

1 What are the issues a small company like Ardmac faces when implementing TQM in a period of rapid growth?

2 Ardmac's 'multi-pronged strategy' comprises seven elements, including safety and 'local presence'. Evaluate this strategy and suggest other elements which might be considered.
3 Why should the construction industry find difficulties implementing TQM?

Acknowledgement

The author is grateful for the contribution made by Kevin McAnallen in the preparation of this case study.

Texas Instruments Europe Leadership and commitment to total quality and business excellence

Texas Instruments Incorporated is a global semiconductor company and the world's leading designer and supplier of digital signal processing and analog technologies, the engines driving the digitalization of electronics. Headquartered in Dallas, Texas, the company's businesses also include material and controls, education and productivity solutions and digital imaging. The company has manufacturing or sales operations in more than 25 countries. Texas Instruments Incorporated employs more than 35,000 people worldwide and has net revenues in excess of $8bn.

Innovation – a driving force for the growth of the company

The 'chip' has revolutionized our everyday lives. It has increased what we are able to do, the speed at which we can do it, and has created profound benefits for society.

The integrated circuit was invented at Texas Instruments in 1958, one of many significant inventions contributing both to the growth of TI and the electronics industry worldwide – an industry destined to grow to $2 trillion by the year 2000. TI's technological innovations, in addition to the integrated circuit, include the first hand-held calculator, the single-chip microcomputer, forward-looking infrared vision systems and the first quantum-effect transistor. These innovations have been the catalyst for the different businesses of TI, their growth, our contributions to society and the way we all live, learn, work and play.

Texas Instruments – global resources serving European customers

TI began in Europe in Bedford, England, back in 1956, the first US-based company to manufacture semiconductors in Europe. Today TI Europe, a wholly owned subsidiary of TI Incorporated, has responsibility to manage all operations in the European region in 15 different countries and employs more than 2300 people. The semiconductor business accounts for over 90% of TI Europe's revenue and over 90% of its people in Europe.

Each of TI's businesses is organized on a worldwide basis, with regional managers in Europe, Japan and Asia Pacific reporting back to a worldwide manager. The responsibility of the regional organizations is to be close to their customers, understanding their requirements, cultures and languages. Operations include application, research, design development, engineering, manufacturing, marketing, sales, order fulfilment and support.

In short, TI's objective is to be a 'transnational' company, combining global efficiency with the highest degree of regional and national responsiveness. Over more than 35 years, strong local presence has earned TI a reputation as a truly European partner, satisfying the needs of its customers.

The majority of TI products and services provided to its customers in Europe are sold to end equipment manufacturers, who incorporate the products into their own systems for resale. This entails many parallel channels to market for TI's products, from direct sales to indirect distributors and agents. For example, out of the 100,000 users of semiconductors, TI Europe serves around 500 customers directly, through market segment dedicated account managers and technical specialists. Other customers are served through independent third-party distributors.

The semiconductor industry has over 300 suppliers competing for market share through product innovation, excellence of execution and lowest operating costs. Its customers expect price reductions on an ongoing basis, as they are also operating in fiercely competitive global markets. TI's objective is to help them produce world-class products, enabled by TI technology. This requires very close partner relationships to achieve the benefits of a 'virtual vertical integration' between the organizations.

TI Europe is strategically well placed, since it researches, designs and manufactures much of its own raw materials and uses the creativity of engineering innovation to continue to bring application solutions to its customers.

Total quality culture – a cornerstone of TI's philosophy

During the 1990s it became clear to TI that, whilst technological innovation was vital to future success, it was insufficient on its own. The company had to find a way to enable its customers to gain access to the innovations and be supported and satisfied in that process. The adoption of total quality was TI's chosen route to becoming more customer orientated, whilst retaining technological excellence.

The journey began in the 1980s with the first concepts and has developed over time into the way TI people do business with customers and each other. Total quality has permeated all TI companies, thousands of people having received continuous training, and it has become the TI way of life. The TQ journey took a major step forward in 1993 when the EFQM model was adopted for TI Europe.

Quality is now manifested in everything TI does, from original design to manufacturing and after-sales service. It is based on a rigorous approach comprising teamwork, people involvement and continuous improvement through understanding customer needs and ensuring that products and services fully meet them.

In Europe, TI developed, very rapidly, a total quality process, 'Total Quality Culture' (TQC), and learned quickly.

To support the programme and priorities of its worldwide businesses, each organization developed a total quality facilitation unit (TQ Promotion Centre) and quality steering team, as well as training and communication processes to advance the total quality journey. Several of the roadmaps have now been in place for ten years.

More recently, the European dimensions of TI business have strengthened and many core business processes now extend across businesses and across country borders. Cross-fertilization, transfer of expertise becoming a 'learning organization', and harmonization of the TQC processes have become paramount.

Use of the EFQM business excellence criteria

The approach was refined by adopting a common programme of continuous improvement against the EFQM criteria, under the banner of 'Total Customer Satisfaction Through Business Excellence'. As part of this programme, all of TI Europe's business and support organizations' self-assessment were to fundamentally transform the company and shape the organization for the future.

TI Europe had performed unsatisfactorily for several years, the European market and its customers had changed fast, and Europe had become more a part of the global market. Customers wanted fewer suppliers, but closer relationships, together with competitive costs for products and services, including advanced technologies that would help them win in the new global market place. For companies to succeed they had to understand these changes and proactively adapt to ever-changing customer needs. The past approach of cost reductions in TI Europe had not been enough to make a real impact and put the company back on the road to growth and sustained profitability. It needed a substantially different approach.

The twelve-month assessment using the EFQM criteria showed clearly the radical changes needed in the company's processes and structure. There was also a need for a tool to drive the efforts towards excellence and competitiveness, a tool that would provide a common language and the 'glue' between the diversified businesses. The EFQM methodology was chosen to help completely rethink the structure and execute a major re-engineering plan across the region that included five key tactics:

● Disengage from non-strategic, labour-intensive and uncompetitive manufacturing activities – to be able to invest in strategic, high value-adding activities with focus on core competencies.

TI in Europe

☐ European Business Centres

☆ Manufacturing Sites

△ European Distribution Centre

○ Customer Support

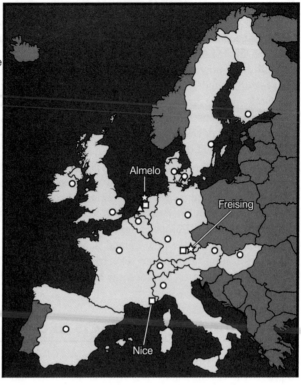

Figure C2.1 *TI Europe business centres today*

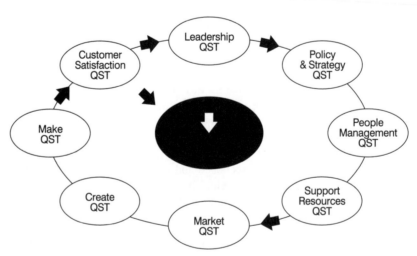

Figure C2.2 *TI Europe organization chart. TI Europe Strategic Leadership Team (ESLT) based on the EFQM criteria*

- Obtain better synergy and rationalization through business organization consolidation into business centres (Figure C2.1).
- Refocus marketing on sustainable, profitable growth and penetration gain.
- Operate as one single 'virtual' European entity across Europe to the extent allowable by legislation.
- Align support and infrastructure functions to the business centre needs.

A key element of the new TI Europe was its management structure, entirely based on the EFQM criteria so as to ensure maximum synergy between its component teams, a clear, common focus on TQ business excellence and a common purpose and direction with a clear, shared vision (Figure C2.2). The TI Europe Strategic Leadership Team (ESLT) is comprised of all the business managers and the chairmen of eight quality steering teams (QSTs), each of which is responsible for one or more of the EFQM criteria. The ESLT is led by the European President who is part of the worldwide Strategic Leadership Team.

Adopting the EFQM model has not only changed the way TI Europe is structured and operates – more importantly, it has helped to turn the company around

The TI Commitment

Mission

Texas Instruments Exists To Create, Make, And Market Useful Products And Services To Satisfy The Needs Of Customers Throughout The World.

Principles

We Will Accomplish This With 'Excellence In Everything We Do'

- Perform With Unquestionable Ethics And Integrity
- Achieve Customer Satisfaction Through Total Quality
- Be A World-Class Technology/Manufacturing Leader
- Provide Profitable Growth/Fair Return On Assets
- Achieve Continuous Improvement With Measurable Progress
- Be a Good Corporate Citizen

Values

We Expect The Highest Levels Of Performance And Integrity From Our People. We Will Create An Environment Where People Are Valued As Individuals And Treated With Respect And Dignity, Fairness And Equality. We Will Strive To Create Opportunities For Them To Develop And Reach Their Full Potential And To Achieve Their Professional And Personal Goals.

Figure C2.3

significantly. TI is once more gaining market share, has substantially reduced overhead costs, has reduced the number of business units, created a 'Virtual Europe Team', invested $500m in value-added technology and achieved significant growth and profitability levels that position the company well for a competitive future.

Leadership and the quality policy

TI's management understanding of the quality approach dates back to 1964, when TI Founder Patrick Haggerty publicized the mission statement alongside the TI principles and values (Figure C2.3). Sometime later, following their awareness training by recognized leaders of the quality movement (Crosby, Juran, Deming) in the late 1970s and early 1980s, and visits to role model companies, TI management recognized the need for a major change to the company's culture. The technology-driven approaches that apparently served the electronics industry well during its infancy (1960s and early 1970s) needed to be replaced by a customer-led, process-focused culture for the 1980s and 1990s. Such a significant cultural change, while eventually destined to involve everyone in the corporation, needed clear leadership to set the objectives, define the strategies and nurture its initial development and tactics of execution. This resulted in a substantial change of the behaviour of managers in inspiring and driving the organization towards total quality.

The measure of success of these leadership efforts is the extent to which TI has managed to develop its culture and achieve the desired level of 'Business Excellence', a total quality approach to the execution of business strategy.

TI requires its managers to lead the total quality process 'from the front', since it believes that management by example is the most effective technique for achieving significant cultural change and that strong leadership is pivotal to the pace of improvement.

Texas Instruments has a worldwide quality policy (Figure C2.4) which has been in place since the early 1980s. Quality steering teams (QSTs) throughout the corporation

---

Texas Instruments Quality Policy

We will achieve business excellence by:

- Encouraging and expecting the creative involvement of every tier.

- Listening to our customers and meeting their needs.

- Continuously improving our processes, products and services.

Chairman, President and CEO

Figure C2.4

TI Europe Vision Statement

We Will Excel In Our Business By Providing
Our Customers With Innovation Solutions
And Becoming The Preferred Supplier
In Those Markets We Target

Figure C2.5

continue to 'cascade' the requirements of this policy to all employees. Through the
European QST structure (Figure C2.2) higher level statements are made relevant to
staff by creating individual business and regional vision statements (Figures C2.5 and
C2.6). Specific business excellence goals are further deployed through a policy
deployment process.

Communication to staff has always been a high priority for TI managers at all levels.
More recently this communication has been reviewed through surveys and refined by
increasing the focus on total quality culture (TQC) priorities and processes. The main
mechanism for communication is via business/department meetings, addressed by
senior executives and managers from Corporate and Group organizations (2 per year),

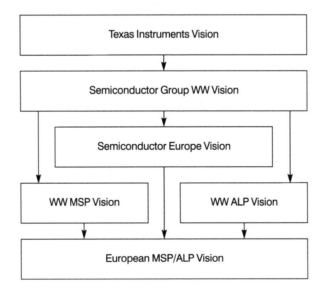

Figure C2.6 *Cascading vision statements*

European organizations (4 per year), individual Business (4 per year) and Departments (4–12 per year). In addition, ongoing awareness and communications programmes are run using posters, newsletters, in-house TQC magazines, badge stickers, pocket reminders and satellite broadcasts to reaffirm the core messages.

Questions

1 What are the particular features of implementing TQM/Business Excellence in a large company in the IT sector?
2 Evaluate the Leadership, Commitment and Policy aspects of the approach used in Texas Instruments.
3 What role could/should quality function deployment (QFD) play in a company like Texas Instruments?

Acknowledgement

The author is grateful for the contribution made by Werner Hofmann in the preparation of this case study.

Process and systems

Part Two

Process and systems

C3

Process management at D2D

Company background

This case study refers to Design To Distribution Ltd (D2D) which, until 1996, was a wholly owned subsidiary of International Computers Ltd (ICL). The company is now no longer part of that organization but the study still reflects best practice in many aspects of process management.

Based in the UK, D2D procured and manufactured high-technology products ranging from personal computers and UNIX workstations to mainframes, retail point of sale terminals and scanners. In addition they made and assembled printed circuit boards (PCBs), which were distributed worldwide, and supported after-sales services through repair and refurbishment.

Investment in manufacturing technology and development and use of state-of-the-art systems, including Just-In-Time techniques and Flexible Manufacturing Systems, had:

- Given D2D a world-class capability, which enabled customers to maintain their competitive edge in an extremely turbulent market place.
- Resulted in showcase facilities which customers and equipment suppliers used as role models.

D2D gained external recognition by winning prestigious awards such as the UK Best Factory, British Quality Award, a European Quality Award prize, and the European Quality Award itself.

Organization overview

D2D was based in the following main sites:

- Kidsgrove, Staffordshire (1100 people)
- Ashton-under-Lyne, Manchester (300)

- Bradwell Wood, Staffordshire (250)
- Byley, Cheshire (100)
- Stevenage, Hertfordshire (250).

It had four main organizations:

- Ashton manufacturing
- Kidsgrove manufacturing
- Refurbishment and Special Manufacturing (R&SM)
- Supply.

History

Changes in D2D's manufacturing operations included development and investment in production lines, facilities and staff, accompanied by significant improvements in productivity and efficiency. There was a strong commitment to total quality.

In 1990 the company entered into a strategic partnership with SUN Microsystems (the first non-ICL customer) to supply PCBs. There were further moves into the contract electronics market by other customers being secured. These customers used the recognized expertise of D2D to produce sub-components of their own brand of computer systems. The company's main business were:

- Bare printed circuit boards
- Printed circuit board assembly
- System assembly and test
- Refurbishment and special manufacturing
- Literature and software operations
- Distribution
- Electro-magnetic conformance
- Procurement.

Core processes in D2D

D2D realized in the early 1980s that to be a cost-effective, competitive, and indeed world-class organization, it must ensure that all processes are understood, measured and in control. Starting in 1987 everyone was trained in process management and improvement, and shown how they are part of a supplier–process–customer chain.

Customer-care training was delivered to everyone to reinforce this, and to re-emphasize that:

- The supplier–process–customer chains are interdependent.
- The processes all support the delivery of products or services to customers.

Part of everyone's training was to emphasize that all work is a process and that all activity can be modelled as a supplier–process–customer chain. Almost 3500 people received this process training.

Table C3.1

Critical process	Related success factors
System, product and service delivery, including customer satisfaction and performance measurement, for each of our six business streams	1 Total Solution Capability 2 Product Quality 3 Service Quality 6 Time to Market 9 Preferred Partner
Prospective customer/strategic partner identification	5 Organizational Capability
Competitive technology status and benchmark identification	5 Organizational Capability 6 Time to Market 8 Lowest Cost Ownership
People satisfaction – Investing in People process	5 Organizational Capability
Process improvement reviews	4 Process Quality
Supplier partnership improvement	7 Procurement Capability 8 Lowest Cost of Ownership
Cost reduction	8 Lowest Cost of Ownership
Self-assessment	10 Technical Capability
Recognition	5 Organizational Capability 9 Preferred Partner
Deployment	All Success Factors

New employees or part-time staff were trained in customer care during their induction training, together with suppliers and vendors. All processes within the company had been identified, all had appropriate measures and were modelled or flowcharted. Strategic and business reviews were used to identify the processes critical to the success of the organization. Information identified from the processes and reviews, including that from customers, competitive and market data, vendors and employees was used in the achievement of customer satisfaction and good business results. Table C3.1 shows the identified list of critical processes, and the related success factors.

How processes were identified

D2D's quality training, given to everyone, defined a process as the mechanism whereby inputs provided by suppliers are changed into outputs provided to customers. Every process had a performance measurement, targeted to ensure continuous improvement.

Operators of every process were properly trained, had any necessary work instructions available, and also had the appropriate tools, facilities and resources to perform the process at optimum capability. This applied to all processes throughout the organization, whatever the outputs, including those in Finance and Human Resources.

Manager and employee teams reviewed performance of all D2D's processes on daily, weekly, monthly, quarterly and annual cycles. The process management required that all processes had appropriate measurements, targets and benchmarks, and process performance was continually refined by the monthly Non-Financial Business Reviews, the annual target agreement process and the annual strategy agreement process. Manager and employee teams agreed strategic objectives annually and reviewed them quarterly. The objectives identified the business areas and markets within which D2D operated, and the products and services provided.

The critical process list was determined by the senior management team at the annual strategy review, supported by the quarterly strategy updates and the monthly business reviews. The management team analysed business performance and methods of management in detail.

A bi-annual self-assessment against the Business (EFQM) Model was conducted. This identified the need to review process management methods, and to re-evaluate top level (critical process) measures periodically. D2D flowcharted and documented the major processes as part of its quality management systems and self-assessment was a major input to the review of D2D processes.

Resolving interface issues

D2D had a consistent process that defined how interfaces should be established, which had been used and continuously refined from 1981. For each process, the process owner agreed measures for the process and the delivery requirement with his/her customers. These could be internal or external processes. Where possible, a scorecard was agreed. Customers were asked to provide data, feedback and information on each failure to conform to their requirement, and the feedback was compared with the internal performance measures of the supplier. The process owner within D2D and the customer (who may or may not be within D2D) mutually agreed the appropriate corrective action, with timescales. Failure to agree at any stage escalated the problem to a higher management review which could ultimately reach the monthly review held by the Managing Director and his team.

Evaluating the impact on the business

D2D knew that if it delivered products or services that did not conform to customers' requirements in terms of cost, quality or service, it would lose customers. D2D also knew that, if it did not continually ensure delivery, it would not retain existing or win new customers. In other words, processes that are not controlled cost business, profit and customers.

D2D used customers' satisfaction data from feedback, such as scorecard reviews, delivered quality audits, or customer surveys to continuously measure internal business process performance. There were also meetings of Customer Services, salespeople, senior designers, senior manufacturing managers and deliverers who focused on process and product performance.

Measuring the cost of quality highlighted the internal cost impact if processes failed to achieve required levels of performance. This measurement covered all processes, including non-manufacturing. The cost and efficiency of all processes was measured and reviewed weekly and monthly, including the Finance, Human Resource and Sales organizations. The cost of quality was then used to identify problem areas and to prioritize corrective actions.

Measuring the cost of quality as a percentage of revenue, month by month, showed a steady reduction, although the company constantly discovered new sources of non-conformance cost. The performance of all critical processes was measured, in terms of D2D's market share and customer satisfaction performance.

Process ownership and standards of operation

Processes were owned in D2D by the people responsible for the output of the process. This principle applied from the single tasks performed by the individual operator or member of staff, to the ownership of the D2D business by the Managing Director.

Ownership of a process was given to the person agreed by appropriate management and employees as having the best ability, based on training, skills and experience, to optimize and maximize the performance of that process. This was part of the

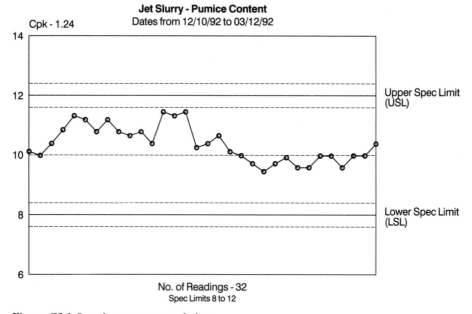

Figure C3.1 *Sample process control chart*

continuous drive to give the responsibility, authority and resources to the person best able to do any given task.

All processes were developed and refined, and measures of the performance of the processes agreed between customers and suppliers. The agreed standard took into account meeting the full customer requirement, at the most cost-effective method of operation, in comparison with competitors and benchmark standards. For D2D's build and assembly processes this included agreeing control limits for the application of Statistical Process Control (Figure C3.1).

The standard for all processes, stated that all appropriate processes would improve towards and achieve a process capability index (Cpk) of 1.6. A Cpk of 1.6 implies a very high level of control of the process (less than 3 ppm failure rate) and many of D2D's processes reached this level of control. The drive towards 6 sigma levels of control was also part of the quality improvement process.

The monthly quality reviews examined the performance of each process against the measures agreed at the beginning of the year. Each area was measured on delivery, efficiency, effectiveness and process yield performance, based on customer requirements and benchmarks.

Process measures used in process management

Business and customer satisfaction performance measures set the requirements for each process, and company measures on Business Results, Customer Satisfaction, People Satisfaction and Impact on Society covered all process requirements throughout the organization. These measures included customer requirements, plus measures of the effectiveness and efficiency of the process.

Process owners regularly reviewed these measures, as appropriate to the process, and agreed new targets as the requirements changed or new benchmarks or competitive information became available.

Specific manufacturing process measures included:

- Solder paste height
- Chemical concentration in solutions
- Component placement accuracy
- Test yields
- Failures from thermal screening and configuration.

Specific supply process measures included:

- Delivery on time
- Error-free deliveries
- Pre-notification to customers of the delivery
- New product introduction cycle times.

Measures were selected which were important when processes were developed, and continually refined to ensure that the most appropriate measures were being used, based on the performance or external benchmark information.

For example, the solder paste height measurement was been carefully calibrated against Japanese, American and European manufacturers to identify precisely:

- How measurements were made.
- Where measurements were made.
- What measures were taken.

Similar benchmark comparisons were made for non-manufacturing processes in, for example, document distribution (speed and accuracy of the distribution process), human resource management (absenteeism and staff turnover) and finance (speed and accuracy of invoice placement).

D2D selected test yield measures to remove as many faults in the products as early in the manufacturing cycle as possible, thus applying the principle of prevention of errors for all processes, product service and support.

Application of quality systems standard in process management

Allied Quality Assurance Procedure (AQAP) 1 registration was achieved in 1981, and ISO 9002 within D2D in 1988. AQAP was the quality system required to allow a vendor to sell to defence installations. To achieve registration to the ISO 9000 requirements D2D needed evidence of a comprehensive management review structure, supported by documentation and auditing processes to confirm the understanding and control of the business process.

The British Standards Institution (BSI) audited D2D's system every six months, and provided an external benchmark for the effectiveness of their own auditing system. Benchmarks for discrepancies raised were made with other large organizations, such as IBM, Avis Rentacar, Elida-Fabergé and Kodak. D2D was shown to have the lowest number of uncorrected non-conformances of all benchmarked companies, and the most advanced relationship with the registration authority.

Audits covered all parts of the organization, and the results of the audits were reviewed locally every month. The company business results review covered the performance of audits and the clearance of non-conformances; there were at least six informal audits per month.

Review of process performance and targets for improvement

Prevention-based feedback loops were built into all processes and all faults reported by customers were proactively managed for analysis and resolution.

People made improvements to processes as part of their everyday work, or by one of the following mechanisms:

- At regular local team meetings.
- Directly to their supervisor or manager.
- DELTA and local suggestion schemes.
- Team brief or DONUT meetings.

Quality team leaders and members were all trained in:

- Ishikawa root cause analysis
- Pareto diagrams
- Force field analysis
- Paired comparison.

The use of quality circles was initiated in 1983. Teams of individuals met voluntarily every week, during working hours, to discuss and improve the processes in their area. The value and importance of team involvement was regularly examined.

Corrective action teams were trained in DFICE methodology:

- Define the problem.
- Fix it.
- Investigate the root cause.
- Correct the root cause.
- Evaluate the corrective action.

Customers told D2D what they expect via:

- A bi-annual ICL customer survey
- Scorecards
- Customer Service feedback
- Visits to the factory
- Our visits to the customers
- Delivered Quality Audits
- Customer reply cards
- Delivery phone calls.

This data was collected for input to the annual target setting process to continually ensure that appropriate measures were being used.

D2D developed a Quality Modelling System (QMS) for processes, to understand what the performance should and could be in comparison to actual performance. The QMS was a powerful software tool that allowed D2D to feed predicted yields and failure rates at all stages into a model of the manufacturing line. This yielded theoretical output targets for delivered quality. A detailed 'what if' analysis was carried out to establish where improvements were theoretically possible.

The model also allowed 'what if' analyses to be undertaken to simulate the effects of process changes. The basic structure is detailed in Figure C3.2. The Quality Modelling System was reviewed at design and site business result reviews.

Suppliers with whom D2D had a very close relationship played a large part in the improvement process. Their input was obtained via joint management improvement

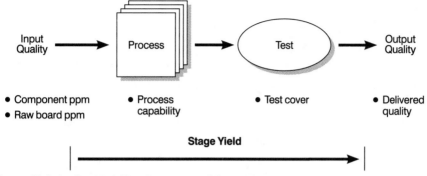

Figure C3.2 *Quality Modelling System – model structure*

teams, on new products and market trends, competitive performance of their own and competitors' products, and improved methods of using their products throughout the review and improvement processes.

D2D's benchmarking processes provided systematic analysis of all processes and use was made of competitive benchmark data wherever it was available. The target was always to be better than benchmark.

Performance targets were typically based on:

- Customer requirements
- Appropriate world class standards
- Machine and equipment capability
- Previous performance
- Process attributes and variables.

New targets were agreed on the basis of existing targets or changes to the customer requirement, aimed at meeting the customer requirement 100% of the time, in the most efficient, cost-effective manner. Team and individual targets were agreed in the appraisal process, and provided objectives throughout the organization to ensure 100% deployment.

The target performance for processes throughout D2D was zero defects, whatever the processes. This included all areas: sales, human resources, finance, information systems, etc.

Review of processes critical to the success of the business

All of the key/critical processes were reviewed by the senior management team every month at the Non-Financial Business Review.

Major processes were systematically reviewed by the local management teams, with input from customers, suppliers, employees and consultants with special skills, as appropriate. These analysed ongoing performance against the identified requirements to ensure improvement plans were in place for all attributes of the process. As with all

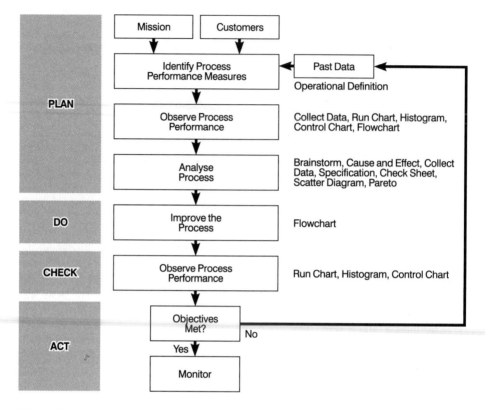

Figure C3.3

processes, the Plan-Do-Check-Act cycle was applied, as in Figure C3.3. For example, the recognition process was continuously reviewed against the feedback from employees, and was refined many times.

Challenging targets

Comparison was made with competitors in major business streams in several ways – external surveys, conferences, visits and published papers – to obtain details on the achieved performance and perceived requirement of customers. D2D's internal reporting systems yielded feedback on customer expectations.

This information was used to continuously review targets and process measures, and constantly improve towards 100% process yields and zero defects in delivered quality. Firstly the pilot process and its measurement was planned and established. The pilot process and its performance was then checked in actual operation.

This approach was applied to all target agreement processes, against the benchmark competitors, identified in the business strategy. The approach itself was subject to a quarterly process review.

Questions

1 Evaluate the approach to process management adopted by D2D, in relation to the company's concern for Customer Care.
2 Discuss the links between the use of SPC, process capability and process ownership at D2D.
3 How would the work on review of processes, their performance and targets for improvement translate into an organization in the service sector?

Acknowledgement

The author is grateful for the contribution made by Dayvon Goodsel in the preparation of this case study.

TQM in BT plc

Company background

Crucial to BT's success has been a commitment to quality which began in 1986 and has become part of everyday life across the company. Amongst other things, this has resulted in BT businesses winning the European Quality Award and the UK Quality Award for Business Excellence in the 1990s.

The company employs around 120,000 people. 'Project Sovereign' in 1991 reorganized the company into three customer-facing divisions, Business Division, Consumer Division and Global Division, supported by a large infrastructure division (Networks and Systems). Between 1992 and 1997, during which time TQM-based self-assessment has been used extensively, BT shed over 130,000 people; achieved without any compulsory redundancy. Further 'globalization' organizational developments have taken place recently.

Despite unprecedented levels of competition, BT's business has continued to grow substantially and the company still retains around 83% of the total market share. There is an ongoing strategy – to stimulate the market, i.e. the use of the telephone. In the 13 years from 1984 to 1997, BT's turnover has grown from £4 billion to over £15 billion. It has some 8000 sites across the world (7500 in the UK of which only about 300 have more than 50 people).

The introduction of TQM into BT

In 1986 BT chose total quality management as a means of focusing on customer requirements as well as encouraging teamwork, a positive attitude to problem solving and commitment to continuous improvement. Supplementing TQM, launched at the same time and providing the cornerstone for everything they do, were the BT values. These define the desired culture of the organization:

- We put our customers first.
- We are professional.
- We respect each other.
- We work as one team.
- We are committed to continuous improvement.

Led by the Chairman, Sir Iain Vallance, total quality was implemented through a series of workshops involving all managers and then cascaded to everybody in the company through the 'Involving Everyone' workshops. This was further supplemented by the Leadership Programme which concentrated on managers' leadership styles and teamworking behaviours, as the company organization was completely redesigned 'to put customers first'.

BT's commitment to continuous improvement led to the launch of Project Breakout, in 1993. This comprehensive review of key business processes provided improvements aimed at generating new revenue, growing markets, working more efficiently, delighting customers and running business processes that would make BT more competitive.

Underpinning all BT operations is the Quality Management System, first certified to the ISO 9001 standard in 1994. This remains the largest single corporate-wide registration in the world. BT UK is also certified to ISO14001 and IiP.

The introduction of a 'balanced scorecard' approach in 1995 served to translate BT's strategy into action through a set of key objectives, measures and targets which were integrated into the Corporate Scorecard (see Chapter 13). Through this, BT ensured that achievements in the four quadrants of the scorecard fed off each other to form a circle of continuous improvement so that:

- Delighting customers helps generate revenue and returns for investors.
- Increased revenue helps fund investments in processes and learning.
- Better processes and learning help BT's people to delight customers.

As part of the planning and objective-setting process, scorecards are now central to the way in which BT's senior executives focus and set direction right across the company. They are also a natural complement to the use of the European Foundation for Quality Management's Excellence Model, providing a focus for the improvement opportunities identified through annual self-assessments.

Self-assessment against the EFQM model for TQM/Business Excellence has been the main driver for company-wide improvement since it was first used in 1992. Most parts of the business now use this model to identify strengths and areas for improvement, within the business planning and objective-setting process, helping BT to raise standards in every aspect of its business.

BT introduced the BEM because it was facing many challenges from the market – changes in demand, technology advancements, etc. It also had many initiatives ongoing: ISO 9000, TQM, Customer Facing Restructuring, etc. Many of these were in danger of being tangential, and offered no measures of success. Having looked at the US Baldrige Award model, Chairman Sir Iain Vallance was a leading figure and founder member in the establishment of the EFQM and the launch of the European Quality Award and the TQM model as a way to measure the 'Enablers' and the 'Results'. He has since brought people into the top of the company with the same views and commitment as himself, including Sir Peter Bonfield, Chief Executive.

Experiences with TQM/Business Excellence

The TQM/Business Excellence model in BT is deployed in three stages: awareness, understanding and use:

Awareness	This is fairly universal with every single manager receiving a letter from the Chief Executive and information card about the BEM and self-assessment.
Understanding	This is (at a minimum) across all divisions at MD, Director and General Manager levels. In most directorates, understanding of the BEM goes down at least one more level (there are six management layers in total).
Use	The BEM was first adopted using a self-assessment workshop approach to deliver a score, strengths and areas for improvement across the major divisions. This achieved understanding and buy-in and enabled (sometimes for the first time) Board members to work together as a team on business issues. This workshop approach continues across BT, where appropriate.

Resourcing the BEM/self-assessment approach has not been seen as a problem in BT, as it has been introduced in the least resource-intensive way, i.e. workshops. People saw the full assessor training as a development opportunity – to widen people's awareness and look at their own organization – and it was not seen as a cost. People regarded the process as a tremendous learning experience and a privileged thing to do.

The costs of running BT's dedicated Business Excellence practitioners has been shown to be less than the rate of using an external consultancy, and the opportunity costs of other people's time is discounted as 'this is the way we run our business'. This view has also helped any 'management attitude' resistance issues, as the top-down approach has communicated senior management's seriousness and commitment. A positive decision was taken to use the Excellence Model and self-assessment as a managerial tool at local levels to align behaviours and ensure involvement in improvement.

The Business Excellence Team is committed to discovering what is crucial 'at the coal face' and to finding a way of delivering this. The key, of course, is to find what it is that people will derive benefit from. For example, in one area a BEM workshop was used to focus on strategy as the manager felt that this was the greatest need for his group.

BT has recognized the following general benefits from the use of self-assessment. It provides:

- a rigorous and structured approach to business improvement, applicable at all levels, ranging from individual business units up to the organization as a whole
- an assessment based on facts and not on individual perception
- a means to achieve consistency of direction and consensus on what needs to be done
- a means to integrate quality initiatives into normal business operations
- a means to measure progress over time
- a means to focus improvement activity
- a check between what the organization needs to achieve and its current plans
- a means to benchmark internally as well as against other organizations.

Customers

BT finds it difficult to assign directly cause and effect between TQM and business benefits, as it feels it 'pulls everything together'. The BEM has enabled BT to get the best out of all the other things that were going on – best practice became better known, e.g. how to deal best with a customer on an enquiry desk. Self-assessment caused the exchange of ideas regarding satisfying and delighting customers.

Customer satisfaction results in BT are impressive and the BEM has provided both a mirror and a window through which to improve results. For example, customer loyalty was not high and, therefore, work was done to 'delight' customers. The BEM and self-assessment were very instrumental in this change from satisfied to very satisfied to loyal customers, including gaining an understanding of the drivers of customer satisfaction.

The difference in perception and other measures is interesting. For example, 99.5% of all telephone services are delivered on the agreed date, but the perception can be much lower than this. The company has, therefore, moved over from internal measures to external perception measures.

People

People satisfaction results in BT rose over three years to the highest levels reached, at a time when people were leaving in large numbers. The company communicates much better, particularly regarding the strategy, which is very clear. People don't even mind bad news, if they know it is coming – everyone accepts that markets and technology are changing, that tomorrow will be different and that 'we will have to change'.

When BT engaged an 'Investors in People' (IiP) process, this fell nicely under the Business Excellence work which has provided all the foundations for IiP.

Financial

Attributing business results directly to the use of TQM/Business Excellence is difficult for BT, but nine out of ten BT managers, when asked in a survey if the business had improved as a result of BEM and self-assessment, answered emphatically yes. 'Everyone from Sir Peter Bonfield down has recognized that it has improved the business.'

BT awards based on TQM/BEM

BT made an early decision to have high-profile company awards, based around Business Excellence success. These are full 75-page documents to mirror the UK and European Award methods exactly. Applicants are site-visited by the assessor team if the assessment score is 500 points or above. Awards are given as follows:

'Achievement'	350 points
'Bronze'	500 points
'Silver'	600 points
'Gold'	700 points

BT Northern Ireland and Yellow Pages have won Gold BT awards and Business Division and BT Payphones have won Silver.

After several years of mandatory self-assessment, the company has softened this approach and business units now carry out self-assessment because they wish to do so. The majority do.

Plans for the future

The BEM has been used in many different ways, in addition to self-assessment, and the approach has become much more holistic. For example, many of the business unit boards use the BEM as a structure for their Board meetings.

'The BEM is as near to BAU (business as usual) as we can get.' Self-assessments are done annually and Business Excellence is a way of life for the majority of managers in the divisions. As the mandatory requirement softened, self-assessment became self-perpetuating.

The Business Excellence Team support whichever method of self-assessment divisional managers prefer, to make sure that the strengths and areas for improvement for tomorrow are identified. The aim is to make the BEM far more forward looking.

The BEM will continue to be used throughout BT to help the business units identify key agenda items and the major areas for improvement in their businesses in the following year.

The clear message from BT is that TQM, Business Excellence and self-assessment will continue to be an integral part of everything it does to further improve the performance of the whole business.

Questions

1 What role has the Quality Management system and the ISO 9001 standard played in BT's total quality journey?
2 Evaluate the deployment of the TQM/Business Excellence model in BT.
3 How could BT have improved its understanding of the success of the TQM/Business Excellence approach?

Acknowledgement

The author is grateful for the contribution made by Mike Bateman in the preparation of this case study.

C5

Self-assessment at Hewlett-Packard Ltd

Company background

Worldwide, Hewlett-Packard employs 120,000 people with a turnover of more than $42 billion, and a presence in every country. In the UK, Hewlett-Packard Ltd employs 6500 people and has a turnover of £2.25 billion.

The company has been using self-assessment as part of its total quality approach for more than ten years. During this period the UK Sales Company has grown by three times whilst maintaining the same cost base and number of employees. This growth is faster than the market and, therefore, the market share has grown.

Why self-assessment was introduced

Hewlett-Packard has its own proprietary self-assessment model, known as the Quality Maturity System. The QMS was developed as a measurement and improvement tool in Hewlett-Packard in the Far East and has been in use for over ten years. It has been mapped against the US Baldrige Quality Award Model and the Business Excellence Model (BEM), for which there has been found to be a 93% overlap – a high degree of correlation.

The QMS has various roots, including the Baldrige framework, but the latter was rejected as it did not at the time address the business results area. The QMS now has 70% deployment in Hewlett-Packard even though its use is optional. The latest QMS, which was developed by over 60 people from within the company around the world, constitutes a set of 'open questions' and involves a site visit and a two-day meeting with a company peer review team.

The triggers for introducing the BEM within Hewlett-Packard Ltd, were:

● customers and suppliers were asking about it
● to assess a different methodology and compare with the QMS
● as an external validation of the Hewlett-Packard QMS process
● to reinforce the self-assessment 'brand' in local Hewlett-Packard organizations.

The reason that Hewlett-Packard Ltd adopted self-assessment in the first place was that the management team felt that they were achieving business results without knowing exactly why. The Managing Director, therefore, brought the idea into the UK company to develop an understanding of the linkages between what they were doing (enablers) and the results. There was no crisis at the time and the major driver was this desire to understand the causes and effects, and to put in place structured business management.

The use of the QMS and the BEM helped to give the required understanding, for example how planning related to process and results, and it helped to focus on the need for:

● good process management
● improvement of processes.

The introduction of TQ/Business Excellence was done at two levels:

i) Every employee from the Chief Executive down was trained on how to improve processes:
   – Plan, Do, Check, Act (PDCA)
   – Basic quality improvement tools
   – How to get and run a process improvement project.
   This led to a great deal of process improvement activity as 75% of the employees were trained.
ii) The management board took on the role of the 'Quality Board' and each director took ownership of one criterion, or one of the six key business processes:
   – Leadership and participation
   – Customer focus
   – Business planning and control
   – Product generation
   – Order generation
   – Order fulfilment.

The focus is on these top-level processes and the processes at the 'ground level', which are subject to ISO 9000 based systems-type control. The company is now working with a standards assessment body on self-assessment cf. ISO 9000.

Experience with self-assessment

As in many organizations, quality was seen as additional to 'the day job' in the early days in Hewlett-Packard Ltd. There was 'buy-in' to the MD's ideas in only 40% of the managers, but over the last 10 years or so this has moved nearer to 100%. The resistance was overcome by the Hewlett-Packard quality fraternity coming together to move from a conformance approach to a business results oriented one. When one or two Hewlett-Packard businesses became quite successful, in terms of business results, managers began to see the benefits. The people system, 'The Hewlett-Packard Way', creates a culture of people seeing value in what they are doing/being asked to do and to learn from other parts of the organization. Hence, the successes led to the spread of the QMS approach.

Self-assessment, using the Hewlett-Packard peer review teams, caused the spread of best practice within Hewlett-Packard and the reviewers act as facilitators of cross-fertilization and improvement across the global organization. There are global databases, for example, for exchanging information.

In the first three years of quality and self-assessment using the QMS, a lot of cost (waste) was taken out of the organization. This moved on to address the issue of growing the business (three years) and finally into the customer focus (three years).

Customers

Compared with its own industry, Hewlett-Packard, Ltd's customer satisfaction ratings are amongst the best, and maintain a consistently high level.

People

Hewlett-Packard people's view of quality is that it contributes to the business. 70% of the people are involved and employee satisfaction in 70% of the areas measured is better than the industry results.

Other people benefits seen from the TQ/Business Excellence approach are the increase in professionalism of management and the use of self-assessment to automatically assess where the business is. Additionally, many process improvement methods have become a natural way of working, e.g.:

- teams problem solving
- use of tools
- flowcharting.

These have become familiar and their use more informal – needing less visibly structured facilitation.

Hewlett-Packard Ltd management still sees the need for a corporate quality group (now called the Business Excellence Centre) for continued innovation in quality/BE.

Financial

As mentioned earlier, above-industry average growth in the business and improvement in productivity are associated with the quality journey, the QMS, self-assessment and business excellence.

Current status and plans for business excellence/self-assessment within the company

Every business management team in Hewlett-Packard is encouraged to go through the latest version of self-assessment to the QMS every two years. Increasingly, parts of the assessment tool kit are now being used tactically at lower levels, in a fragmented way, to involve more people at the team level. This has also been extended to target largest business partners and suppliers, i.e. where there are good partnerships.

The BEM is integrated into the business planning cycle and the self-assessment outputs feed the annual planning process. It is used very much to drive strategic business improvement.

Hewlett-Packard Ltd intends to continue to use its QMS and the BEM together; the latter will be particularly helpful in the area of 'Resources' which is not directly addressed by their own QMS.

The Societal Results criterion will also be useful to strengthen the Hewlett-Packard measures in this area. The company has found the external assessment of the various award processes very useful and will adopt some of these methodologies in its own QMS reviews, e.g. site visits.

The whole approach will be kept alive in Hewlett-Packard by:

- Sponsorship from the top – the MD, who is also a 'European Sponsor for Quality' in Hewlett-Packard.
- Continuously challenging the things that are done and developing new angles and approaches.
- 'Deeper deployment', more informal use, e.g. use of the QMS questionnaire as a precision weapon to solve problems, to get away from the formal assessment every two years.
- Training of new managers in the QMS, BEM and self-assessment methods.

The clear message from Hewlett-Packard Ltd is that Business Excellence and self-assessment will continue to be, and become even more, an integral part of everything the company does to deliver sustained excellent business performance.

Questions

1 What are the key aspects of Hewlett-Packard's approach to self-assessment?
2 Why has self-assessment been successful in Hewlett-Packard?
3 Evaluate the current status of Business Excellence/self-assessment in Hewlett-Packard and the company's plans for the future.

Acknowledgement

The author is grateful for the contribution made by David Gee in the preparation of this case study.

Part Three

The tools and improvement cycle

The employee value plan – the benchmark for British Aerospace, Military Aircraft and Aerostructures

Industry and company background

The international aerospace and defence industry has undergone and is still undergoing major change. The spate of mergers and acquisitions in the USA has continued to focus European defence and aerospace companies on ways to improve performance. British Aerospace aims to establish a position of strength based on centres of excellence for future consolidation at European or global levels. The nature of the aerospace and defence market means that, at any given time, British Aerospace may simultaneously partner with a company on one or more programmes whilst also competing aggressively against it on other programmes.

British Aerospace employs about 45,000 people. There are strong links and partnerships across the world, particularly in the USA and Europe. Military Aircraft and Aerostructures (MA&A) is the largest business unit employing over 18,000 people on seven sites and making a major contribution to the £8.5 billion turnover of the company.

In the UK market, MA&A's prime contractorship aspirations face continuing competition. In the emerging markets of the future, such as information warfare and surveillance, they face potential competition from companies new to the sector. Within the market place, the intensity of competition continues to grow as reduced UK home defence budgets force all suppliers to export as a compensation for lost home volume. New ambitious companies and nations are also entering world markets, offering lower costs and comparable skills. This has forced aerospace and defence companies to focus on the delivery of improved value to customers and to broaden their portfolio to cover land, sea and air systems.

Customer reaction

The result of shrinking defence budgets and the high cost of new replacement aircraft means that governments are exercising their full range of options to fulfil their needs. Their options can be roughly split into three categories:

Do nothing

An order may be cancelled, delayed or reduced and reliance put on a partner country to carry out the required task that the order was set to fulfil. This, obviously, is the worst possible option for Military Aircraft and Aerostructures.

Make do with existing equipment

Governments may decide to maintain and manage the aircraft and equipment in their fleet in order to extend their in-service lives for as long as possible. This option offers potential business in the form of life extension and upgrade work. Competition is heavy in this sector, however, from defence electronics companies.

Buy 'new' aircraft types

This option covers the purchase of second-hand aircraft, derivatives of existing types, or brand new aircraft. Governments who decide on this course offer the widest scope for MA&A's business. To be successful, however, they need to continually develop their products in line with market needs and seek ways to make entirely new aircraft developments affordable to the customer.

The organization

Towards the end of the 1990s, MA&A's value planning process identified the need for significantly improved performance to take account of shareholder demands, fixed-price contracts and increasing competition in the market place. To meet the demands of this ever-changing business environment, a new organization structure for MA&A was announced.

For some time MA&A had been slowly evolving towards a more project-focused organization. The move in this direction recognized the importance of customers, improved awareness of project targets and ensured that the organization was positioned to allow a smooth transition towards any industrial restructuring options which may occur in the future.

The ultimate aim was to provide a more financially accountable and customer-focused project organization supported by process-driven functional excellence, dispensing with non-value-added tasks. The increased project focus also underpinned the introduction of new business processes under an Operational Efficiency Improvement (OEI) programme.

Significant benefits were produced as a result of the changes. These included:

- Clearer focus on the customer.
- Improved business performance.
- A clearer product focus.
- More effective deployment of common business processes.
- More effective management of the MA&A value chain, from design and development through to supporting the customer.
- Clearer budgetary responsibility at all levels.

- Reduced organizational duplication, e.g. finance reporting, resource management, etc.
- Less confusion of job roles.
- Clearer individual and team accountabilities.

As MA&A's structure developed to give a greater focus on projects and Integrated Project Teams (IPTs), people found themselves working in one of three 'areas' of the business: *Customer Projects*, *Internal Supply* and the *Functions*. These are shown in Figure C6.1.

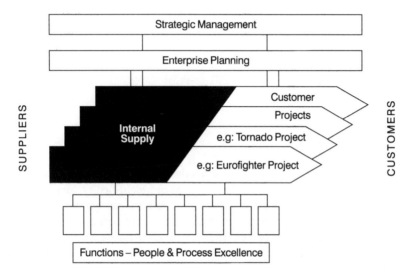

Figure C6.1 *The MA&A organization*

The external *Customer Projects* within MA&A are shown on the right of the diagram which covered the spectrum of the military and civil projects. Each Project Board assumed full profit and loss accountability for the project's performance, including responsibility for customer satisfaction and programme execution.

Internal Supply consisted of three new project boards to supply the aircraft projects with detailed parts, technical facilities and specialist 'know-how'. They are shown on the left of the diagram and represent parts of the customer value chain, which are inappropriate to allocate to or segregate across the separate aircraft projects.

The three new project boards were part of the internal supply chain for each aircraft project and each operates as a separate cost centre.

The *Functions* shown at the base of the diagram retained key responsibilities for developing the processes which the projects use and for facilitating the consistent application of best practice across the organization. They were about ensuring that the organization maintains a world-class capability in its people, its processes and its technologies.

A new area of Enterprise Planning was included in the Functional organization. Its role was to ensure a clear understanding of the resources needed to meet customer programmes – to predict longer-term needs and balance resources as appropriate.

Becoming a benchmark company – the five values

The business environment existing, and projected into the future, of increasing globalization and competition, meant that the interests of the business could only be assured by being the best, the benchmark. A major change programme, 'Benchmark BAe', provided the focus for the required change using a framework of five values, which would be applied everywhere across the business. Everything MA&A do is based around these values, giving focus and vision for the challenges which lay ahead. Every Business Unit within British Aerospace uses the values as their focus, which means people throughout the company are all working towards the same goals.

The five values captured the goals of conduct of the business to be realized in five key areas in becoming the benchmark:

- Customers
- People
- Performance
- Partnerships
- Innovation and Technology.

To provide direction and energy, supporting these values 19 benchmark actions were given priority across the company. These actions are identified in Figure C6.2. Each Business Unit's progress against the 19 benchmark actions was monitored at a corporate level on a monthly basis on a 'Success Board', which used a traffic-light system to mark achievements. This Success Board could be viewed on the Intranet, the creation of which itself was one of the 19 actions, and the MA&A management committee used monthly review systems to monitor progress across the Business Unit.

All of the 19 actions were, therefore, woven into MA&A's plans for each of the values. The plans themselves were restructured around the values and Business Plans became Value Plans. An 'Employee Value Plan' was produced each year for all employees that identified the full range of actions required to further the company's vision to 'Become the Benchmark'.

As will be shown, the values extend beyond the initial 19 benchmark actions. To support deployment of the values, Value Champions were appointed, usually Management Committee members, supported by Value Teams. The 'Employee Value Plan' documented what had been done and what had to be done to fulfil the values within MA&A.

Extracts and examples from the plan are given below under the five values:

- **Customers – Our Highest Priority**

  We will delight all our customers, both internal and external, by understanding and exceeding their expectations.

  Progress has been made on the journey towards improved customer satisfaction. Many teams within Military Aircraft & Aerostructures have started to use the Customer Value self-assessment tool kit ACE (Achieving Customer Excellence) and EFQM to help define and create actions plans.

Customers	People	Performance	Partnerships	Innovation & Technology
The Customer Programme To enable everyone to know, understand and delight their customers, both internal and external. The programme includes: • Customer Value Self Assessment Tool • Customer Care Policy • Links to Reward and Recognition • Communications – Achieving Customer Excellence (ACE) • Training and Development.	**PDP for Everyone** To provide the opportunity for all BAe employees to have ongoing and relevant development. **Leadership Development inc. Leadership Framework** To have focused leadership development. **Involvement Process** To provide the opportunity for individuals to contribute and be listened to. **Fair and Equitable Employer** To become a Benchmark employer. **Profit Sharing Scheme** To give a tangible reward to all employees which is related to the profitability of the Company.	**Value Planning Process** To develop and deploy a Value Plan for each Business Unit. **Value Adding** To provide a tool (Value Based Management) to help us to optimize the value of each business. **EFQM** To provide a common measure of, and tool for, achieving 'business excellence'.	**Partnership Sourcing Policy** To improve supplier performance, rationalize number of suppliers and develop strategy for procurement of raw materials. **Create Benchmark Culture Industrial Partnership** To commit to creating a Benchmark culture within existing and future partnerships. **Partnership Personnel Policy** To adopt people policies which achieve increased performance with our industrial partners. **Champion for Collaboration** To improve the way we trade internally. 'BAe first' culture. **Corporate Communities Policy** To build on internal best practice on work being done with the community. **Government Communication and Relationship Plan** To improve the relationship with the Government.	**Innovation Forum** For EDs, MDs and 'factholders' to challenge existing patterns of thinking in order to shape the strategic direction of our business. **Chairman's Awards for Innovation** To promote innovation by recognizing and publicizing people and teams. **Process for Innovation** To establish best practice processes and enhance and duplicate them around the business. **British Aerospace Intranet** To provide a British Aerospace internal communication and information system.

Figure C6.2 *British Aerospace benchmark functions*

We are now seeing a situation where the 'Know, Understand, Delight and Measure' principles of ACE are becoming embedded within our day-to-day operations.

As planned, the Management Committee has held monthly meetings to review both the deployment of the Customer Value and to discuss current customer issues that face the business. Positive results achieved from these meetings have so far included the development of a cross-project Customer Strategy and the beginning of a customer-focused training and development programme.

Achieving customer satisfaction is the achievement of success. With so many strong competitors in the market place, it is necessary for us to stand out. We need to go that extra mile to show that British Aerospace puts the customer above all else – offering positive attitudes, productive relationships and better value than any other company.

● **People – Our Greatest Strength**

All our people will be encouraged to realize their full potential as valued members of the British Aerospace team.

People will always be the basis of MA&A's success. The aim of the People value is to provide all of our people with the opportunity to maximize their potential and use their skills and abilities to position the organization for the future.

Already in this document we have seen some of the changes, both in terms of the market and the organization, facing people within MA&A. This value sets out what we need to do to meet future challenges and the increasing pace of change within our business.

Our people strategy has been developed to take account of a wide variety of influences, including:

– The need to increase customer satisfaction.
– The impact and requirements of new technology.
– The impact of current and future joint venture and partnership arrangements.
– A changing social environment.
– Changing political, economic and legislative considerations.

- **Performance – Our Key To Winning**

We will set targets to be the best, continually measuring, challenging and improving the way to do things, both as individuals and as members of our teams.

To be the best we must focus all our efforts into winning in a very competitive world. Our key drivers are:

– Increasing shareholder value so that they continue to invest in the British Aerospace of the future.
– Achieving all our targets by performance against our MA&A Value Plan and our own Operational Value Plans.
– Delighting our customers – by delivering a quality product/service when the customer needs it.
– Growing our business – by securing new orders and continually innovating and re-investing.
– Adding value – through our people and partnerships.
– Achieving our vision to be the Benchmark.

Shareholder value

Increasing shareholder value (and share option schemes allow many of us to be shareholders) puts the emphasis on the value of the Company and the amount of cash we can generate.

Achieving our targets

Our MA&A Value Plan, supported by around 40 individual team Operational Value Plans covering Project Teams, Functional Teams, Value Teams and Sites, sets performance targets that are both challenging and achievable if we all work smarter within the organization.

Year on year improvement targets have been set on each Project and these will only be achieved by building improvement into the plans for all our activities.

As the Value Planning process develops, more people are now actively challenging our traditional ways of working and setting their own targets for continual improvement.

Recognizing the dynamic customer and programme requirements, we are introducing a three-monthly rolling update to the Value Plan. It will allow all of

us to respond to the demands and priorities of the business. By regularly reviewing our Value Plan and using key indicators that measure our performance against it, we can ensure a continuous focus on our principal objectives and apply extra effort or priority where necessary.

Adding value

Our aim is to add value to the business by releasing the full potential of all our people working in integrated, focused and empowered teams, which have both the opportunities and resources to achieve their collective targets.

We will seek improvement in performance through removing unprofitable tasks, for example cross-checking and monitoring of our partners and suppliers where they work as integrated members of the team.

Achieving Benchmark Performance

The EFQM Business Excellence Assessment model has been used throughout MA&A and we have contributed to the development of the British Aerospace Business Excellence Review process (BER), modelled on the EFQM. Both these processes are complementary and allow us to focus on benchmark performance covering leadership, policy and strategy, people management/satisfaction, resources and processes, impact on society, customer satisfaction and business results.

Annual assessments provide opportunities for improvement which are incorporated into Value Plans, for example:

- Focusing on key business processes with ownership across MA&A being established in 1998.
- Linking our performance measurement into the Key Business Drivers and Key Processes.
- Ensuring that the Value Plan involves people and is understood and integrated with regular reviews and actions where necessary.
- Establishing a structured way of measuring customer perception.

Growing our business requires us to seek out new orders in markets around the world. We will only achieve success if we can compete in terms of cost, quality and timeliness compared with other companies offering equally attractive products and services.

● **Partnerships – Our Future**

We will strive constantly to be our customers' preferred supplier, our suppliers' preferred customer, a respected partner in our industrial alliances and a source of pride to our Government and our local communities.

In Military Aircraft & Aerostructures we are involved in a wide range of internal and external partnerships. These include:

- Other Business Units
- Within the Business Unit
- Industrial Partnerships

- Research Partnerships
- Suppliers and Subcontractors
- Community
- Education.

The Partnership value recognizes that working in true partnerships can create benefits throughout our business in relationships of all kinds.

Understanding the needs and expectations of our partners is crucial to our future success. We need to analyse our current levels of satisfaction and achievement and develop joint improvement plans and targets for continuous improvement.

Internal partnerships

Approximately 15 per cent of our annual sales are conducted through inter-Business Unit trading. MA&A is both a customer and supplier in such trading relationships.

A multi-Business Unit team concluded that guidelines on internal partnership conduct should be agreed in order to improve the efficiency of trading within British Aerospace. Key aspects for the guidelines include:

- A special emphasis on retaining core competencies.
- Ensuring that British Aerospace Business Units treat each other with respect.
- The transfer of best practice and ensuring that due regard is given to the interests of the Company as a whole.

The importance of partnerships is clear. Through them we can not only reduce costs, but work together on projects which would be untenable if we were on our own. We must develop these partnerships to the benefit of our organization. As competition gets stronger, they will provide us with the widest base of expertise and resources to meet the challenges of the market head on.

- ● **Innovation and Technology – Our Competitive Edge**

  We will encourage a hunger for new ideas, new technologies and new ways of working – to secure sustained competitive advantage for our Company.

  Everyone thinks about their individual role in our Company – what the internal and external influences on that role are and where it fits in to the bigger picture. We all have ideas about how our role can be improved to deliver better results. Your ideas might involve small gradual changes or they may be much grander than that – perhaps a fundamental rethink of a product, process, support or business practice. Many ideas will involve customers, suppliers, partners or other British Aerospace people.

  The Innovation and Technology value aims to utilize the good ideas of our people to maximize our intellectual wealth, so that we become the benchmark in all that we do. Innovation – the successful exploitation of new ideas – supports all the other values and is something we can all play a part in.

  There are four actions currently being pursued to sustain and nurture the growth of innovation within British Aerospace:

- The Chairman's Award for Innovation
- The Innovation Forum
- INTRANET/Link-BAe
- Process for Innovation.

As we progress it is clear that these four actions are inextricably linked and the impact that the Innovation and Technology value has in supporting and advancing the other values within MA&A will continue to grow in the future.

We need to continually innovate in the way that we work in both our processes and products to stay ahead of the competition. We will maintain a significant investment to assure our position in the future.

The company won the UK Award for Business Excellence in 1999.

Summarizing

The business environment within which British Aerospace and the Military Aircraft and Aerostructures Business Unit operate has undergone dramatic and rapid change. The need to reduce costs while growing the business was of prime importance and senior management believed that the only way of doing this was to develop the way MA&A worked so that the resources were used in increasingly intelligent ways. In short, they needed to work smarter.

A change programme, directed at creating a benchmark business, identified and used five values to focus change in key areas: their customers, their people, their performance, their partnerships and on innovation and technology. An annual Employee Value Plan allowed people to see what had been achieved and what was planned to be achieved in the future and helped the business to live up to its values. Using the benchmark actions drove the company to live up to its values and to reap the business benefits from its projects.

Questions

1 What are the main tenets of British Aerospace MA&A's goal of becoming a Benchmark company and how could these be adapted for an organization in the public sector?
2 Evaluate the 'Employee Value Plan' and offer constructive criticism and suggestions for further improvement.
3 Suggest additions/alternatives for the performance measures and targets listed as key drivers for the company.

Acknowledgement

The author is grateful for the contribution made by John Walley and Steve Unwin in the preparation of this case study.

Part Four

Organizational, communications and teamwork requirements

Business excellence through speed and teamwork in Philips Electronics

Philips – a global company

Royal Philips Electronics is eighth on Fortune's list of global top 30 electronics corporations. The company is active in about 100 businesses, varying from consumer electronics to domestic appliances, and from security systems to semiconductors.

Philips is among the world's top three producers in many of its businesses, including lighting, monitors, shavers and colour picture tubes for TVs and monitors. Translated into figures, the company produces over 1.5 billion incandescent lamps every year, and some 30 million picture tubes; and each day, the factories turn out a total of 50 million integrated circuits. PolyGram, a 75 per cent subsidiary, is the world's largest music corporation.

Worldwide, Philips:

- employs about 265,000 people
- has some 240 production sites in over 40 countries and sales and service outlets in 150 countries
- has research laboratories located in six countries and staffed by some 3000 scientists, and is responsible for some 10,000 inventions
- has a global network of some 400 designers spread over 25 locations
- shares are listed on 16 stock exchanges in nine countries.

The strength of Philips' global operations is reflected in its (value-base) leadership position in many of the markets in which it is active:

	World	Europe
Lighting	1	1
Consumer Electronics	3	2
Corded/cordless phones (in units)	1	1
Shavers	1	1
Steam irons	2	2
Semiconductors	9	4
Colour picture tubes	1	1
Laser optics	2	1
Medical imaging equipment	3	2
PolyGram (music)	1	1

Company history and achievements

The foundations for what was to become one of the world's biggest electronics companies were laid in 1891 when Gerard Philips established a company in Eindhoven, the Netherlands, to 'manufacture incandescent lamps and other electrical products'.

The company initially concentrated on making carbon-filament lamps and by the turn of the century was one of the largest producers in Europe.

Developments in new lighting technologies fuelled a steady programme of expansion, and, in 1914, it established a research laboratory to study physical and chemical phenomena, so as to further stimulate product innovation. Marketing companies had already been established in the USA and France before the First World War, and in Belgium in 1919, and the 1920s saw an explosion in their number.

It was at this time that Philips began to protect its innovations with patents, for areas taking in X-ray radiation and radio reception. This marked the beginning of the diversification of its product range. Having introduced a medical X-ray tube in 1918, Philips then became involved in the first experiments in television in 1925. It began producing radios in 1927 and had sold one million by 1932. One year later, it produced its 100 millionth radio valve, and also started production of medical X-ray equipment in the United States.

Philips' first electric shaver was launched in 1939, at which time the Company employed 45,000 people worldwide and had sales of 152 million guilders.

Science and technology underwent tremendous development in the 1940s and 1950s, with Philips Research inventing the rotary heads which led to the development of the Philishave electric shaver, and laying down the basis for later ground-breaking work on transistors and integrated circuits. In the 1960s, this resulted in important discoveries such as CCDs (charge-coupled devices) and LOCOS (local oxidation of silicon).

Philips also made major contributions in the development of the recording, transmission and reproduction of television pictures, its research work leading to the development of the Plumbicon TV camera tube and improved phosphors for better picture quality.

It introduced the Compact Audio Cassette in 1963 and produced its first integrated circuits in 1965. The flow of exciting new products and ideas continued throughout the 1970s: research in lighting contributed to the new PL and SL energy-saving lamps; other key breakthroughs came in the processing, storage and transmission of images, sound and data where Philips Research made key breakthroughs, resulting in the inventions of the LaserVision optical disc, the Compact Disc and optical tele-communication systems.

Philips established PolyGram in 1972, and acquired Magnavox (1974) and Signetics (1975) in the United States. Acquisitions in the 1980s included the television business of GTE Sylvania (1981) and the lamps business of Westinghouse (1983).

The Compact Disc was launched in 1983, while other landmarks were the production of Philips' 100 millionth TV set in 1984 and 300 millionth Philishave electric shaver in 1995.

The 1990s were a decade of major change for Philips. The Centurion programme was introduced to return the company to a healthy footing, businesses were sold, activities stopped and cutbacks made in employment. Today, the company is still actively reorientating itself to face the demands of the 21st century. In line with Philips' theme – 'Let's make things better' – the emphasis is firmly placed on providing the products that people really want to buy, on establishing the basis for substantial long-term profits, and on maximizing shareholder value.

Managing the company

Royal Philips Electronics is managed by the Board of Management, which also looks after the general direction and long-term strategy of the Philips group as a whole.

The Supervisory Board monitors the general course of business of the Philips group, advises the Board of Management and supervises its policies.

These policies are implemented by the Group Management Committee, which consists of the members of the Board of Management, chairmen of most of the seven product divisions and some other key officers.

The Group Management Committee, which is the highest consultative committee, also serves to ensure that business issues and practices are shared across Philips.

The Philips brand

The Philips name and shield logo is among the world's most recognized trademarks. Together they form Philips' most important asset, for while manufacturers make products, it is a brand that consumers buy . . . and keep on buying. Brand recognition is not enough, however. Consumers must have a clear idea of what the brand stands for

– they must be able to see the 'personality' of Philips and understand its values and standards.

This is why the company has invested in a worldwide brand management programme in order to better understand consumers' needs, desires and dreams and incorporate these into the product creation process; to communicate with consumers in a consistent way; and to progressively develop a common brand language and culture throughout the company.

First steps in this programme have included the setting up of a marketing competence centre and a global consumer intelligence unit, together with the introduction of dedicated brand champion managers for the different regions of the world.

The aim of these and other measures is to unleash the power of the Philips brand; to build on an awareness established over 100 years to enable it to become one of the top three brands in every market in which the company is present.

'Let's make things better'

'Let's make things better' is Philips' company theme – both a rallying cry and a public commitment; it is the creed to which the company has committed itself and it exemplifies the company's aspirations.

'Let's make things better' can mean making better products, systems and services, of course. However, of greater importance to Philips, it is far more a case of making things better, in the sense of contributing to improving the quality of people's work and lives. The theme developed as a corporate pledge from the appreciation that consumers are far more individualistic than ever before in their attitudes and demands. They have their own tastes and preferences and they are unique individuals, which is how they want to be treated – and not as one of the masses. 'Let's make things better' is Philips' commitment to improving the quality of their lives on an individual basis; to strive to make things better for each and every one of them.

Philips quality – journey to world-class level

The quality journey is regarded by Philips as a race without a finish line. As businesses grow and mature, new benchmarks appear and new targets are set. Nearly all Philips organizations are ISO 9000 certified, which lays the foundation for continuous improvement or 'Let's make things better', all the time.

The 'Philips Quality Award' (PQA-90) was the next challenge after ISO 9000, with its focus on process management. Those units that achieved the desired PQA-90 level and thus obtained the PQA-90 Award defined the next steps towards world-class performance.

From the world-class quality models, including the Malcolm Baldrige National Quality Award, Philips chose the EFQM model for Business Excellence as the most comprehensive and suitable one for the entire Philips organization. In this way, Philips continued to have a single model which serves as a uniform reference and external standard.

The PQA-90 programme taught Philips the value of self-assessment and made people in the company aware of the value of mutual learning through peer auditing. In a similar way they have applied the EFQM model within Philips under the theme of: *'Reaching the BEST'* (Business Excellence through Speed and Teamwork). This is presented in the Philips Business Excellence (PBE) Policy, their 'approach to Total Quality', as follows:

Business Excellence
We aim to be one of the best companies in the world: the best to trade with, work for, and invest in.

- Customers are fully satisfied by the quality of Philips' products and services.
- Employees can develop and use their full potential.
- Shareholders get a premium return on their investment.
- Suppliers like to work with us as this generates superior value for both.
- In the larger community, we contribute to the quality of life.

To achieve our goals we will deliver excellence in every way based on the PBE model.

... through Speed ...

Superior customer value of products and services is attained through world-class performance of business processes. Excellence process performance is the result of systematic improvement, both by incremental steps and by breakthroughs. To achieve excellence performance, we will accelerate our speed of learning.

... and Teamwork ...

Competence and knowledge are the foundation for excellence. We utilize company talents fully by working in teams and learning from the best internal and external practices. Open communication both within and between teams, departments, businesses and divisions will mobilize all our capabilities.

The Philips way to achieve Business Excellence is known as:

BEST – Business Excellence through Speed and Teamwork

The words are familiar and the goals are understood but it is the *BEST* process that represents a breakthrough in leadership for Philips. *BEST* is a management process that drives the company to world-class performance levels through improvement and alignment of all business it processes.

The relentless pursuit of excellence, the drive for continuous improvement, the commitment to make things better, to constantly seek better and breakthrough ways to manage the enterprise – these are principles guiding Philips today. Reaching for the *BEST* is for:

- *Customers* – Philips recognizes that its customers want products and services to be the very best, just as Philips wants to be their first choice.
- *Suppliers* – Philips knows that close co-operation with suppliers will enable it to improve the whole supply chain.
- *Employees* – they want to be part of a winning team. Sharing in the success of the company gives a sense of achievement and inspires people to take on new challenges.
- *Shareholders* – Philips' shareholders demand consistently high performance based on the company's resolve to be the best.
- *Society* – the larger society, of which Philips forms a part, expects the company to contribute to the quality of life.

Speed and teamwork are an important part of the *BEST* equation for Philips:

Speed
Improvement programmes can be clear, correct and focused but, just like business processes, if they are too slow, they don't deliver results ahead of the competition. By carefully considering its working methods and finding ways to work smarter, Philips knows it can reduce the cycle-time of business processes. Shorter process cycle-time also accelerates the speed of learning.

Teamwork
Philips recognizes that it can only be the best with teamwork, sharing knowledge and communicating with each other. In Philips, teamwork is the key to competitiveness and the route to achieving the full potential. By sharing best practices and providing mutual support, Philips is able to outperform competitors.

(*See Explanatory Note 1 at the end of the case study.*)

In Philips, business excellence, speed and teamwork are the hallmarks of business today and provide the road map to success. They define what the company has to do to thrive and prosper. The *BEST* process also specifies how to implement these imperatives, how to direct and focus the efforts – it is the engine that drives the implementation of what the company wants: a secure and prosperous position, now and in the future.

BEST – the Philips way to business excellence

BEST is a high-performance change engine that embraces the characteristics of the Philips Quality system and surpasses the PQA standards. *BEST* reinforces the significance of the tools and concepts of Philips Quality for building the winning organization. Philips believes that the *BEST* way to business excellence is through the continuous four-step cycle of Plan, Do, Check, Act (PDCA – Figure C7.1), both at the strategic and operational level:

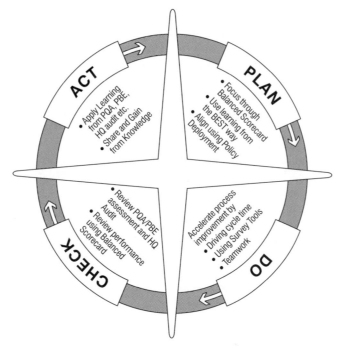

Figure C7.1 *The Plan, Do, Check, Act (PDCA) cycle in Philips*

- **Plan: Translate strategy into action**

  Philips knows that clarity about the goals and the way to achieve them is essential to transform a common vision into a shared reality. Management teams identify, prioritize and align key goals through Balanced Scorecards and Policy Deployment. The goals and the actions to achieve the goals as well as targets and dates are specified and agreed upon at all levels.

  The Balanced Scorecards specify the business priorities based on a cause-and-effect analysis. This analysis takes into account the requirements of all stakeholders, and incorporates the learning from reviews.

  Policy Deployment in Philips communicates and translates these priorities through successive organizational layers, ensuring that all employees pull in the same direction towards clearly defined and cascaded goals.

- **Do: Manage processes**

  In Philips, processes are recognized as the drivers of business results:

  - Cycle time is a powerful driver of process improvement. Reduction of cycle time drives the expansion of a process's capability.
  - Process survey tools reveal priorities for improvement and indicate what should be done next.
  - Cross-functional teams co-operate across functional boundaries with the total business chain as their common focus.

The way Philips improves business results, therefore, is to improve the performance of its business processes. Management teams identify their main business processes and organize cross-functional teams to improve and maintain process performance. Team competitions promote working in process improvement teams.

● **Check: Review processes and results**
Review of business performance shows, in business-specific terms, how results have been achieved. The ability of Philips to learn and improve continuously is seen as its most sustainable competitive advantage:
– Operational progress is reviewed with the Balanced Scorecard.
– The PBE model is used to assess improvement of the total business.
– Headquarter audits assess *BEST* leadership.

● **Act: Respond to the review**
Conclusions from the review lead to consolidation of achievements and start a next cycle of improvement.
Applying the learning from audits and reviews closes the improvement cycle. Knowledge management makes current understanding available throughout the company.

Systematic practice of these steps integrates the management of improvement with the management of the business. Philips recognizes that hands-on leadership is essential and *BEST* leaders are required to give their teams the inspiration, information and instruments to be creative and self-directive.

The *BEST* tools

In Philips, *BEST* merges the management of improvement with the management of the business through four tools that tie improvement efforts to business results:

BBS – Business Balanced Scorecards
PST – Process Survey Tools
PBE – PBE Assessments
HQA – Headquarter Audits.

The *BEST* competencies

It is recognized that the success of the *BEST* way in Philips is dependent on how well the organization is led and how well it learns, i.e.:

● Knowledge management
● Professional competence and
● Leadership competencies

are vital.

The Balanced Scorecards

Balanced Scorecards are used in Philips to identify and monitor the drivers of results and facilitate faster, more informed decision making. The Business Balanced Scorecard (BBS) focuses on the factors that are critical for business success and presents them in a chain of four perspectives (Figure C7.2).

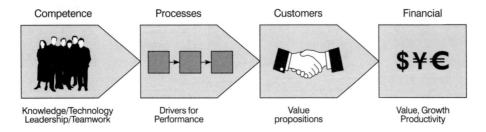

Figure C7.2 *The four perspectives of the BBS*

Philips concentrates on developing the competencies that are required to manage business processes that provide products and services that satisfy customers who, by buying the products, determine the financial results. The BBS enables Philips to explore and monitor the cause-and-effect relationships between these four perspectives, financial indicators showing what to achieve in the common language of money. Indicators in the other three categories show how the desired results will be achieved. In other words, understanding what drives top performance is the basis for deciding how to achieve top results in Philips.

(See Explanatory Note 2 at the end of the case study.)

Process survey tools

A Philips survey gives a team a tool to assess their business process and develop an improvement plan based on their assessment. The team assesses elements that need to be in place in order to raise process performance on a ten-step scale, from basic to world-class performance.

Philips has found a Process Survey to be a powerful tool because:

- Step descriptions indicate what should be done to reach the next level and can readily be translated into a specific improvement plan.
- The maturity profile indicates weak and strong areas and suggests improvement priorities.
- The maturity profile enables sharing of best practices through comparison with other processes and other units.

PBE assessments

PBE assessments against the 'new' EFQM Excellence Model (Figure C7.3) identify areas for improvement and put enablers and results in an all-encompassing perspective.

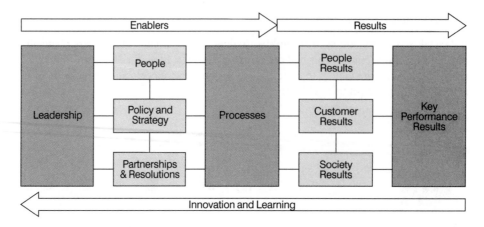

Figure C7.3 *The EFQM excellence model*

Building on the positive experiences with self-assessments and peer audits in the PQA programme, the PBE model is used in a similar way, albeit with a stronger link to the regular performance management process.

Headquarter audits

In a headquarter audit (HQA), peers assess how a business management team provides leadership in achieving business excellence using the world-class standard specified in the PBE model. They look into the way a Business Centre manages its internal processes and its constituent businesses:

- Are the right measures defined?
- Are cause-and-effect relationships that are characteristic for the business identified?
- Are business processes assessed?
- Are cycle times reduced?
- How is learning shared?
- Is the PDCA cycle applied to the *BEST* process itself?

By asking such questions the managers/auditors help their colleagues to review the effectiveness of their *BEST* Policy and validate the results of their self-assessment. Further objectives are to share learning across the organization and to strengthen the commitment of top management.

(See Explanatory Note 3 at the end of the case study.)

Knowledge management

Philips recognizes that knowledge management (KM) – the proficiency with which a company creates, acquires and disseminates knowledge and turns it into a business competence – is the basic source of competitive advantage. Knowledge can be made accessible through information systems with directories of experts (Philips Yellow Pages) and databases of best practices. But information technology, although vital, is merely an enabler. People are only inclined to offer and seek knowledge when they can interact freely, motivated by a shared vision. Trust and teamwork are the fundamental enablers of KM in Philips. Good managers, knowing that, raise the capability of the organization by creating a collaborative environment in which explicit and tacit knowledge is actively shared.

Knowledge management is the result of several developments. On the demand side in Philips is: business process management, global competition, speed of change; whilst on the supply side is: information systems using Intranet, peer audits using the PQA or PBE model, balanced scorecards that explore cause-and-effect relationships, survey tools that facilitate benchmarking, leadership competencies which include coaching.

Applying the lessons learned in Philips is the completion of the PDCA cycle and knowledge management means to expand 'applying the lessons learned' to 'sharing the lessons learned and learning from the lessons others learned'.

Professional competence

Philips has numerous examples of professional excellence. The financial function, the manufacturing function, the purchasing function, the logistics function, all have developed or adopted frameworks for raising their performance. Significant resources have been dedicated to raising the level of professionalism of these communities. However, it is recognized that this is not enough and that world-class performance requires breakthroughs in cross-functional business processes such as product creation, demand generation and order fulfilment. The goal of *BEST* is to integrate improvements across the business chain and thereby make professionalism more relevant for the stakeholders.

Leadership competencies

The recently defined leadership competencies in Philips describe the behaviour of the individual manager that is required to achieve business excellence:

Task-oriented competencies
- Determined to achieve excellent results (translates vision into challenging goals).
- Focuses on the market (understands the market and external environment).
- Finds better ways (uses every opportunity to improve business processes).

People-oriented competencies
- Demands top performance (is role model for top performance).
- Inspires commitment (persuades the team to share the vision).
- Develops self and others (coaches and manages knowledge).

In Philips, *BEST* leaders integrate the management of improvement with management of the business.

Communicating *BEST*

The Philips Intranet site is available to guide people in finding the training, tools, publications, best practices, links to other sites and information to support them in implementing *BEST*. The site, called Philips Yellow Pages, provides the opportunity to easily contact people and learn about their fields of experience. Employees are encouraged to e-mail to an address and, by automatic reply, they receive a registration form.

The Philips magazine *Quality Matters* serves as a platform for the communication of best practices across the entire Philips organization, and informs Philips management about new developments and guidelines in *BEST*.

Both the Intranet site and *Quality Matters* contain announcements of new publications to support *BEST*, as well as reply forms for ordering materials and publications, and for subscribing to *Quality Matters*.

Explanatory notes

1 Philips Quality Teams

A Philips Quality Team is a group of people, in any business, at any level, who join together to improve the way they work by focusing on their process(es). Management makes sure they have the time, place, knowledge and authority to analyse their processes, identify problems, find answers and implement solutions.

The Philips Quality Network creates the conditions under which the Philips Quality Teams can flourish. The network consists of the Corporate Quality Council, the Quality Councils of the division and business units and the Quality Steering Groups of plants. They are responsible for driving the change process and monitoring progress.

Quality Support Managers assist their Quality Council or Steering Group by preparing policy, proposing initiatives and supporting the PBE process. They help managers to coach their teams by organizing workshops and providing problem-solving tools. They support teams by facilitating teamwork and problem solving.

2 Business Balanced Scorecards (BBS)

The illustrations of balanced scorecards in Figures C7.4 and C7.5 are taken from a Philips Business Unit. The first scorecard is a Strategy Review example (Figure C7.4); the second is an Operations Review example (Figure C7.5). (*Note*: The data is for illustrative purposes only.)

Traffic light reporting

Colours are used to indicate how the actual performance compares with the target entitlement:

Green   –   meeting entitlement
Yellow   –   performance is in line with the plan
Red   –   performance is below plan.

Balanced Scorecard (illustrative data)		Check Points		
Critical Success Factor	Performance Indicator	Target '99	Target '01	Target '03
Financial				
Economic Profit Related	Euro (min)	145	250	330
Sales	Euro (min)	1822	1950	2200
Ifo	%age of sales	12.50%	13.50%	15.00%
Working capital	Turnover speed	4.5	5.3	6.2
Productivity	Sales/wagebill	3.1	3.5	3.9
Cashflow	Euro (min)	250	380	470
Customers				
Market share	%age	19.00%	20.50%	22.30%
Delivery performance	ICSL	93%	95%	97%
Customer complaints	Max time to closure - days	21	14	10
Sales of new products	%age of total sales	tbd	tbd	tbd
Brand index	Absolute value - nominal	110	110	110
Survey results	Score	7.5	8	8.5
Processes				
BEST Marketing	Survey tool score	3	6	8
BEST Purchasing	Survey tool score	3	6	8
BEST Manufacturing	Survey tool score	4	7	9
Cycletime reduction	%age from last check point	30	30	30
Competence				
Organisation capability	PBE achievement	tbd	tbd	tbd
Leadership assessment	Approached action plan	Complete	Complete	Complete
BEST training	%age of target group complete	90%	95%	95%
QIC participation	%age of population	25%	40%	50%

■ Below Plan   ☐ Meeting Plan   ▨ Meeting Entitlement

Figure C7.4 *Strategy review*

In this business unit example, the columns headed 'target' state the expected performance that can be below what is actually required. For instance for some processes, the '99 Process Survey score is expected to be below 3. It is therefore reported red although it is foreseen in the plan.

Indicators at the level of a business

These may include:

Financial
Economic Profit Realized
Income from Operations
Working Capital
Operational Cash Flow
Inventory Turns
Productivity

Processes
Process Survey Tool Score
% Reduction in Process
Cycle Time
Number of Engineering Changes
Capacity Utilization
Order Response Time
Process Capability (Cpk)

Customers	Competence
Ranking in Customer Survey	PQA/PBE Score
Market Share	Leadership Competence
Repeat Order Rate	% Patent-protected Turnover
Complaints	*BEST* Training Days/Employee
Brand Index	QIC participation

Indicators below business level

Many business indicators can be deployed to next levels in Philips.

Other indicators cannot meaningfully be consolidated and will only be reported at operational level. For instance: Yield, Cycle Time, Defects (PPM), Mean Repair Time, Back Orders, and Incorrect Delivery.

Balanced Scorecard (illustrative data)		**Check Points**			
Critical Success Factor	Performance Indicator	Target Q1	Target Q2	Target Q3	Target Q4
Financial					
Economic Profit Related	USD min	6	12	20	28
Sales	USD min	109	231	363	500
Ifo	%age of sales	9.0%	8.7%	9.3%	10.0%
Working capital	%age of sales	13.5%	13.3%	12.8%	11.1%
Productivity	USD	0.11/0.43	0.11/0.42	0.10/0.41	0.10/0.40
Cashflow	USD min	16	20	30	55
Customers					
Market share	%age	10.9%	11.1%	11.2%	11.3%
Delivery performance	CSL	85%	85%	90%	93%
Partnership Programme	%age of sales	0%	0%	5%	10%
Brand index	Absolute value	1.40	1.36	1.33	1.31
Survey results	Score	7.1	7.2	7.4	7.5
Processes					
BEST Marketing	Survey tool score		1.5	1.5	3
BEST Purchasing	Cost reduction	-0.5%	-1.0%	-1.5%	-2.5%
Cycle time	Export Surabaya - days	45	40	37	35
	Malu GLS - days	30	27	23	21
BEST Manufacturing	Survey tool score	3.5	4.5	5.0	6.0
Competence					
Organization capability	PQA 90 achievement	0	0	1	3 units
Leadership assessment	Approached action plan	20%	30%	65%	Complete
BEST training	%age of target group complete	45%	70%	90%	90%
QIC participation	%age of population		15%	15%	20%

■ Below Plan   □ Meeting Plan   ▨ Meeting Entitlement

Figure C7.5 *Operations review*

3 Headquarter Audits

Objectives

The objectives of the headquarter audits are:

- To help the auditees review the effectiveness of their implementation of the Philips Business Excellence Policy by identifying strong points and areas for improvement.

- To validate the results of the self-assessment of the organization (optional).
- To provide an opportunity for shared learning across PDs.
- To strengthen the visible commitment and involvement of top management.

Scope

The scope of the audit is: how the headquarters manages its internal processes and its interfaces with the constituent businesses to provide leadership in business excellence throughout the entire organization.

Auditees

Headquarters of the divisions (PDs) and the company HQ are audited. The list of audits to be conducted is reviewed annually by the Philips Quality Policy Board and approved by the Group Management Committee (GMC).

The PDs are responsible for organizing similar audits at the Business level.

Audit team

The audit team consists of 3 to 4 auditors. All members are either members of a PD Management Team or of the GMC.

A GMC member will act as the lead auditor. Most of the auditors are experienced in PQA auditing and trained in PBE.

A PD/CQB Quality Manager acts as facilitator and, to ensure some continuity, one or two of the auditors are taken from the previous audit team.

Reference for the audit

The PBE model is the reference for the audit. As a one-day audit does not allow a comprehensive audit result on all PBE criteria, the audit focuses on the enabling factors of PBE (about two-thirds of the audit time is spent on the enabling factors).

Primary focus

The audit team's primary focus is on the implementation of the *BEST* approaches as a customized subset of the enablers defined in the PBE model. The most important *BEST* approaches focus on policy deployment and process management through the concepts of balanced scorecards and process survey tools.

Timing

The Headquarters Audits are conducted once a year, attuned to the performance review cycle. If another (award-based) audit has been planned for an organization in the same period, the HQ Audit can be shifted. The schedule of the audits is agreed and reviewed in the Philips Quality Policy Board and GMC. The audit takes one whole day plus the evening before.

Audit briefing pack

One week before the audit, an audit briefing pack must be made available to the auditors. This pack enables the auditors to prepare for the audit, to select the issues to focus on and to select the persons to be interviewed.

The pack includes:

- Organization charts.
- An introduction to the organization, its processes and improvement programme.

It is also strongly recommended to include:

- PQA or PBE self-assessment scores and material underlying some or all of the subcriteria.
- Improvement plans and information on improvement teams.

Typical programme

First evening – Presentation by CEO, including Q & A of auditee
                  Audit team meeting to select focus areas

Next day   – Teams of 2 auditors meet with individuals or groups
                 Working lunch for the audit team
                 Audits by 1 or 2 auditors who walk around
                 Meeting to reach a consensus
                 Presentation of the audit report, discussion of main issues
                 Evaluation and closing discussions.

Presentation by the auditee

A short presentation to the auditors is made, focusing on:

- Improvements since the last audit (if an audit has taken place before).
- Explaining the improvement plan and its links to the various inputs.
- How resulting improvements of the main processes are measured.
- Linking these improvements to the business results.

Audit report by the auditors

The audit reports contain:

- Strong points and areas for improvement, preferably addressed per PBE criterion.
- If applicable: validation of the self-assessment.

Distribution of the audit report is restricted to the auditees and the members of the audit team.

An evaluation of the audit process is sent by the facilitator to the head of CQB.

The audit team will not communicate any findings outside the group of participants without the prior consent of the audited organization.

Auditor's preparation for the audit

The facilitator takes the initiative for the audit according to the overall schedule agreed by the GMC. He/she:

- Fixes the date approximately six months in advance.
- Clarifies roles and tasks within the audit team.

- Determines who will be interviewed during the audit (audit plan).
- Discusses the overall business issues this particular organization is facing, based on the different frames of reference the auditors may have.
- Ensures that the overall purpose of the audit is to help the auditee.
- Ensures attention is paid to details to achieve excellence – the unit is expecting a thorough audit – it does not expect the auditors to cover all points, but expects them to probe certain areas in depth.

Auditee's preparations for the audit

These should include:

- Prepare the organization for the upcoming audit: communicate the objectives of the audit and the expected working approach of the audit team.
- Prepare the presentation for the audit team.
- Have a meeting room available where the auditors can meet undisturbed during the audit day.

Questions

1 Describe the 'quality journey' in Philips, drawing a chart of activities which a company in a similar industry could follow if it was beginning the implementation of TQM.
2 Evaluate the approach taken by Philips and offer constructive criticism and suggestions for further improvement.
3 What role has teamwork played in the development of Business Excellence (*BEST*) in Philips?

Acknowledgement

The author is grateful for the contribution made by Paul Morgan in the preparation of this case study.

Part Five

Implementation

C8

BBC Broadcasting & Presentation

At the heart of all TQM initiatives is the customer–supplier relationship. Given that this relationship is an integral part of the day-to-day processes that connect customer and supplier at each stage of the business, the importance of realigning processes with the TQM philosophy is key to its success. In Chapter 13 seven steps were proposed to effect the continuous cycle of commitment, communication and cultural change that are essential aspects of the TQM model:

- Gain commitment to change.
- Develop a shared mission.
- Define measurable objectives.
- Derive CSFs from the mission.
- Identify critical processes and gain ownership.
- Analyse critical processes into subprocesses and activities and tasks.
- Monitor and adjust process alignment in response to problems.

This is the model that has been adopted in this Business Plan for Total Quality for the BBC Broadcasting & Presentation department.

Context

Broadcasting & Presentation is responsible for the on-air branding and promotion of all the BBC's channels. This includes public service and commercial channels. Broadcasting & Presentation's media planning section schedules this promotion, ensuring that it is appropriately demographically targeted and delivers against the priorities defined in the marketing strategy set by Marketing & Communications. An important objective for this area is the development of a cross-promotional strategy, i.e. how a channel's air time should be managed to promote other, related channels.

The department is also responsible for the detailed planning of programme junctions – the air time between programmes. As part of this process, Broadcasting & Presentation aims to ensure that within the constraints imposed by the skeleton schedule it inherits from Scheduling, programmes run as closely to the published times as possible.

During recent years a major activity has been the launching of new commercial and public service channels. This activity has been responsible for the diversification of the department's customer base and an almost 50% increase in staff numbers (currently almost 600). 25% of the department's income derives from this new business.

In the first step, the Broadcasting & Presentation Senior Management Team revised their mission statement. This need to redefine the department's purpose and aspirations was prompted by an acknowledgement of the dramatic increase in the range and volume of activity undertaken over the recent past, the fact that the department was now servicing many more customers than before and that, for the first time, there were potential competitors in the field for the services that Broadcasting & Presentation provided, at least in the sphere of commercial channel development.

It was also recognized that these environmental factors were generating a need to overhaul how the department was delivering the services it provided to its customers. The development associated with new business was being bolted onto old pre-existing structures and processes which had evolved in an environment in which only two public service channels had existed as opposed to the proliferating multi-channel environment that was emerging.

The mission statement

The mission statement that emerged out of a lengthy process of facilitated debate was:

> We aim to enhance all our brands by helping audiences find, enjoy and value our clients' services.

This mission statement is admirable for its brevity and it does define the department's role – the phrase 'enhance all our brands' clearly states, albeit in highly generic terms, the core business activity. It could, however, be argued that 'enhance all our brands' could equally apply to Marketing & Communications and needs qualifying in terms of the generic activities of promotion, media planning and play-out.

The mission statement takes a long-term view and signals change. For instance, the explicit reference to 'clients' suggests the provision of a service to a customer – this embodies a key concept to which the Senior Team is committed and which will entail a profound cultural change in the way the department performs its activities in future – namely, taking a much more customer-focused approach.

It also takes a long-term view in that it deliberately does not specify that these clients need necessarily be BBC or Joint Venture clients. It is conceivable that, in the future, the current regulatory restrictions that inhibit the department's ability to seek external customers may be lifted – and the department may be pitching for business with external, non-BBC associated companies.

The department's distinctive competency is embodied in the phrase 'helping audiences find, enjoy and value our clients' services'. In the BBC and Joint Venture context, this recognizes a key advantage that Broadcasting & Presentation has over potential competitors and one which enables it to deliver a primary objective of the Broadcast directorate of which it is a part. This is its ability to reach targeted audiences through strategically placed cross-promotion across the three media of television, radio and on-line, thereby encouraging audiences to sample the full range of BBC and Joint Venture services. This aggregation of Broadcasting & Presentation's activities enables it to deliver the key top-level Broadcast directorate objective: 'To make life better for all through broadcasting and all we do to support it.'

It could be argued, therefore, that, with one iteration which incorporates a more detailed definition of the activities undertaken by the business, the mission statement satisfies the essential criteria. With this one revision the mission statement would read:

> Through the unrivalled excellence of our on-air promotion, media planning and play-out services, we aim to enhance all our brands so that audiences find, enjoy and value our clients' services.

Defining measurable objectives

Out of the discussions that arose on the mission it was agreed that Broadcasting & Presentation needed to develop objectives around the following areas:

Objective	Measure
Deliver creativity, innovation and excellence in line with our clients' brand propositions	Number of industry awards; press mentions; high customer satisfaction ratings; focus groups on audience attitudes to channel events and promotions
Review senior team structure and recommend how it might be altered to deliver a more customer-focused approach	Customer focus is an objective for each senior team member; number of days spent per team member on formal training based on delivering customer focus; comparison of customer feedback before and after introduction of customer focus as an objective
As part of an overall HR strategy produce plans for attracting, developing and retaining people with the right skills and motivation to deliver Broadcasting & Presentation's mission	Existence of a written talent plan. Retention of staff defined as key by the Succession plan; staff satisfaction ratings as measured in the staff survey

Objective	Measure
Deliver a communication strategy as to how Broadcasting & Presentation can present itself as delivering a flexible quality service at a competitive price in line with brand proposition	Benchmark with competitor; measure number of forums – external and internal – at which Broadcasting & Presentation communicates the services it offers
Develop a strategy for positioning the department to shape the opportunities and competitive threats presented by new technologies	Number of 'first in field' technological advances adopted by the department; attendance at key technical conferences, etc.; savings and improved efficiencies attributable to the adoption of new technologies

Whilst these objectives connect with the mission, the analysis of critical success factors and related measures that follows suggests ways in which these broad objectives might be more precisely honed. They also suggest that there are other objectives in addition to these that Broadcasting & Presentation might usefully include as future objectives.

Critical success factors and impact on the mission

In reaching critical success factors there needs to be a process whereby all the possible impacts on the mission are enumerated. These can then be categorized into the CSFs – the minimum subgoals that the department must have or needs to achieve its mission. Each CSF has to be necessary and together they have to be sufficient to achieve the mission. A detailed breakdown of categories can be found in the Appendix at the end of this case study, but the core categories are:

- Research into audience perceptions/improved audience understanding
- Systems
- Competition
- Talent
- Growth in customers, i.e. greater diversity
- New technology
- Political/regulatory impacts
- Organizational impacts within the BBC.

CSFs

From these broad categories of impacts we can start to define what Broadcasting & Presentation's CSFs should be. Selecting according to the principle that each CSF must be necessary if Broadcasting & Presentation is to deliver its mission, and that together all the CSFs are sufficient to ensure that the mission is achieved, delivers the following CSFs. Below are relevant key performance indicators:

CSF	KPI
We must have distinctive on-air branding	Qualitative research measuring: ● percentage sample recall of branding and promotions against key competitors ● percentage sample rating of attributes associated with distinctiveness in relation to on-air branding and promotions ● percentage of sample who perceive on-air branding, promotion and continuity voices as having a positive, negative or nil impact on overall channel perceptions
We must have viewers aware of BBC programmes	Qualitative research via tracking studies and focus groups measuring percentage of 'available to view' audience who went on to watch first episode of a series as a result of on-air promotion were guided to a programme by information in an on-air promotion
We need talented and motivated staff	● Departmental percentage turnover rates ● Percentage turnover rates as compared with the rest of Broadcast ● Percentage of Broadcasting & Presentation who rated highly in the 1998 Staff Survey: satisfaction with work environment existence of opportunities for personal growth and development ● Percentage rates of absenteeism: across department as a whole and by staff category ● Percentage of staff involved in Training & Development Initiatives ● Number of staff who won industry awards; number of 'hero-grams' from clients and internal customers
We need satisfied clients	Levels of satisfaction measured by: ● percentage of new business attributable to existing clients ● percentage of clients who commission repeat business ● percentage of clients who rate the service that Broadcasting & Presentation provides as good or excellent in follow-up questionnaires and interviews with clients (direct and via third-party consultancy)
We need new business opportunities	● Percentage of new channel business pitches awarded over competitors to Broadcasting & Presentation

CSF	KPI
We must have robust IT and technical systems	• Number of breakdowns on air, over a minute's duration, attributable to technical or systems failure • Failure of internal systems identified in the departmental Risk Assessment plan as critical to the business affecting output for over an hour, over 4 hours, more than 24 hours

The next stage was to break down these critical success factors into critical processes with defined TQ Performance Measures and then to develop a matrix which enables the business to prioritize the processes that need addressing according to:

i) how many CSFs each process impacts upon
ii) how well each process is currently affected.

An aspect of the TQM approach at this stage is the assignment of ownership of each critical process by a member of the Senior Team. The table below illustrates how this currently applies within Broadcasting & Presentation. Interestingly, what we find when we come to cross-reference CSFs and critical processes is that the critical process which has most ambiguity of ownership is in fact the one that has the highest scoring CSFs attached to it. In terms of the TQ measures, it should be assumed that wherever possible year-on-year data and trends should be used.

Critical process	Owner	TQ performance measures
Develop and manage staff in line with the needs of the business	HR Manager	• Percentage of appraisals completed on time • Percentage of staff attending weekly communication forums • Percentage of overall spend allocated to training and development • Percentage of staff attending training with a specific customer focus • number of training days per staff allocation of training spend on core versus non-core activity
Produce high-quality promotions	Head of Promotions	• Number of industry awards year on year • Number of favourable press mentions per year • Percentage of promotions approved by clients as meeting criteria defined in creative brief • Number of upheld adjudications against promotions by regulatory bodies • Number of trails per promoter per year on year • Cost per promotion year on year

Critical process	Owner	TQ performance measures
Apply audience research to our activities	Shared between Head of Media Planning/Head of Transmission/Head of Promotion	• Number of audience research presentations per year and percentage staff attendance • Percentage of staff actively using research data in day-to-day activities • Percentage of overall budget allocated to research specific to Broadcasting & Presentation
Manage air time across channels	Head of Media Planning	• Number of promotion TVRs (measure of air time value) by service and by channel, year on year • Cross-promotion between services: year-on-year promotion minutage and numbers of TVRs • Number of priority promotions achieved
Identify potential on-air problems that could jeopardize the brand	Head of transmission	• Number of incidents where Broadcasting & Presentation staff intervened in order to ensure compliance with BBC/ITC Guidelines • Number of content alert announcements made by Broadcasting & Presentation • Number of schedule re billings issued per year
Plan the schedule in detail	Head of Transmission	• Number of programmes transmitted more than four minutes later than billed time • Number of programmes started more than one minute early
Transmit programmes	Head of Transmission	• Number of programme breakdowns of over one minute attributable to Broadcasting & Presentation human error or failure of Broadcasting & Presentation equipment • Percentage of programmes transmitted satisfactorily

If we then map critical processes against critical success factors we can identify those processes that most impact on the achievement of CSFs.

Critical processes	Critical success factors						Number of CSFs impacted by CP and Quality
	CSF 1	CSF 2	CSF 3	CSF 4	CSF 5	CSF 6	
	Distinctive on-air branding	High awareness of BBC priority programmes	Talented/ motivated staff	Satisfied clients	New business	Robust systems	
CP1 Transmit programmes				**		**	2A
CP2 Produce high-quality programmes to brief		**	**	**	**	**	5B
CP3 Understand and apply audience research	**	**	**	**	**	**	6C
CP4 Detailed schedule planning			**	**		**	3A
CP5 Manage the air time effectively		**	**	**	**	**	5E
CP6 Train staff	**	**	**				3B
CP7 Monitor competition	**	**		**	**		4D
CP8 Editorialize over output		**	**	**			3B

A = Excellent, B = Good, C = Fair, D = Bad, E = Embryonic Stage

From this we can deduce that the processes which impact most significantly on the CSFs and are done badly or are in an embryonic stage are the ones that most need to be focused on.

No. of CSFs impacted	E Embryonic	D Bad	C Fair	B Good	A Excellent
6			CP3		
5	CP5			CP2	
4		CP7		CP6	
3				CP8	CP4
2					CP1
1					

The matrix suggests that it will be important to develop CP5 (Manage air time effectively) and improve CP3 (Understand and apply audience research). As mentioned earlier, the team needs to start by assigning ownership of this process to one of their number.

CP2 (Produce high-quality promotions to brief) includes a high proportion of CSFs and is currently perceived as being done well, so careful tracking of client satisfaction levels and regular evaluation of competitor output are recommended in order to try to improve performance further. CP7 (Monitor competition) has a relatively high proportion of CSFs and is perceived as being done badly, which makes it a priority.

This model of defining the CF or Critical Process, assigning ownership and establishing measures which can then be acted on to deliver improvement can be carried on down through the organization, ensuring that there is a consistent approach which can engage staff at every level and across all functions. This can be illustrated by breaking down a key process into its subprocesses – the example given is the subprocess involved in producing a promotion to brief.

Critical Success Factor

We must have a high awareness of BBC priority programmes.

Measures: Percentage of 'available to view' audience who went on to view first episode of a series as a result of on-air promotion; percentage recall of promotion among a sample comprising the demographic groups at which the programme was targeted.

Critical Process

We need to produce high-quality promotions.

Measures: Percentage of overall trails commissioned which clients (i.e. Channel Controllers or Marketing & Communications) accept as meeting the criteria of the creative brief; number of industry awards per year; number of favourable press mentions per year.

Subprocess

Team allocated to produce promotion collectively brainstorm creative ideas.

Measure: Percentage of overall ideas that match criteria specified in the creative brief.

Activity

Individual Assistant Producer produces draft script and storyboard to test the ideas generated.

Measures: Delivery against stipulated timescale of the production process. Extent to which execution matches or comes in under budget. (At this stage with major priorities, there is often a check with the client that the criteria in the brief are being met – not a measure in the hard quantifiable sense but an important means of eliciting levels of client satisfaction.)

Task

Individual Assistant Producer develops draft storyboard into off-line version of promotion.

Measures: Delivery according to timescale and budget; extent to which promotion meets required duration; assessment against specific requirements of the creative brief, i.e. suitability pre-watershed; compliance with requirements of regulatory bodies such as Broadcasting Standards Council.

Teams

What this analysis of a subprocess demonstrates is how the Adair model (see Chapter 11) of action-centred leadership and teamwork can function through a hierarchy of quality teams equipped with the agreed measures for evaluating each stage of the process. In the case of Promotion, the benefits of teamworking are apparent in the strong supportive culture that exists in this part of the department, combined with a strong sense of individual ownership for the making of each promotion and the fact that the task is clearly defined in terms of timescales, budgets and available resource. Although not formalized, the process of taking individual output back to the team for critical evaluation – in terms of measurement, the difficult bit – is integrated into the processes of the four core Promotions teams. A fully-fledged TQM approach is not in place because no formal framework exists for it in the department. Embryonically, however, in Promotions there is a culture which is aligned with the overall TQM approach.

Conclusion

What the analysis in this business plan illustrates is that a systematic approach to the business in the public sector is helpful and that the Senior Team has to be committed to the process of change that this implies. Through a process of clarifying objectives, developing agreed measures for the CSFs and critical processes of the department and taking a team-based approach, there is potential for motivating and developing the department's people in a way which would give greater clarity of purpose to the business. It would also transform that customer–supplier relationship which, it is gradually being realized, is at the heart of all Broadcasting & Presentation's activities.

Questions

1 Evaluate the approach used by BBC Broadcasting for general application in the public sector – health, education, armed services, social services, tax collection, etc.
2 Discuss the issues of measurement in an organization such as this one, and evaluate the approach taken to measurement 'recommended' by the BBC.
3 How should the senior team in BBC Broadcasting & Presentation develop their thinking to sustain the momentum of total quality/business excellence?

Acknowledgement

The author is grateful for the contribution made by Helen Rowlands in the preparation of this case study.

Appendix
Detailed breakdown according to category of the impacts affecting the CSFs of the BBC's Broadcasting & Presentation department

Audience research

Interpretation and application of 100 Faces of UK, a major new piece of audience/ marketing research – a way of segmenting the audience in terms that are particularly appropriate to a public service broadcaster – highly relevant to the media planning operation; supporting systems need to be in place to exploit this research fully.

Systems

Major process improvements could potentially be effected within Broadcasting & Presentation if the interfaces between various critical systems were developed. This is being taken forward under Project Darwin – Broadcasting & Presentation needs its priorities in terms of underlying systems improvements to be part of the Darwin agenda; failure to achieve this prioritization could affect the media planning operation in particular.

Competition

The importance of creative, distinctive output that differentiates our clients' channels and service from those of the competition is increasingly important in a multi-channel environment.

Talent

Costs inflating; expansion of channels means demand for most desirable staff; in purely financial terms our competitors are capable of offering more.

Growth in customers, i.e. greater diversity

Need to satisfy more clients, sometimes with conflicting demands; currently customers include Director of Television, Controller BBC ONE, Controller BBC TWO, Chief Executive Broadcast, UKTV Joint Venture, BBC Worldwide, BBC Corporate Affairs, BBC Radio, BBC Education, BBC News and BBC On Line.

New technology

The speed at which audiences take up new channels will impact on the success and survival of those channels – collapse of this business will mean reduced income and enforced redundancies among Broadcasting & Presentation staff; digital/analogue switch; take-up of interactive services; development of new means of delivery could make existing plant and processes redundant.

Political/regulatory impacts

Impact of devolution on drive for greater autonomy from Corporate Centre among the national broadcasters – could undermine effectiveness of media planning strategy and result in on-air brand dilution.

Organizational impacts within the BBC

Incorporation of Resources, currently a major supplier, could result in Broadcasting & Presentation needs being overridden by Resources' commercial imperatives; delegation of professional responsibility only (i.e. not managerial responsibility) for presentation staff in the Nations and in Radio is impeding the pan Broadcast integration of presentation processes; boundary issues, in relation to on-air branding and media planning, unresolved with the newly created Marketing & Communication function; accommodation shortages – the installation of play-out suites and equipment means the department is restricted to its existing location which has little capacity for expansion; the rest of Broadcast HQ staff are in a central location several miles away – potential impact on Broadcasting & Presentation's 'connectedness' with rest of Broadcast; requirement to deliver stringent efficiency cuts could impede the ability to make investments that deliver long-term benefits.

M implementation and policy deployment at ST Microelectronics

Company background and TQM

ST Microelectronics (formerly SGS-Thomson Microelectronics) is a global, independent semiconductor company which designs, develops, manufactures and markets a broad range of integrated circuits and discrete devices for a wide variety of microelectronic applications including telecommunications and computer systems, consumer equipment, automotive products, industrial automation and control systems.

In 1997 the company won the European Quality Award. This marked the progress made in developing as a world-class organization and also coincided with the tenth anniversary of the formation of the company created by the merger of Thomson Semiconducteur and SGS Microellecttronica.

In order to fully appreciate the achievement of the company in these ten years it is first necessary to describe some of the dynamics of the semiconductor industry since these dynamics shaped STM's TQM initiative. Microelectronics is one of the most competitive industries in the world, with more than 200 merchant suppliers, over 100 of them being global players, servicing a market of $130bn that has long-term CAGR of about 16%. Only three European companies are left in the top 20 worldwide ranking. The economic law of microelectronics is 'when the demand goes up – prices fall; when the demand goes down – prices fall'. Technological advance is very rapid; capital intensity is high. Spending on R&D runs at about 14–16% of sales, two to four times higher than most other industries. Every dollar of incremental sales requires a dollar of incremental investment, with the investment usually one year ahead of the sales.

In this environment companies tend to polarize into two groups: the broad line, global companies with market shares in the range of 4–7%; and narrow niche companies with market shares of less than 1%. A notable exception to this group structure is, of course, Intel, which has a narrow product base but a high market share.

In 1987 the two founder companies of ST saw themselves in a difficult position since neither was large enough to become a truly global world-class player and yet both had a reasonably broad product and technology base. The decision was therefore taken to merge the two bodies into one, creating a company which, in 1987, had:

Sales	$851m
Headcount	17,300 people
Profit/loss after tax	($203m)

Whilst this achieved a critical mass, the financial results were not encouraging and much work was clearly needed to transform the company into the organization which was the vision of the senior management team. The first years of the programme were devoted to rationalization and consolidation. At the same time, however, advantage was taken of the complementarity of the product and technology portfolios, customers, market strengths and production capacities. Attention was focused on eliminating the weaknesses and exploiting the strengths. Two of the early key goals were defined as being a rapid increase in sales and market share, together with a slimming down of production sites and the number of employees.

Unfortunately, as the programme developed the market suddenly hit one of the down cycles which the industry experiences and, in 1990, the improvements in financial results halted and, in fact, worsened. Immediately the 'traditional' management action programme was brought into play. There was a rapid 'downsizing' programme which hit people, product portfolio and, ultimately, market share. By examining this process in action, both within ST and other companies, the relationship rapidly dawned of the danger of it developing into a 'vicious spiral'. This brought about a review of the focus of the company and the determination to find a new way of proceeding which would give rise to the term 'virtuous spiral'.

In 1991 ST launched a TQM initiative based on the European Foundation for Quality Management (EFQM) model. In launching this effort there was total commitment from the CEO and all his executive staff. In fact, in December 1991 Pasquale Pistorio, CEO, stated that: 'TQM is a mandatory way of life in the corporation. SGS-Thomson will become a champion of this culture in the Western world.' These words needed to be backed by action and resource – both financial and people. Very quickly there was a framework put in place, based on an analysis, which determined that the key components of successful implementation of TQM should be:

- Organization
- Common Framework
- Local Initiatives
- Culture Change
- Mechanisms
- Policy Deployment.

Also the programme needed to be driven from the top down, not by diktat, but by example.

There was already in existence a corporate mission statement, but it was not closely linked in the minds of the staff with their day-to-day activities. Furthermore, it had been written shortly after the merger and did not totally reflect the needs of the company, the shareholders, the employees or the customers. It was, therefore, revised and became the key launching point for all the decisions which affected the future of the corporation.

The mission statement is both short and clear:

> To offer strategic independence to our partners worldwide, as a profitable and viable broad range semiconductor supplier.

This statement had implications regarding the size and dynamics of the corporation, resulting directly from the structure and investment needs of the semiconductor industry. Following the revitalization of the mission statement, there quickly followed publication of the corporation's:

- Objectives
- Strategic Guidelines
- Guiding Principles
- TQM Principles
- Statement of the Future.

All of these were published in a booklet titled *Shared Values*, which was circulated to all employees worldwide, in their local languages.

These initial efforts by the corporate management team would have been in vain if the necessary resources had not been provided to support the implementation of TQM. A corporate TQM support group was established, budgets were allocated and the executive management, including the CEO, allocated significant time to TQM implementation. In the initial phase, most of the time and effort went into training and communications, with regular bulletins, e-mails and brochures.

The policy deployment process allowed the corporate goals to be cascaded into local goals which were both realistic and challenging. The training programmes, targeted at 50 hours per employee per year, ensured that people had the skills to accept the goals and translate them into local action plans. The management were encouraged to recognize achievements at local, national and international level. Finally, strong efforts were made to break down the walls between the various parts of the organization and create an atmosphere in which cross-fertilization was not only accepted but actively encouraged, until it became a way of life.

These changes were not easily or readily accepted in all parts of the corporation. Whilst the benefits could be seen on an intellectual plane at a cultural level, some groups found it easier to move faster than others. The corporate TQM Vice President, Murray Duffin, described the process as 'pulling down the walls and using the bricks to build bridges'. The difficulty of achieving success cannot be underestimated. STM started with the advantage that many of its European staff had a fundamentally Latin culture and many of the managers had been exposed to American culture, either as a result of working in American companies or interfacing with American customers. Also the semiconductor industry had its own culture which was and still is very strong. None the less, cultural barriers still exist and STM had to find ways of working with many different cultures whilst trying to overlay a common STM culture, ways of working and vision of the future.

Policy Deployment at STM

Policy Deployment (PD) is the primary method used in STM to make TQM 'the way we manage' rather than something added to operational management. In order to make it effective, STM has simplified the approach, combining as many existing initiatives as possible, to leave only one set of key improvement goals deriving from both internal and external identified needs. In this process the management of STM also provided a mechanism for 'real time' visual follow-up of breakthrough priorities to support very rapid progress.

In STM, Policy Deployment is regarded as:

- The 'backbone' of TQM.
- The way to translate the corporate vision, objectives and strategies into concrete specific goals, plans and actions at the operative level.
- A means to focus everyone's contributions in support of employee empowerment.
- The mechanism for jointly identifying objectives and the actions required to obtain the expected results.
- A vehicle to ensure that the corporate quality, service and cost goals are given superordinate importance in annual operational planning and performance evaluation.
- The method to integrate the entire organization's daily priority activities with its long-term goals.
- A process to focus attention on managing STM's future, rather than the past.

Policy Deployment's place in STM's overall TQM scheme of continuous improvement is illustrated in Table C9.1.

A Policy Deployment manual, addressed to all managers at any level of ST Microelectronics, was developed as a methodological and operative user guide for those charged with planning and achieving significant improvement goals. Examples, detailed explanations and descriptions of tools/forms were included in the manual.

Policy Deployment operates at two levels: continuous focused improvement and strategic breakthrough – referred to as Level 1 and Level 2.

The yearly plan is designed by assembling the budget and improvement plan, but also taking into account the investment plan.

All these elements must be consistent and coherent. Current-year business result goals are defined in the budget and the underlying operations and capability improvement goals have to be approached using Policy Deployment. Among all the improvement goals, a very few (one to three per year) are then selected for a more intensive management. These are the breakthrough goals and must be managed using special attention and techniques. Policy Deployment goals have to be consistent with long-term policies, and, finally, everything must be consistent with and must be supported by the investment plan.

Continuously improving performance and capabilities, and especially achieving 'breakthroughs', i.e. dramatic improvements in short times, was the main task that each manager was asked to face and carry out in his/her activities. Once the importance of achieving dramatic goals was clear, the problem arose of how to identify and prioritize them. To assist, STM fixed four long-term policies (broad and generic objectives):

- Become number one in service.
- Be among the top three suppliers in quality.
- Have world-class manufacturing capabilities.
- Become a leader in TQM in the Western business world.

These long-term policies reflected the need to improve *strategic capabilities*. They were implemented progressively by achieving sequential sets of shorter-term goals focused on *operational capabilities*, *operational performance* and urgent requirements, as illustrated in Figure C9.1. STM recognized that a successful enterprise ensures consistency between its short-term efforts and long-term goals.

Table C9.1

Concern	Vehicle	Focus	Responsible	Frequency
Current-year business year	Budget and Operations Reviews, Accounting control	The past/results (Mainly 'What')	Operations management	Monthly/ Quarterly
Prioritize operating results and total capabilities improvement	Policy Deployment Level 1	The future/ processes (Mainly 'How')	Steering committees Action owners All involved personnel	Monthly/ Quarterly
Breakthrough improvements	Policy Deployment Level 2	The near future	Steering committees and all levels of involved personnel	Daily/ Weekly
Ad hoc improvements and problem solving	QIT/PST/ NWT	Past, present and future	Steering committee and team members	As necessary
Continuous improvement at departmental level	Next operation as customer (NOAC) Defects per million opportunities (DPMO)	The internal customer The work product	All department managers and personnel	As necessary

Urgencies	Short term	Medium term	Long term
● Removal of problems ● Catching of opportunities Examples: - Quality problem - Process breakdown - Customer complaint - Important opportunity	● Improvement of operational performance Examples: - JIT - Cycle time - Inventory turns - Defectiveness - Yield - Productivity	● Improvement of operational capabilities Examples: - Concurrent engineering - TPM - Logistics - Self-managing teams - Planning/ Scheduling	● Improvement of strategic capabilities Examples: - Human Resource capabilities - Technological breakthroughs - Multi-processing - Mixed design know-how - Time to market

Figure C9.1 *Example of objectives by different horizon*

Policy Deployment flow in STM

Figure C9.2 is a high-level schematic of the yearly planning flow, relating Budgeting and Policy Deployment in STM.

Figure C9.3 shows the sequential deployment, at different levels, of Policy Deployment goals and action plans, linked to the STM TQM 'Management Amplifier'. This illustrates four key requirements for good policy deployment:

- A negotiation at each level to agree means and goals or targets, illustrated by the 'catch ball' in Figure C9.3.
- The creation of action plans to achieve goals or targets.
- Review of action plan progress, and adjustment as necessary.
- Standardization of improvement to 'hold the gains'.

Figure C9.4 illustrates some of the Policy Deployment tools used to help with means analysis, ownership assignments and progress assurance. These tools were explained in detail in the manual for managers.

Approaches to manage and achieve the STM goals

The yearly plan comprised all the goals and the performances the company had to reach during the year. Goals related to sales volume, profit and loss, inventories, standard costs, expenses, etc., were generally managed by Management Control through the budget. In order to be more and more competitive, however, more challenging goals had to be identified each year and these goals – the ones that constitute the improvement plan – need 'Special Management' through a specific approach. This approach is Policy Deployment, in which a policy can be fully defined as the combination of goals/targets and means (Figure C9.5). The characteristics of the

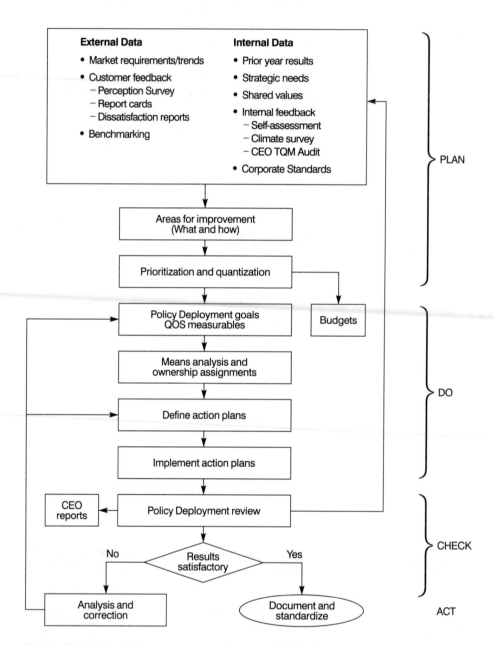

Figure C9.2 *Policy Deployment management process in STM*

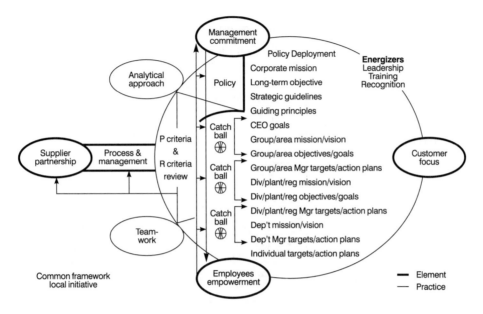

Figure C9.3 *The elements and practice of Policy Deployment in STM*

different approaches to manage the different goals (budget level and Policy Deployment level) are illustrated in Table C9.2.

Policy Deployment applies both to 'What' goals, i.e. mainly results oriented, and 'How' goals that are more related to operational, technological, organizational and behavioural aspects, mainly process oriented (Figure C9.6).

'How' is mainly concerned with improving capabilities and 'What' is mainly concerned with improving results, deriving from improved capabilities.

Drivers for 'What' goals are mainly corporate standards, prior results and Vision statements.

Drivers for 'How' goals are mainly Vision statements, climate survey, self-assessment, customer feedback and strategic plans.

Each level of the company (Corporate, Group, Division) must perform its own 'Whats' deployment and 'Hows' deployment.

'Whats' deployment means both targets and means deployment, where means deployment must be supported and must be coherent with 'Hows' deployment, that is generally related to a longer term Vision.

ST Microelectronics believes that, to be a total quality company, strategy, philosophy, values and goals must be transmitted down the organization, from level to level in a systematic way, to provide focus, clarity direction and alignment. For the company, Policy Deployment is the process through which goals, and the action plans to achieve them, in support of and consistent with the top-level corporate mission, strategic guidelines and objectives, are cascaded to all levels of the organization. Effective Policy Deployment ensures that STM's goals and actions are aligned 'from top floor to shop floor'.

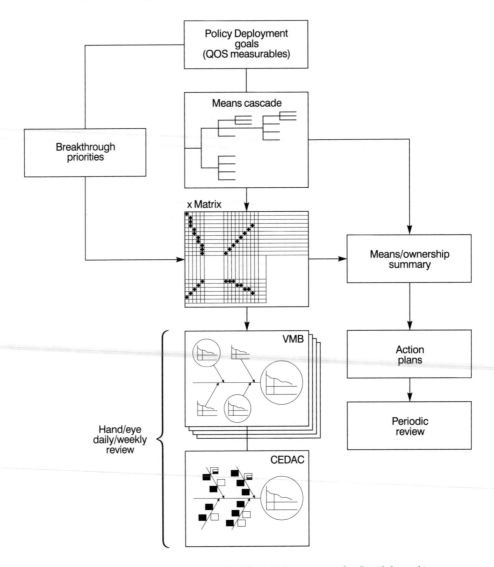

Figure C9.4 *Policy Deployment tools (VMB, Virtual Management for Breakthrough)*

The goal cascade involves a decomposition at each level to get to detailed goals that are readily obtainable. The x-matrix is a tool to aid this decomposition and fix ownership for the detailed goals.

Questions

1 Discuss the TQM implementation framework developed in this case and its application generally to other organizations, including those in the service sector.

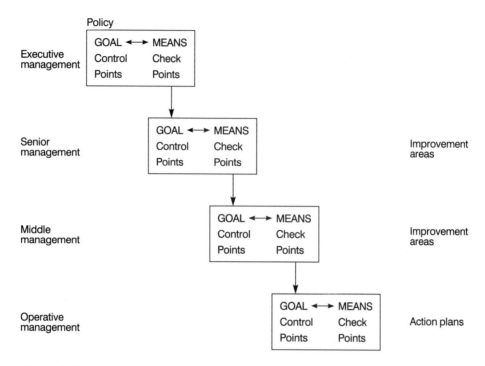

Figure C9.5 *Policy Deployment terminology illustrated*

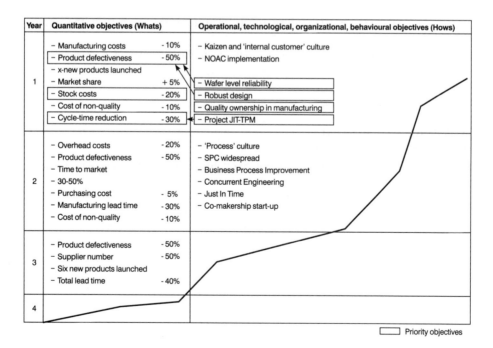

Figure C9.6 *'What' and 'How' goals (examples)*

Table C9.2

		Improvement goal	Improvement approach	Drivers
Budget level	{	☐ Business as usual	☐ Maintenance growth sporadic or undefined	☐ Budgets ☐ Competition ☐ Customers ☐ Sops routine ☐ Tactical opportunities
2 levels of policy deployment	{	☐ Focused improvement (Policy Deployment)	☐ Kaizen	☐ Shared values ☐ Corporate standards ☐ Strategic focus ☐ Self assessment ☐ Benchmarking
		☐ Breakthrough (Policy Deploymnent and visual management)	☐ Quantum	☐ Vital priorities ☐ Benchmarking

2 How does the 'goal translation' approach relate to TQM – what are the linking factors?

3 Show how the approach used by STM could be applied to any change management problem.

Acknowledgement

The author is grateful for the contribution made by Murray Duffin in the preparation of this case study.

Appendix A

Three American gurus

A small group of American quality experts or 'gurus' have, in the past, advised industry throughout the world on how it should manage quality. The approaches of Philip B. Crosby, W. Edwards Deming and Joseph M. Juran, their similarities and differences, are presented briefly here.

Philip B. Crosby

Crosby's four absolutes of quality:

- Definition – conformance to requirements.
- System – prevention.
- Performance standard – zero defects.
- Measurement – price of non-conformance.

He offers management fourteen steps to improvement:

1 Make it clear that management is committed to quality.
2 Form quality improvement teams with representatives from each department.
3 Determine where current and potential quality problems lie.
4 Evaluate the cost of quality and explain its use as a management tool.
5 Raise the quality awareness and personal concern of all employees.
6 Take actions to correct problems identified through previous steps.
7 Establish a committee for the zero defects programme.
8 Train supervisors to actively carry out their part of the quality improvement programme.
9 Hold a 'zero defects day' to let all employees realize that there has been a change.

10 Encourage individuals to establish improvement goals for themselves and their groups.
11 Encourage employees to communicate to management the obstacles they face in attaining their improvement goals.
12 Recognize and appreciate those who participate.
13 Establish quality councils to communicate on a regular basis.
14 Do it all over again to emphasize that the quality improvement programme never ends.

W. Edwards Deming

Deming's fourteen points for management are the following:

1 Create constancy of purpose towards improvement of product and service.
2 Adopt the new philosophy. We can no longer live with commonly accepted levels of delays, mistakes, defective workmanship.
3 Cease dependence on mass inspection. Require, instead, statistical evidence that quality is built in.
4 End the practice of awarding business on the basis of price tag.
5 Find problems. It is management's job to work continually on the system.
6 Institute modern methods of training on the job.
7 Institute modern methods of supervision of production workers. The responsibility of foremen must be changed from numbers to quality.
8 Drive out fear, so that everyone may work effectively for the company.
9 Break down barriers between departments.
10 Eliminate numerical goals, posters and slogans for the workforce asking for new levels of productivity without providing methods.
11 Eliminate work standards that prescribe numerical quotas.
12 Remove barriers that stand between the hourly worker and his right to pride of workmanship.
13 Institute a vigorous programme of education and retraining.
14 Create a structure in top management that will push every day on the above thirteen points.

Joseph M. Juran

Juran's ten steps to quality improvement are the following:

1 Build awareness of the need and opportunity for improvement.
2 Set goals for improvement.
3 Organize to reach the goals (establish a quality council, identify problems, select projects, appoint teams, designate facilitators).
4 Provide training.

5 Carry out projects to solve problems.
6 Report progress.
7 Give recognition.
8 Communicate results.
9 Keep score.
10 Maintain momentum by making annual improvement part of the regular systems and processes of the company.

A comparison

One way to compare directly the various approaches of the three American gurus is in tabular form. Table A.1 shows the differences and similarities, classified under 12 different factors.

Table A.1 *The American quality gurus compared*

	Crosby	Deming	Juran
Definition of quality	Conformance to requirements	A predictable degree of uniformity and dependability at low cost and suited to the market	Fitness for use
Degree of senior-management responsibility	Responsible for quality	Responsible for 94% of quality problems	Less than 20% of quality problems are due to workers
Performance standard/motivation	Zero defects	Quality has many scales. Use statistics to measure performance in all areas. Critical of zero defects	Avoid campaigns to do perfect work
General approach	Prevention, not inspection	Reduce variability by continuous improvement. Cease mass inspection	General management approach to quality – especially 'human' elements
Structure	Fourteen steps to quality improvement	Fourteen points for management	Ten steps to quality improvement
Statistical process control (SPC)	Rejects statistically acceptable levels of quality	Statistical methods of quality control must be used	Recommends SPLC but warns that it can lead to too-driven approach
Improvement basis	A 'process', not a programme. Improvement goals	Continuous to reduce variation. Eliminate goals without methods	Project-by-project team approach. Set goals
Teamwork	Quality improvement teams. Quality councils	Employee participation in decision-making. Break down barriers between departments	Team and quality circle approach
Costs of quality	Cost of non-conformance. Quality is free	No optimum – continuous improvement	Quality is not free – there is an optimum
Purchasing and goods received	State requirements. Supplier is extension of business. Most faults due to purchasers themselves	Inspection too late – allows defects to enter system through AQLs. Statistical evidence and control charts required	Problems are complex. Carry out formal surveys
Vendor rating	Yes *and* buyers. Quality audits useless	No – critical of most systems	Yes, but help supplier improve
Single sources of supply		Yes	No – can neglect to sharpen competitive edge

Appendix B

TQM Bibliography

General quality management and TQM

Bank, J., *The Essence of Total Quality Management,* Prentice-Hall, Hemel Hempstead (UK), 1992.

Crosby, P.B., *Quality is Free*, McGraw-Hill, New York, 1979.

Crosby, P.B., *Quality Without Tears,* McGraw-Hill, New York, 1984.

Dale, B.G. (ed), *Managing Quality* (2nd edn), Philip Alan, Hemel Hempstead (UK), 1994.

Deming, W. E., *Out of the Crisis,* MIT, Cambridge, Mass. (USA), 1982.

Deming, W. E., *The New Economies,* MIT, Cambridge, Mass (USA), 1993.

Feigenbaum A.V., *Total Quality Control* (3rd edn, revised), McGraw-Hill, New York, 1991.

Garvin, D. A., *Managing Quality: the strategic competitive edge,* The Free Press (Macmillan), New York, 1988.

Hutchins, D., *Achieve Total Quality,* Director Books, Cambridge (UK), 1992.

Ishikawa, K. (translated by D. J. Lu), *What is Total Quality Control? the Japanese Way,* Prentice-Hall, Englewood Cliffs, NJ (USA), 1985.

Kehoe, D.F., *The Fundamentals of Quality Management,* Chapman & Hall, London, 1996.

Macdonald, J. and Piggot, J., *Global Quality: the new management culture,* Mercury Books, London, 1990.

Murphy, J. A., *Quality in Practice* (2nd edn), Gill and MacMillan, Dublin, 1992.

Price, F., *Right Every Time,* Gower, Aldershot (UK), 1990.

Sarv Singh Soin, *Total Quality Control Essentials – key elements, methodologies and managing for success,* McGraw-Hill, New York, 1992.

Wille, E., *Quality: achieving excellence,* Century Business, London, 1992.

Leadership and commitment

Adair, J., *Not Bosses but Leaders: how to lead the successful way,* Talbot Adair Press, Guildford (UK), 1987.

Adair, J., *The Action-Centred Leader,* Industrial Society, London, 1988.

Adair J., *Effective Leadership* (2nd edn), Pan Books, London, 1988.

Juran, J. M., *Juran on Leadership for Quality: an executive handbook,* The Free Press (Macmillan), New York, 1989.

Levicki, C., *The Leadership Gene,* F. T. Management, London, 1998.

Townsend, P. L., and Gebhardt, J. E., *Quality in Action – 93 lessons in leadership, participation and measurement,* J. Wiley Press, New York, 1992.

Customers, suppliers and service

Albin, J. M., *Quality Improvement in Employment and other Human Services – managing for quality through change,* Paul Brookes Pub. (USA), 1992.

Cook, S., *Customer Care – implementing total quality in today's service driven organisation,* Kogan Page, London, 1992.

Daffy, C., *Once a Customer always a Customer,* Oak Tree Press, Dublin, 1999.

King Taylor, L., *Quality: total customer service* (a case study book), Century Business, London, 1992.

Mastenbrock, W. (ed)., *Managing for Quality in the Service Sector,* Basil Blackwell, Oxford (UK), 1991.

Zeithaml, V. A., Parasuraman, A. and Berry, L. L., *Delivering Quality Service: balancing customer perceptions and expectations,* The Free Press (Macmillan), New York, 1990.

Design, innovation, and QFD

Adair, J., *The Challenge of Innovation,* Talbot Adair Press, Guildford (UK), 1990.

Fox, J., *Quality Through Design,* MGLR, 1993.

Juran, J. J., *Juran on Quality by Design,* Free Press, New York, 1992.

Marsh, S., Moran, J., Nakui, S. and Hoffherr, G. D., *Facilitating and Training in QFD,* ASQC, Milwaukee, WI (USA), 1991.

Zairi, M., *Management of Advanced Manufacturing Technology,* Sigma Press, Wilmslow (UK), 1992.

Quality planning, JIT, and POM

Ansari, A. and Modarress, B., *Just-in-time Purchasing,* The Free Press (Macmillan), New York, 1990.

Bineno, J., *Implementing JIT,* IFS, Bedford (UK), 1991.

Harrison, A., *Just-in-Time Manufacturing in Perspective,* Prentice-Hall, Englewood Cliffs, NJ (USA), 1992.

Juran, J. M. (ed), *Quality Control Handbook,* McGraw-Hill, New York, 1988.

Muhlemann, A. P., Oakland, J. S. and Lockyer, K. G., *Production and Operations Management* (6th edn), Pitman, London, 1992.

Voss, C. A. (ed), *Just-in-Time Manufacture,* IFS Publications, Bedford (UK), 1989.

Quality Management Systems and Processes

Born, G., *Process Management to Quality Improvement,* John Wiley, Chichester (UK), 1994.

Braganza, A. and Myers, A., *Business Process Redesign – a view from the inside,* International Thomson Business Press, London, 1997.

British Standards Institute: *ISO/CDI 9001:2000 Quality Management Systems,* BSI, London, 1998.

Federal Information Processing Standards (FIPS), *Publications 183 and 184,* National Institute of Standards and Technology (NIST), Gaithesburg (USA), 1993.

Hall, T. J., *The Quality Manual – the application of BS5750 ISO 9001 EN 29001,* John Wiley, Chichester (UK), 1992.

Rothery, B., *ISO 9000,* Gower, Aldlershot (UK), 1991.

The Baldrige and European Quality Award criteria

Brown M. G., *Baldrige Award Winning Quality: how to interpret the Malcolm Baldrige Award criteria* (2nd edn), ASQC, Milwaukee, WI (USA), 1992.

EPQM (European Foundation for Quality Management), *The European Excellence Model for 1999.* Brussels, 1999.

Hart, W. L. and Bogan, C.E., *The Baldrige: what it is, how it's won, how to use it to improve quality in your company,* McGraw-Hill, New York, 1992.

Mills Steeples, M., *The Corporate Guide to the Malcolm Baldrige National Quality Award,* ASQC, Milwaukee, WI (USA), 1992.

National Institute of Standard and Technology, *USA Malcolm Baldrige National Quality Award 1999 Criteria for Performance Excellence,* NIST, Gaithesburg (USA), 1999.

Quality costing, measurement and benchmarking

Bendell, Tony, *Benchmarking for Competitive Advantage,* Longman, London, 1993.

British Quality Foundation, *The X-Factor – winning performance through Business Excellence,* BQF/EC for BE, London, 1999.

Camp, R. C., *Business Process Benchmarking: finding and implementing best practice,* ASQC Quality Press, Milwaukee, WI (USA), 1995.

Dale, B. G. and Plunkett, J. J., *Quality Costing,* Chapman and Hall, London, 1991.

Dixon, J. R., Nanni, A. and Vollmann, T. E., *The New Performance Challenge – measuring operations for world class competition,* Business One Irwin, Homewood (USA), 1990.

Hall, R. W., Johnson, H. Y. and Turney, P. B. B., *Measuring Up – charting pathways to manufacturing excellence,* Business One Irwin, Homewood (USA), 1991.

Kaplan, R. W. (ed), *Measures for Manufacturing Excellence,* Harvard Business School Press, Boston, MA (USA), 1990.

Kaplan, R. S. and Norton, P., *The Balanced Scorecard,* Harvard Business School Press, Boston, MA (USA), 1996.

Kinlaw, D. C., *Continuous Improvement and Measurement For Total Quality – a team-based approach,* Pfieffer & Business One, (USA), 1992.

Macdonald, J. and Tanner, S.J., *Understanding Benchmarking in a Week,* Institute of Management, London, 1996.

Porter, L. J. and Rayner, P., 'Quality costing for TQM', *International Journal of Production Economics,* **27,** pp. 69–81, 1992.

Spendolini, M. J., *The Benchmarking Book,* ASQC, Milwaukee, WI (USA), 1992.

Talley, D. J., *Total Quality Management: performance and cost measures,* ASQC, Milwaukee, WI (USA), 1991.

Zairi, M., *Benchmarking for Best Practice,* Butterworth-Heinemann, Oxford (UK), 1996.

Zairi, M., *TQM-Based Performance Measurement,* TQM Practitioner Series, Technical Communication (Publishing), Letchworth (UK), 1992.

Zairi, M., *Measuring Performance for Business Results,* Chapman and Hall, London, 1994.

Zairi, M., *Effective Benchmarking – learning from the best,* Chapman and Hall, London, 1996.

Tools and techniques of TQM (including SPC)

Bhote, K. R., *World Class Quality – using design of experiments to make it happen,* AMACOM, New York (USA), 1991.

Carlzon, J., *Moments of Truth,* Ballinger, Cambridge, Mass. (USA), 1987.

Joiner, B., *Fourth Generation Management,* McGraw-Hill, 1994.

Neave, H., *The Deming Dimension,* SPC Press, Knoxville (USA), 1990.

Oakland, J. S., *Statistical Process Control: a practical guide* (4th edn), Butterworth-Heinemann, Oxford (UK), 1999.

Price, F., *Right First Time,* Gower, London, 1985.

Ryuka Fukuda, *CEDAC – a tool for continuous systematic improvement,* Productivity Press, Cambridge, Mass. (USA), 1990.

Wheeler, D. J., *Understanding Variation,* SPC Press, 1993.

Wheeler, D. J., *Understanding Statistical Process Control* (2nd edn), SPC Press, 1992.

Shingo and Taguchi methods

Bendell, T., Wilson, G. and Millar, R. M. G., *Taguchi Methodology with Total Quality*, IFS, Bedford (UK), 1990.

Lagothetis, N., *Managing for Total Quality – from Deming to Taguchi and SPC*, Prentice-Hall, Englewood Cliffs, NJ (USA), 1990.

Ranjit, Roy, *A Primer on the Taguchi Method*, Van Nostrand Reinhold, New York, 1990.

Shingo, S., *Zero Quality Control: source inspection and the Poka-yoke system*, Productivity Press, Stamford, Conn. (USA), 1986.

TQM through people and teamwork

Adair, J., *Effective Teambuilding* (2nd edn), Pan Books, London, 1987.

Blanchard, K. and Herrsey, P., *Management of Organizational Behaviour: Utilizing Human Resources* (4th edn), Prentice–Hall, Englewood Cliffs, NJ (USA), 1982.

Choppin, J., *Quality Through People: a blueprint for proactive total quality management*, Rushmere Wynne, Bedford, (UK), 1997.

Dale, B. G., Cooper, C. and Wilkinson, A., *Total Quality and Human Resources – a guide to continuous improvement*, Blackwell, Oxford (UK), 1992.

Larkin, T. J. and Larkin, S., *Communicating Change – winning employee support for new business goals*, McGraw-Hill, New York, 1994.

Katzenbach, J. R. and Smith, D. K., *The Wisdom of Teams – creating the high performance organisation*, McGraw-Hill/Harvard Business School, Boston, MA (USA), 1994

Kormanski, C., 'A situational leadership approach to groups using the Tuckman Model of Group Development', *The 1985 Annual: Developing Human Resources*, University Associates, San Diego, CA, (USA), 1985.

Kormanski, C. and Mozenter, A., 'A new model of team building: a technology for today and tomorrow', *The 1987 Annual: Developing Human Resources*, University Associates, San Diego, CA, (USA), 1987.

Krebs Hirsh, S., *MBTI Team Building Program, Team Member's Guide*, Consulting Psychologists Press, Palo Alto, CA (USA), 1992.

Krebs Hirsh, S. and Kummerow, J. M., *Introduction to Type in Organizational Settings*, Consulting Psychologists Press, Palo Alto, CA (USA), 1987.

McCaulley, M. H., 'How individual differences affect health care teams', *Health Team News*, **1** (8), pp. 1–4, 1975.

Masaaki, I., *Kaizen: the key to Japanese competitive success*, McGraw-Hill, New York, 1986.

Myers–Briggs, I., *Introduction to Type: a description of the theory and applications of the Myers–Briggs Type Indicator*, Consulting Psychologists Press, Palo Alto (USA), 1987.

Scholtes, P.R., *The Team Handbook*, Joiner Associates, Madison, NY (USA), 1990.

Schutz, W., *FIRO: A Three-Dimensional Theory of Interpersonal Behaviour*, Mill Valley WSA, CA (USA), 1958.

Schutz, W., *FIRO: Awareness Scales Manual,* Consulting Psychologists Press, Palo Alto, CA (USA), 1978.

Schutz, W., *The Human Element – Productivity, Self-esteem and the Bottom Line,* Jossey-Bass, San Francisco, CA (USA), 1994.

Tannenbaum, R. and Schmidt, W. H., 'How to choose a leadership pattern', *Harvard Business Review,* May-June, 1973.

Tuckman, B. W. and Jensen, M. A., 'States of small group development revisited', *Group and Organizatonal Studies,* **2** (4), pp. 419–427, New York, 1977.

Wellins, R. S., Byham, W. C. and Wilson, J. M., *Empowered Teams,* Jossey Bass, Oxford (UK), 1991.

Whitley, R., *The Customer Driven Company,* Business Books, London, 1991.

Cross-functional process improvement

Dimaxcescu, D., *The Seamless Enterprise – making cross-functional management work,* Harper Business, New York, 1992.

Francis, D., *Unblocking the Organizational Communication,* Gower, Aldershot (UK), 1990.

Hammer, M. and Champy, J., *Re-engineering the corporation,* Nicholas Brearley, London, 1993.

Harrington, H. J., *Total Improvement Management,* McGraw-Hill, New York, 1995.

Rummler, G. A. and Brache, A. P., *Improving Performance: how to manage the white space on the organization chart* (2nd edn), Jossey-Bass Publishing, San Francisco, CA (USA), 1998.

Senge, P.M., *The Fifth Discipline,* Century Business, London, 1990.

Senge, P. M., Roberts, C., Ross, R. B., Smith, B. J. and Kleiner A., *The Fifth Discipline Field book – Strategies and tools for building a learning organization,* Nicholas Brearley, London, 1994.

TQM Strategy and Implementation

Ciampa, D., *Total Quality – a user's guide for implementation,* Addison-Wesley, Reading, Mass. (USA), 1992.

Collins, J. C. and Porras, J. I., *Built to Last,* Random House, London, 1998.

Fox, R., *Six Steps to Total Quality Management,* McGraw-Hill, NSW (Australia), 1991.

Hardaker, M. and Ward, B. K., 'Getting things done – how to make a team work', *Harvard Business Review,* pp. 112–119, Nov/Dec., 1987.

Hiam, A., *Closing the Quality Gap – lessons from America's leading companies,* Prentice-Hall, Englewood Cliffs, NJ (USA), 1992.

Labovitz, G., Chang, Y. S. and Rosansky, V., *Making Quality Work – a leadership guide for the results-driven manager,* Harper Business, London, 1993.

Morgan C. and Murgatroyd, S., *Total Quality Management in the Public Sector,* Open University Press, Milton Keynes, (UK), 1994.

Munro-Faure, L. and Munro-Faure, M., *Implementing Total Quality Management,* Pitman, London, 1992.

Saylor, J. H., *Total Quality Management Field Manual,* McGraw-Hill, New York, 1992.

Scherkenbach, W. W., *Deming's Road to Continual Improvement,* SPC Press, Knoxville (USA), 1991.

Schuler, R. S. and Harris, D. L., *Managing Quality – the primer for middle managers,* Addison-Wesley, Reading, MA (USA), 1992.

Spenley, P., *World Class Performance Through Total Quality,* Chapman and Hall, London, 1992.

Tennor, A. R. and De Toro, I. J., *Total Quality Manager – three steps to continuous improvement,* Addison-Wesley, Reading, MA (USA), 1992.

Tunks, R., *Fast Track to Quality,* McGraw-Hill, New York, 1992.

Whitford, B. and Bird, R., *The Pursuit of Quality,* Beaumont, Herts. (UK), 1996.

Index